SHADOW DIVERS EXPOSED
BY GARY GENTILE

THE REAL SAGA OF THE
U-869

Bellerophon Bookworks

Bellerophon Bookworks
P.O. Box 57137
Philadelphia, PA 19111

Additional copies of this book may be purchased from the same address by sending a check or money order in the amount of $25 U.S. for each copy (plus $3 postage per order, not per book, in the U.S. Inquire for shipping cost to foreign countries). Alternatively, copies may be purchased from the author's website, and paid by credit card:

http://www.ggentile.com

The author took the front cover photograph of the British J-class submarine, which lies off the coast of Melbourne, Australia.

International Standard Book Numbers (ISBN)
1-883056-24-1
978-1-883056-24-7

First Edition

Printed in the U.S.A.

CONTENTS

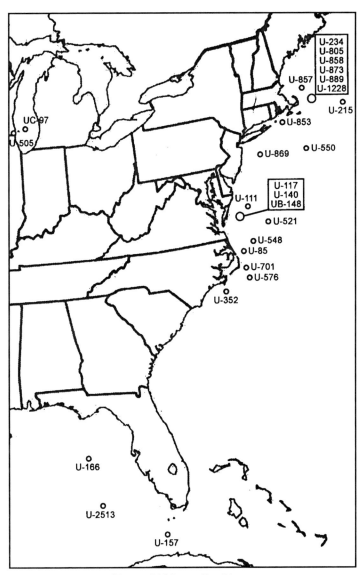

Charted U-boat Positions

At the present time, twenty-four U-boats from two world wars are known to exist off the coast of the eastern and southern United States. In addition, the *UC-97* lies at the bottom of Lake Michigan, and the *U-505* is a museum in Chicago, Illinois. Not shown is the *UB-88*, which lies off San Pedro, California.

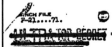

UNITED. STATES FLEET
HEADQUARTERS OF THE COMMANDER IN CHIEF
NAVY DEPARTMENT
WASHINGTON 25, D. C.

3 January, 1945.

U/Boat Intelligence Summary (Continued).

- -

     (b) Outbound:

         A U/Boat (U-069) now estimated in the central
North Atlantic has been ordered to head for a point about 70 miles
southeast of New York approaches. (1729/29). During November this
U/Boat was used in Kurier tests (radio flash transmissions) in the
Skaggerak.

> (Note: This is the first U/Boat in the
> western Atlantic to be sent
> south of the Gulf of Maine
> since U-518 operated off Hatteras
> in September.)

   3.   CANADIAN FRONTIERS

         One U/Boat (U-806 - Hornbostel) is estimated
on patrol in the Halifax - Gulf of Maine area having been told
21 December that U-1230 "is presumably in the same op area as
you are.". A fresh U/Boat (U-1232 Dobrats) which previously had
been reporting weather, is currently estimated in the vicinity
of Sable Island probably moving into the Halifax area. They
have been told that from recent experiences (U-1221) "successes
may be expected only directly off Halifax; act accordingly".
The defense was described as "little weary patrolling without
asdic. Off Halifax none, elsewhere little day and night air."
(2031/22).

         U-1231 (Lessing) is estimated south of Grand
Banks returning from a Halifax patrol. She was told 27 December
that if operations in the vicinity of Anticosti Island were no
longer possible because of the season, she was to operate off
Halifax harbor.

> (Note: (1) The 7219-ton British MV, SAMTUCKY,
> in HHX-327 was torpedoed off Halifax
> and beached 21 December. HMCS
> CLAYOQUOT, an AM, was torpedoed and
> sunk 15 miles off Halifax 24 December
> while on A/S search prior to the
> sailing of XB-139 for Boston.
>
> (2) An RCAF Liberator attacked a periscope
> southeast of Halifax 25 December. Oil
> bubbles and wreckage were reported.)

545

-2-

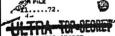

UNITED STATES FLEET
HEADQUARTERS OF THE COMMANDER IN CHIEF
NAVY DEPARTMENT
WASHINGTON 25, D. C.

17 January, 1945.

U/Boat Intelligence Summary.

1. 　　CENERAL SITUATION

　　　　U/Boats continue inshore operations at focal points of shipping. Commanders are showing more ability in handling their boats as they gain confidence in schnorchel and the immunity it affords from aircraft attack. The number at sea in the Atlantic remains fairly static at 35 to 40 U/Boats. Of particular interest was the attack on 16 January by TG 22.8. (4 DEs) on the southern weather reporter, whom they had been stalking the past two weeks, and which resulted in her probable sinking. Another U/Boat is on weather patrol in the central North Atlantic, one is off Halifax and one is probably still patrolling west of Gibraltar Strait. Three are in transit in the central North Atlantic, two homebound from Canadian waters, and one outbound, heading for the New York area. Approximately 24 U/Boats, about half of which are in transit, are estimated in the vicinity of Britain. There are still no U/Boats estimated in the Atlantic south of 30N. Four U/Boats with cargo for Germany are homebound in the Indian Ocean; a 1200-tonner is still estimated *homebound on patrol off* ～～～～～～～～～～ Australia. Most outbound U/Boats in the Atlantic are now receiving important messages in special individual ciphers, none of which has been broken.

2. 　　WESTERN ATLANTIC

　　(a) 　New York:

　　　　　The U/Boat heading for the New York approaches, U-869 (Neuerburg), is presently estimated about 180 miles SSE of Flemish Cap. She reported her position in about 56N 27W 6 January and was told to "continue southward cruise". She is expected to arrive in the New York area at the beginning of February.

-1-

555

F-21.....73.

UNITED STATES FLEET
HEADQUARTERS OF THE COMMANDER IN CHIEF
NAVY DEPARTMENT
WASHINGTON 25, D. C.

25 January, 1945.

U/Boat Intelligence Summary.

1.   GENERAL SITUATION

        Unprecedented successes for inshore operations reported by four U/Boat commanders off the harbors of Halifax, Gibraltar, Cherbourg and in the Irish Sea have resulted in immediate decorations for these C.O.s and a definite note of exultation evidenced in ComSubs' congratulatory despatches. The coastal waters of the British Isles remain the main target for from 20 to 25 U/Boats slightly over half of which are in passage. Two U/Boats are estimated patrolling off the eastern Scottish coast, four between St. George's Channel and the Irish Sea, and three in the English Channel with another about to arrive there. One U/Boat was sunk off Land's End 21 January by a British destroyer. Eight are outbound in the vicinity of the Shetland-Faeroe Passage. One U/Boat may be south of Newfoundland heading for New York approaches, although her location is uncertain due to a mix up in orders and Control assumes she is heading for Gibraltar. Three U/Boats are reporting weather from the North Atlantic. None is estimated in the Atlantic south of 35N. There are four U/Boats in the Indian Ocean enroute to Germany. Another will refuel one of them and then return to Batavia. The 1200 tonner recently patrolling off Australia has been ordered to return to Batavia and is expected to arrive about 3 February.

2.   WESTERN ATLANTIC

   (a) New York

       The intentions and location of U-869 (Neuerburg) who was ordered to the New York area 29 December are obscure since Control sent her a conflicting message 19 January saying that she was expected to arrive in U-070's area, off Gibraltar, about 1 February. Based on the signals she received it appears likely that U-869 is continuing toward her original heading off New York. On the other hand a reply to Control's message of 19 January (referred to above) would seem to be in order unless U-869 shifted radio watch without orders and missed this signal.

      (Note: The CORE will begin sweeping for this U/Boat shortly prior to proceeding against the U/Boats reporting weather in the North Atlantic.)

ESF ATTACKS 7/44 - 5/45

1 #	Date	Location	Comments	Ev
6685 C	7/20/44	40-01N/73-27W	Haste, HH	I/H
6685 A	7/20/44	40-00N/73-29W	PC 1212, mousetrap and DC	I/H
6685 B	7/20/44	40-00N/73-29W	Blimp K-61. DC	I/H
7521	1/11/45	40-00N/73-29W	PC 1265	I
7541	1/15/45	39-44N/73-02W	HMCS Winnipeg (10 1/2 miles from U-Who.	I
7546	1/15/45	40-07N/72.44	PC 1209. DC	I
7662	2/6/45	38-58N/72-00	Breckinridge, DC,	H
7697	2/9/45	40-08N/73-40W	PC 1170, mousetraps	I
7714	2/11/45	39-34N/73-32W	PC 1246	I
7715A	2/11/45	39-30N/72-58W	USS Koiner, Sound contact, DC/HH	I
7715B	2/11/45	"	Howard Crow	I
7746	2/15/45	40-30N/74-01W	PC 1264, mousetraps and DC.	H
7759	2/17/45	38-58N/72-25W	SS Harpers Ferry, explosion, then gunfire.	J
7789E	2/20/45	"	Blimp K-77, DC	H
7789D	2/20/45	40-17N/73-42	Blimp K-30, DC	H
7789F	2/20/45	"	Blimp K-98, DC	H
7789C	2/20/45	40-31N/73-27W	USCG Trition, mousetraps	H
7802	2/22/45	40-12N/73-44W	HMCS Battleford	H
7825	2/25/45	38-45N/73-53W	Uniontown, HH & DC	H
7829	2/26/45	39-46N/72-17W	Natchez	I
7850	2/17/45	34-30N/8-13W	Fowler. DC. U-869.	H/B
7865	2/20/45	40-03N/73-15	Haste, sound contact, DC & HH	I
7866	2/22/45	39-41N/72-25W	Haste, Sound contact, HH	I
7902	3/9/45	39-50N/72-53W	Escorts of ON-236.Co-ordinates exactly over charted wreck.	H
Incid #	Date	Location	Comments	Ev
7920	3/10/45	40-30N/72-54W	Wyffels	I
7923	3/12/45	39-28N/72-43W	Mervine, DC	H
7969	3/17/45	42-55N/53-46W	Sutton. HH. U/W explosion. Water 80 ft in air.	J

Attack reports that Barb Lander tabulated in 1994.

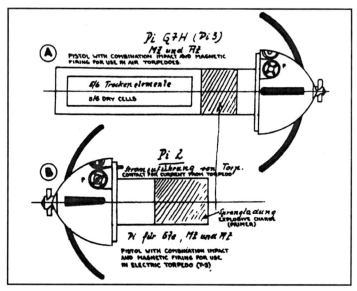

Ⓐ *Pi G7H (Pi 3)*
MZ und AZ
PISTOL WITH COMBINATION IMPACT AND MAGNETIC
FIRING FOR USE IN AIR TORPEDOES.

6/6 Trockenelemente
6/6 DRY CELLS

Pi 2
Stromzuführung vom Torp.
CONTACT FOR CURRENT FROM TORPEDO

Sprengladung
EXPLOSIVE CHARGE
(PRIMER)

Ⓑ *Pi für G7e, MZ und AZ*
PISTOL WITH COMBINATION IMPACT
AND MAGNETIC FIRING FOR USE
IN ELECTRIC TORPEDO (T-3)

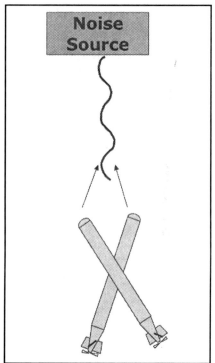

PROLOGUE
Dirty Politics

"The law isn't the only guide to the conduct of human affairs."

- Ross MacDonald

Prepare for Boarding!

A watershed incident occurred on Saturday evening, August 1, 2005.

In preparation for an early morning departure, Harold Moyers and Greg Masi loaded their dive gear onto Moyers' 42-foot boat, the *Big Mac*. The boat was docked at the South Jersey Marina in Cape May, New Jersey. Five other divers had yet to arrive.

Their work done, Moyers and Masi lounged on the deck, chatting and smoking cigars before going to sleep. At about 8:00 p.m., a Coast Guard semi-rigid inflatable boat pulled into an empty spot about four slips away from the *Big Mac*. Three Coast Guard officers jumped off the inflatable, tied mooring lines to the dock cleats, then strode purposefully to the stern of the *Big Mac*.

The lead man looked at Moyers and Masi, and said, "Captain Moyers?"

Moyers raised his hand.

Firmly but courteously, the officer said, "Where are you going tomorrow, Cap?"

Without hesitation, Moyers said, "The *U-869*."

The three "coasties" exchanged looks with each other. Their faces displayed genuine surprise at Moyers' open admission.

The lead officer informed him that salvage of a military wreck was illegal, and that he could not be permitted to engage in an illegal activity.

Moyers told the coasties that he wished to cooperate with them one hundred percent, but that he knew the law. He was going to the site only to take video footage for an upcoming convention of the Destroyer Escort Sailors Association. The Coast Guard did not have the authority to stop him from doing so.

He also informed the officers of the U.S. Coast Guard Historians web page, which acknowledged Moyers with having unearthed the truth about the sinking of the *U-869*.

The expressions on the faces of the officers conveyed their appreciation of Moyers' frank explanation. The lead coastie excused himself to make a cellular phone call. He walked along the dock a ways and spoke to someone on the phone.

While he was engaged in conversation, one of the other coasties said, "You dudes got set up."

The officer in charge strode back with the phone to his ear, and asked Moyers for a phone number at which he could be reached. Moyers gave his cell phone number to the coastie, who repeated it for the person on the line. The officer disconnected, and told Moyers that someone would call him within the hour.

The coastie was openly friendly. He thanked Moyers for his cooperation, and said that he hoped that he had no problems in getting out the next day. All three officers departed.

Twenty minutes later, Moyers received a phone call from Lieutenant Eric Mathies, from the U.S. Coast Guard Atlantic Group in Norfolk, Virginia. He switched on his speakerphone, and asked Moyers to repeat his intentions. He said that he had read the Coast Guard Historian's website, and that his story checked out.

Informer with Malice Aforethought

Moyers asked, "How did you guys know that I was going to the U-boat?"

Lieutenant Mathies laughed, "We had a confidential informant report you." He read the pertinent part of the military shipwreck act, and wished Moyers a successful trip. He also told Moyers that he would help him to file a request pursuant to the Freedom of Information Act, in order to ascertain who had lied to the Coast

Guard about the nature of his trip.

The informer had claimed that Moyers intended to loot the wreck.

Several days later, Moyers called Lieutenant Mathies. The lieutenant gave Moyers a FOIA contact at the Coast Guard information office in Washington, DC: Donald Taylor. Moyers called Taylor. Taylor informed Moyers that he would have to send a formal request in writing, but that he was wasting his time. Informers enjoyed legal protection; their names were never revealed. Nor were they ever punished for providing misleading information, no matter how erroneous.

How absurd is it that a person or persons can use the Coast Guard as a cat's-paw in a private persecution without first having the Coast Guard investigate the reliability of the informer and the source of his information; and worse, without the informer suffering any recrimination for raising a false alarm that caused the expenditure of taxpayers' dollars?

Moyers described to Taylor how a person with a grudge had stretched the thin resources of Homeland Security even thinner. Taylor was sympathetic, but he assured Moyers that bureaucracies are not easily changed, and that he had no chance of ascertaining the name of the informer, even though Moyers had been victimized at the Coast Guard's expense, and even though the Coast Guard had been victimized at the taxpayers' expense.

Will the Real Culprit Please Stand Up?

When Pat Rooney heard about the Coast Guard boarding incident, he called Moyers at once and apologized effusively for being indirectly responsible. He was desperately afraid that Moyers would blame him for causing the trouble. Rooney explained to Moyers that, two days prior to the boarding, he was on a dive trip with Richie Kohler. As they were returning to port, Rooney happened to mention that Moyers was going to the U-boat on Sunday to obtain photographic evidence of the damage holes in order to support his thesis of the depth-charge attack.

Kohler became livid. In his anger, he shouted statements such as, "Why can't he leave well enough alone?" and "Why does he have to stick his nose into it?" He also claimed that he and John Chatterton had the proverbial "smoking gun" - parts of the *U-869's* torpedo that circled back and detonated against the pressure hull, causing the U-boat's demise. Possibly he was overreacting because he and Chatterton had recently given an interview in which they stated categorically that the *U-869* was sunk by its own torpedo. The interview was included in the paperback edition of *Shadow Divers*.

After the boarding incident, Rooney asked Kohler to confirm his suspicions that Kohler had something to do with the call to the Coast Guard.

Kohler instantly became defensive. He told Rooney, "I ain't no cop caller. And if you want to guess who called, you don't have to guess too hard." He sort of admitted complicity, but he would not give Rooney the name of the caller.

Taylor agreed that the escapade was a waste of Coast Guard resources. He suggested that Moyers write to his congressional representative, who might be able to force the release of the informer's name. Moyers did so, but has received no reply.

Great Reception

Moyers had already tracked down Lieutenant Commander Charles Judson, the skipper of the *Koiner*. Now he intended to speak with other crewmembers who were involved in the attack against the *U-869*.

The DESA convention was held in Albany, New York in September 2005. Moyers gave his presentation on the night of the twelfth. The destroyer escort sailors were enthralled by his presentation of the facts. The convention gave him the opportunity to obtain first-hand accounts from crewmembers of the *Howard D. Crow* - information that was not available from archival sources - and to speak with crewmembers of the *Joyce*,

Gandy, and *Peterson* (the destroyer escorts that sank the *U-550* - see Appendix Four for details).

The crewmembers enjoyed the presentation and underwater video so thoroughly that they presented Moyers with a fine letter of appreciation.

Moyers stated, "The wife of Basil Philipy said the nicest thing of all. She told me that ever since this information was revealed, her husband has been a new man."

Raison D'être

For years, northeast wreck-divers have been out-raged by misinformation that has been disseminated to the media, particularly about the *U-869*, but about other diving incidents as well. Their voices will be heard in the following pages.

The Coast Guard investigation failed to achieve the goal of the informer who did not have the courage to claim credit for his action. But the punch below the belt provided the primary incentive for writing this exposé: the proverbial straw that broke the camel's back.

I did not read *Shadow Divers* when it was first pub-lished. I thought that I had no need to read it, for I knew the story of the *U-869* firsthand, and I knew all the people who were involved with the wreck. I had been diving with them for years. Most were my friends.

Even though I had heard through the grapevine that the book contained inaccuracies, I did not - I *could* not - know the true depth of the inaccuracies until, gal-vanized by the Coast Guard boarding incident, Moyers finally convinced me to take an active stance in telling the real story that *Shadow Divers* either omitted, dis-torted, or created.

Forewarned, I read *Shadow Divers* with a high-lighter in one hand, so I could mark all the passages to which I took exception. Were I to write in the style of *Shadow Divers*, I would state that I went through a gross and a half of highlighters in the process of perus-al - but that would be an exaggeration. One highlighter was enough to mark two to three *hundred* passages that required redress. I saw additional erroneous passages every time I opened the book.

I would be treating my faithful readers unfairly if I did not admit some personal bias. I have been passionately involved in shipwreck research and deep wreck-diving for more than thirty years. Some of the inaccuracies and factual differences that I found annoying may not seem quite so important to all my readers. For that reason, I have placed many of the less noteworthy inaccuracies in Appendix Five, which the casual reader may choose to ignore. Some of these inaccuracies are historical in nature. My observations and corrections can be corroborated from a number of sources: either historical documents or honest and reliable witnesses.

Dewey, Cheatham, and Howe

Food producers are required by law to list the ingredients on the package in which goods are sold. The food must contain those ingredients or else strong penalties apply. It is unfortunate for the reading public that book publishers are not legally required to adhere to such standards of honesty. Food for thought and public consumption is every bit as important as food for the human body. Yet all too often, truth in publication is a dispensable concept that yields to the pursuit of sales. The government provides no protection from fraud in leisure reading.

Random House, the publisher of *Shadow Divers*, promoted the book as nonfiction. Dust jacket blurbs advertised the book as a "true adventure" and a "true tale." According to the dictionary, "true" means "consistent with fact or reality; not false or erroneous," plus "real; genuine" and "reliable; accurate."

Books are organized in libraries according to the Dewey decimal system. In this system, three-digit numerals are assigned to specific subject categories. According to information that the publisher provided, *Shadow Divers* was listed as military history. The book will be found in the nonfiction section. A library patron should be able to assume that a book belongs in the category in which it was filed, and that the information that is contained in the book conforms to the advertisements on its cover.

Shadow Divers does not merit such a Dewey decimal number because it fails to meet the criteria of historical nonfiction. The book fits none of the definitions of "true." Literary integrity was dismissed in order to make an ordinary story about ordinary people doing ordinary things seem extraordinary. Such a book was a wanton disservice to an ingenuous public.

Nyuk, nyuk, nyuk!

With all due respect to the author of *Shadow Divers*, I have written *thirty* books on shipwrecks and wreck-diving. I believe that this lifetime endeavor gives me more of a professional background in the field than Robert Kurson, whose only previously published titles were *The Official Three Stooges Encyclopedia: the Ultimate Knucklehead's Guide to Stoogedom*, and *The Official Three Stooges Cookbook.*

Some of my uninformed readers may be disappointed to learn that the heroes of *Shadow Divers* were mere caricatures in a book that was to a large extent fictitious. I apologize in advance for knocking their white knights off their charging steeds, and for letting the truth get in the way of a story that has been offensively sensationalized.

Denial is a common flaw in human nature. A few readers will be unwilling or unable to accept the documented facts and the testimony of witnesses that contradict the conceits that *Shadow Divers* implanted in their minds. Some people can believe only what they hear or read first, no matter how improbable the yarn. They are mentally constrained by the sanctity of the first printed word they encounter, and sternly object to subsequent denunciation.

Once a belief becomes indelibly imprinted, these people are then unable to make the intellectual leap to reconsider the facts, and cannot accept any alternative view of events no matter how persuasive the evidence.

These people will never allow the truths in the present exposé to replace their cherished notions and idols. They may even become angry with me as the author for attacking the fantasies in which they have come to believe. They must suffer the failings of their own personalities.

Tight Knit Community

The bitter rivalries that are depicted as the norm in *Shadow Divers* are actually aberrations, much like crime in society. Crime makes front-page boldface headlines, while baking contests are relegated to small print in the back pages of metropolitan newspapers. Many high-circulation magazines are driven by sex scandals, but the overwhelming majority of people maintains loving and long-lasting relationships.

Portions of *Shadow Divers* read like a supermarket tabloid, dwelling artificially on conflict to create an interesting story that was otherwise mundane in comparison with more exciting events in which the Shadow Divers took no part: much like tallest pygmy concept. This plot device led to a thwarted view of wreck-diving in general, and to individual wreck-divers in particular. The *U-869* was but one shipwreck among hundreds that have been discovered in recent years. That the others did not receive the same amount of publicity and promotion does not make them any less historically significant.

The reader should know that divers are not necessarily a special breed of people. For the most part, they are everyday people leading everyday lives. The exploration of the underwater world provides a means to escape the ordinary aspects of their lives. Some divers seek extraordinary adventure, and those who do tend to band together with others who have similar interests. Strong friendships result.

Many of these friendships last throughout a person's lifetime. Some friendships fall into neglect only because a person quits diving or moves out of the area. Those who remain active form close bonds of brotherhood (and sisterhood). The brothers and sisters of the northeast wreck-diving community were appalled at the falsities in *Shadow Divers*. They cried out against a book that had gone uncontested.

The purpose of *Shadow Divers Exposed* is to set the record straight, and to put the saga of the *U-869* in real historical perspective.

CHAPTER ONE
Destruction of the *U-869*

*"Life is a matter of luck, and the odds in favor of success
are in no way enhanced by extreme caution."*
- *Erich Topp (U-552)*

Mortality Incognito

On February 11, 1945, an incident of violence
occurred off the U.S. eastern seaboard: the depth-
charging of a German U-boat.

By this time in the war such incidents were commonplace. But this particular incident was extraordinary, perhaps unique, in that of all the people who were
directly involved, those who had firsthand knowledge of
the consequences were killed almost immediately, while
those who lived to tell about their part in the attack
were unaware of the outcome.

Sixty years passed before Harold Moyers discovered
the truth.

The Baying Wolves Breed

The Fuhrer's U-boats were sacrificial components
of the mad dictator's bid for world domination. In Adolf
Hitler's grand game of political chess, they amounted to
nothing more than underwater pawns whose sole reason for existence was to cause widespread death and
destruction as a means of achieving his wild ambitions.
Hitler's nefarious scheme for conquering the free peoples of the world entailed the demolition of all the forces
that were opposed to his vision of a social organization
in which everyone was subjugated to Nazism, with him
as supreme commander.

Hitler's dream of conquest was the world's night-
mare. Initially, his U-boat fleet was small: it was limited, in fact, by the terms of the Armistice. The size of
Germany's naval fleet was restricted to a percentage of
the fleets of the Allied nations. In the mid-1930's, when

the Fuhrer's invasion plans were formulating, he know-ingly violated the articles of capitulation by clandes-tinely increasing his U-boat fleet, in anticipation of waging war against neighboring civilized nations.

Production increased slowly at first because of the need to conceal the illegal operations. When the Allies eventually learned of the violations, there was little they could do to enforce the treaty short of a declaration of war. Diplomacy works only among rational beings, not against charging tigers.

Expansion of the U-boat arm lagged behind Hitler's timetable for war. Against good advice, Hitler com-menced hostilities with an inadequate fleet of U-boats. When his army invaded Poland - on September 1, 1939 - the number of U-boats that he needed for his offen-sive against the Allies was seriously lacking. Estab-lished construction facilities were then enlarged, and new facilities were erected, but throughout the war, production never overtook demand. The fleet remained inadequate because the Allies sank U-boats at such an alarming rate.

Although Hitler built more than 1,200 U-boats - four times as many as the United States built - his U-boats sank only twice the tonnage that American sub-marines sank. Germany typically had about the same number of U-boats on patrol as the U.S. had at any given time. U.S. submarines would have sunk more ships if they had not run out of targets as the Japanese retreated to the home islands.

The Fuhrer's Right Arm

In July 1935, Admiral Karl Doenitz was appointed to command Hitler's U-boat arm. Second to Hitler, he was the person who was most responsible for waging the U-boat war against the merchant marine, and he did so with intense dedication and enthusiasm. Doenitz may not have been as fanatical a Nazi as Hitler, but he supported Nazism nonetheless.

To claim that he was not a Nazi because he did not belong to the Nazi party is like claiming that American submariners were Republicans although their President was a Democrat. It was simply German tradition that officers not be politically active. Nonetheless, all members of the U-boat arm were volunteers who chose to fight for the cause of the Fatherland, which was clearly an aggressive stance toward expansionism and lebensraum.

Doenitz has been treated sympathetically in history, despite the fact that he engaged in unrestricted submarine warfare. In this sense, "unrestricted" meant the act of torpedoing unarmed vessels without first giving the passengers and crew the opportunity to abandon ship prior to destruction. In other words, according to the rule of restricted warfare, it was permissible to sink merchant vessels but not to kill the people onboard.

Rules for warfare are as absurd as rules for mugging and murder. Yet the London Submarine Agreement of 1930 banned the employment of unrestricted submarine warfare - similar to the way in which other agreements banned the use of poison gas and dumdum bullets.

Doenitz began to develop strategies and tactics for unrestricted submarine warfare as soon as he assumed command of the U-boat fleet. His entire campaign was focused on the concept. Although his apologizers are quick to note that American submarines also engaged in unrestricted submarine warfare, they generally neglect to mention that it was not until two years after Doenitz initiated the scheme.

Considering that Doenitz conspired with Hitler to go to war, it is surprising that history has treated him so well, especially in light of well-known facts: he was clearly anti-Semitic, he was a staunch believer in Aryan superiority, he hated Bolshevism, he gave speeches in support of his views, and he lent fervent support for Hitler's wholesale killing spree and military conquest of the world.

Historically, Doenitz's inhumane transgressions have been played down. He broached no insubordination among his officers and men. When Oskar Kusch removed a portrait of Hitler from the officers wardroom, and ridiculed the Fuhrer as an insane megalomaniac, he was tried by a tribunal, found guilty of sedition and defeatism, and summarily executed. Doenitz made no attempt to interfere and have his sentence commuted to reduction in rank and imprisonment.

Heinz Hirsacker returned from a lackluster patrol in which he failed to engage the enemy because of fierce and overwhelming countermeasures. Doenitz deemed that Hirsacker was not aggressive enough to command a U-boat. He had Hirsacker arrested for cowardice in the face of the enemy. Hirsacker was tried and condemned to death. No one pleaded for clemency in his behalf. He committed suicide before his execution.

One is not likely to read that toward the end of the war, Doenitz knowingly sent U-boats on suicide missions - even to the point of ordering his U-boats to ram enemy vessels in a last-ditch effort to sink them. It is ironic that this overly aggressive stance impeded the progress of the American and British invasion of Germany, thereby allowing the Russians to reach Berlin ahead of their English-speaking allies, and contributing to the segregation of the city.

The *Laconia* Affair

Doenitz was tried at Nuremberg for committing criminal acts of war. The prosecution castigated him mostly for issuing the *Laconia* order.

On September 12, 1942, under the command of Werner Hartenstein, the *U-156* torpedoed and sank the passenger liner *Laconia.* In addition to the passengers and crew, there were 1,800 Italian prisoners of war on board. Hundreds of survivors jumped into the sea where they were attacked by sharks. When Hartenstein heard survivors shouting in Italian, and realized that his Allies were dying, he notified U-boat Control and launched a massive rescue operation without receiving authority to do so. He plucked survivors out of the water and took lifeboats in tow. Once he took the initiative, Doenitz had little choice but to back his decision by ordering nearby U-boats to lend assistance.

Hartenstein transmitted a message in plain English in which he requested aid from the Allies. He promised not to attack any rescue vessels provided that he was not attacked. The British thought the transmission was a ruse to lure vessels to destruction. A British plane dropped depth charges next to the *U-156*, causing damage. Hartenstein put the survivors back in the water, cut the towline to the lifeboats, and crash-dived. Later, rescue operations were recommenced in haphazard fashion, but most of the *Laconia's* survivors drowned or were eaten by sharks.

Hitler was furious. He lashed out with such strong condemnation of the way the affair was handled that Doenitz was forced to issue instructions that read, in part, "No attempt of any kind must be made at rescuing members of ships sunk."

His defenders claimed that Doenitz fought a humanitarian war. One might ask, How does one fight a humanitarian war whose purpose is to subjugate people who do not wish to be killed or enslaved?

Doenitz was found guilty of war crimes. He was sentenced to ten years and ten days in prison. He served every day of his sentence.

Last of the Litter

The *U-869* was among of the last of the Fuhrer's U-boats that was completed in time to see service in the war. Its construction was completed in 1944 at the Deschimag yard in Bremen, Germany. A Type IX-C-40 measured 250 feet in length and 22 feet abeam. Its displacement tonnage approximated 1,545 tons submerged, and 1,232 tons on the surface.

The offensive armament of a Type IX-C-40 consisted of twenty-two torpedoes that could be launched from six tubes: four in the bow, two in the stern. For defense on the surface, it was armed with four 20-millimeter anti-aircraft guns, and possibly one or more 37-millimeter guns, or perhaps even 15-millimeter guns.

The uncertainty is due to the ongoing changes in

tactics near the end of the war, and consequent alterations in gun configurations. No guns are extant on the wreck. Possibly they were dragged off the hull by clam dredges or fishing trawls before divers first visited the wreck. (See Appendix One for more on damage caused by dredges and trawls.)

The number of torpedoes may have been reduced to fourteen for the final patrol. Extra torpedoes were carried outside the pressure hull under the outer hull or skin. These had to be hefted through the torpedo loading hatches by means of block and tackle. A U-boat was unable to dive during this lengthy procedure, making it a sitting duck for antisubmarine aircraft.

For propulsion, the U-boat was fitted with two diesel engines and two electric motors. Because the diesel engines consumed enormous quantities of air, they could be operated only when the U-boat was on the surface, or when it was running at periscope depth with the snorkel extended. Maximum speed on the surface was about 18 knots. When the U-boat was submerged, its two propellers were driven by a pair of electric motors that drew their power from large storage cells. Top speed underwater was about 7 knots.

On electric motors, the U-boat could proceed at 4 knots for fifteen hours before the energy that was stored in the batteries was depleted. The range at 4 knots was sixty miles. The U-boat's endurance was longer at reduced speed: theoretically, it could travel one hundred twenty miles at 2 knots. Once exhausted, the batteries had to be recharged by the diesel engines.

Even without propulsion, the amount of oxygen that the crew consumed limited overall submergence endurance to between thirty-six and forty-eight hours.

From Predator to Prey

The *U-869* was under the command of Kapitanleutnant Hellmut Neuerburg. The U-boat traveled from Germany to occupied Norway, where it docked at Kristansand. When it departed for its first war patrol - on December 8, 1944 - it had orders to proceed to an operational area off the U.S. eastern seaboard: a distance that measured 4,500 miles along the chosen route.

Theoretically, the *U-869* was capable of traveling 432 nautical miles in 24 hours on diesel engines, or 168 miles on electric motors. In reality, its daily progress was far less, because the sky was thick with alert Allied aircraft, and because numerous aggressive Allied vessels patrolled the sea. As a result of this constant surveillance and harassment, a U-boat was forced to travel submerged most of the time. It never traveled on the surface during the day, when its distinctive profile was easily spotted. Nor could it travel all night on the surface, because enemy aircraft and warships were equipped with radar, which spotted a U-boat even better than human eyes did during the day.

The snorkel, which permitted a U-boat to proceed with its hull submerged, thus reducing the size of its profile, was not too small to be detected. At high speed, the snorkel created a wake that was visible from the air by day; at night, the snorkel could be detected by evermore sophisticated radar. When a U-boat was submerged, it could then be detected by sonar.

It is commonly misunderstood that a U-boat traveled at full speed on its diesel engines when it ran with its snorkel extended. In reality, a U-boat used only one diesel engine for propulsion; it used the other diesel engine to recharge the batteries for the electric motor. As soon as a U-boat was chased beneath the surface, it started draining the batteries that were in most cases only partially recharged. Furthermore, the snorkel tube and the submerged hull created hydrodynamic drag that prevented a U-boat from achieving its highest operational speed. The snorkel assembly could be damaged at too high a speed.

A plethora of Allied warships and aircraft patrolled the North Sea and the North Atlantic Ocean. They traveled almost completely unopposed. U-boats had to slink through the sea and maintain a constant vigil in order to survive. Whenever a plane was spotted in the air, or the silhouette of a vessel was observed on the horizon, prudence demanded that a U-boat crash-dive. If it was detected from the sky, aircraft homed in on the U-boat and delivered harassing depth-charge attacks. The pilots then radioed for surface support. Navy vessels converged on the last reported position, detected the U-boat on sonar, then tracked and attacked it to submission, putting it on the defensive.

Once located, the submerged U-boat was harried incessantly with hedgehogs and depth charges. It was forced to go deep and engage in avoidance maneuvers in order to avert destruction. Even if the U-boat managed to escape unharmed - or with only minimal damage - it had to wiggle like a worm on an angler's hook, turning this way and that. These radical turns and reduction in speed slowed its approach to its destination.

The gray wolf was now the hunted instead of the hunter. The *U-869* took a circuitous route that was intended to decrease the chance of enemy contact, or to avoid it altogether. This route carried the U-boat north of Iceland, westward through the passage between Iceland and Greenland, then south into the North Atlantic. This distance measured some 2,000 miles, and took thirty days to travel. The forward progress of the *U-869* averaged 60 nautical miles per day.

After an entire month at sea, the *U-869* was not even halfway to its operational area.

Ultra Decrypt

The most closely guarded secret of World War Two was code-breaking intelligence.

Every U-boat carried a deciphering machine called Enigma. Outgoing messages were encoded by a complicated system of wheels and disks prior to transmission. Incoming messages had to be decoded by Enigma before they could be read.

Polish and British mathematicians broke the German machine ciphers early in the war. For some time afterward, Britain did not let anyone - including the U.S. - know that it was reading German transmissions.

British radios monitored transmissions from U-boat Control to the various U-boats at sea, as well as transmissions from individual U-boats to U-boat Control.

These messages were forwarded to code breakers at Bletchley Park, in London. Intelligence experts deciphered the messages, collated the information, and wrote analyses for use by military authorities, none of whom knew where the intelligence originated. Decoded messages were dispatched to appropriate commands. These decoded messages, or decrypts, were stamped Ultra Top Secret (which meant above and beyond Top Secret). Thus the British were able to read operational orders, U-boat movements, attack reports, and so on.

Communiqués between Doenitz and his wolf packs not only offered insights into the way in which the Admiral was running the U-boat war, but they provided the exact location of any U-boat that transmitted its position to U-boat Control. In addition, high-frequency direction-finding technology (known as HF/DF, or huff-duff) was used to obtain radio fixes on a U-boat's transmission location.

The position of every U-boat was plotted on a gigantic plotting board. Constant updates permitted staff officers to note each U-boat's current position, to track its course, and to project its track by extrapolating its speed and bearing.

The New Ally

After the U.S. entered the war, the Brits shared this information with Naval intelligence experts. The Navy established a Submarine Tracking Room in Washington, DC; it was the American counterpart of the British facility at Bletchley Park.

Eventually, there grew a need for the greater organization and dissemination of Ultra decrypts. In May 1943, the U.S. Navy created a separate antisubmarine command that was known as the Tenth Fleet. The Tenth Fleet was staffed by some fifty personnel, but had no ships.

Adjacent to the Submarine Tracking Room was a

"Secret Room." This room was kept locked at all times. Only five people had keys to this room: the lieutenant in charge (John Parsons), his assistant John Boland, two yeomen, and "the Navy's principal U-boat tracker, Kenneth Knowles." The Secret Room was where all the U-boats' positions were plotted from Ultra decrypts. Commander Knowles then transferred these positions to the Submarine Tracking Room "without revealing the source of his information."

A Submarine Tracking Officer was assigned to make course interpolations that were based not only on enemy transmissions, but on reported sightings. In the plotting room, the STO drew tracks on a huge wall chart. These tracks were updated continuously as new intelligence was received or intercepted. This system enabled the STO to extrapolate the time at which a particular U-boat might arrive at a specified location. He would then disseminate this information to Navy hunter-killer groups that consisted of small aircraft carriers and heavily armed escorts. These hunter-killer groups would crisscross the predicted coordinates, and pounce on the unwary U-boat with a multitude of planes and fast escort vessels that dropped depth charges and hedgehogs with incredible accuracy. It was this awesome offensive power that placed U-boats on the defensive.

Track Record

On January 6, 1945, Neuerburg sent a radio message to U-boat Control in which he gave his position as 56° North latitude, 27° West longitude. U-boat Control acknowledged receipt of the message, and replied with instructions to furnish the status of his fuel reserve. According to post-war analysis of U-boat Control's diary, Control expressed "some concern about the submarine as she should have been considerably further south-west."

Neuerburg radioed the requested report. U-boat Control ordered the *U-869* to "continue southward cruise." According to a Tenth Fleet intelligence summary, "She is expected to arrive in the New York area at the beginning of February." The operational area was further refined to "about 70 miles southeast of New York approaches."

More than a month before its arrival, the commander of the Eastern Sea Frontier knew the ultimate destination of the *U-869*. Forewarned was forearmed. The U.S. Navy waited patiently for the appearance of the Fuhrer's lone wolf.

The Message Muddle

U-boat Control pondered the inadequate speed and exorbitant fuel consumption of the *U-869*. After due deliberation, it ordered a change in the U-boat's operational area to Gibraltar. Allied radio listeners intercepted this message, but apparently Neuerburg did not. He continued toward New York unaware of the change of orders.

The STO made an assessment of the situation. He concluded that the "*U-869* shifted radio watch without orders and missed this signal."

According to an Ultra decrypt that was dated January 25, the *U-869* was then "south of Newfoundland heading for New York approaches, although her location is uncertain due to a mix up in orders and Control assumes she is heading for Gibraltar."

While U-boat Control was waiting for the *U-869* to announce its entry to the Mediterranean Sea on or about February 1, Naval forces in the Eastern Sea Frontier were preparing a reception off the coast of New Jersey: "The *Core* will begin sweeping for this U/Boat shortly prior to proceeding against the U/Boats reporting weather in the North Atlantic." The *Core* was a baby flattop that was attended by a bevy of destroyer escorts. The flotilla was known as a hunter/killer group. Despite Ultra intelligence, the *Core* group was unable to connect with the *U-869*.

The *U-869* maintained radio silence as it proceeded to its doom.

Outward Bound

On the morning of February 11, 1945, fast convoy CU-58 departed from New York Harbor, bound for the eastern Atlantic. Nine warships escorted the heavily armed freighters and tankers. Two of these warships were destroyer escorts: the *Howard D. Crow* (DE-252), under the command of Lieutenant John Nixon; and the *Koiner* (DE-331), Lieutenant Commander Charles Judson in command. The officers and crew on the *Howard D. Crow* were in the service of the U.S. Coast Guard. The men on the *Koiner* were U.S. Navy personnel.

The convoy proceeded on a baseline bearing of 143° from Ambrose light. The convoy zigzagged periodically by making course changes to port and starboard of the base course. A zigzag target was difficult to strike because a U-boat skipper had to lead the target with his torpedo: that is, he had to predict the point at which the course of the target and the course of his torpedo would intersect. He did this by estimating the speed and direction of the target, then by calculating the point of intersection on a computer. When a target zigzagged, both its direction and its forward progress changed unpredictably.

A standard torpedo traveled like a bullet: in a straight-line course that could not be altered once it was launched. The Germans countered the zigzag tactic by introducing a FAT torpedo that ran straight for a set period of time, then made a series of back and forth loops until it struck something (or ran out of propellant). The FAT torpedo was used against convoys. They also had an acoustic torpedo that zeroed in on propeller cavitation and could change its course in flight. The acoustic torpedo was employed against attacking warships. (For an in-depth discussion of torpedoes, see Appendix One.)

Contact!

At 4:39 in the afternoon, Howard Denson, the sonar operator on the *Howard D. Crow*, detected a suspicious object in the distance. The sonar unit "pinged" whenever its signal echoed off a hard object. Denson alerted the anti-submarine warfare officer, Ensign George King. Because the ping was solid, indicating that the object was made of steel, King was so certain that the object was an enemy submarine that he ordered immediate preparations for a hedgehog attack without waiting for confirmation from the captain.

The destroyer escort peeled away from the convoy to investigate. Fourteen minutes after the initial contact, she approached the moving object and fired a full load of hedgehogs: twenty-four Mark 10 projectiles, which stood in a box like quills on the back of a hedgehog (or its North American counterpart, the porcupine).

Unlike depth charges, which detonated at a pre-set depth, hedgehogs detonated only when they struck a solid object. If the hedgehogs failed to detonate, the implication was that they had not struck anything solid (although a detonator malfunction was a possible explanation). Soft sand generally was not firm enough to detonate a hedgehog.

The hedgehogs were launched ahead of the vessel, like miniature missiles in a cluster with an elliptical pattern. Each hedgehog carried a warhead that contained 38 pounds of high explosive. Eighteen hedgehogs flew from the launching box; six failed to fire. According to the *Howard D. Crow's* deck log, the attack caused "explosions beneath surface."

A hedgehog landed on a hard target in the water column! (Although the plural form was used in the deck log, surviving witnesses stated that only one hedgehog detonated.)

In the carpenter's workshop, Robert Quigley was not aware that an attack was being launched. The detonations were so powerful that he believed that a torpedo had struck the ship. When he ran onto the deck, he saw an oil slick spreading on the surface of the sea. He asked his bunkmate Ted Siviec, "What's happening?"

Siviec had just fired the hedgehogs and was busy throwing the duds over the side. "We're attacking a sub."

Lieutenant Nixon sounded the general alarm. The warship came to life like a disturbed hornet's nest, as officers and men raced to battle stations.

The submerged target seemed to be attempting to slink away from its powerful opponent. The destroyer escort maneuvered into position for another attack.

In order to protect the merchantmen in her charge, it was not necessary for the warship to *destroy* a lurking U-boat. It was necessary only to keep a U-boat submerged until the convoy passed safely out of range. Lieutenant Nixon transmitted a request for assistance from another escort.

At 5:17, the *Howard D. Crow* dropped four depth charges that resulted in "air bubbles and oil slick." Siviec recalled that the oil slick was half a mile in length.

The headphones were practically glued to Denson's head. He listened for every nuance in the sonar pings. The destroyer escort maneuvered like a pugilist in the boxing ring, turning in accordance with Denson's instructions as he gauged the strength and direction of the echoes that were returned to his headset.

By 5:44, the *Howard D. Crow* was in position for another attack on the target, which appeared to be moving slowly along the bottom. Before the submarine could creep away, the destroyer escort dropped three more depth charges with identical results.

The *Koiner* detached herself from the convoy and charged into the fray. At 6:31, as the *Howard D. Crow* stood by, continuously pinging the target, the *Koiner* dropped a pattern of depth charges on a target that was no longer in motion. She dropped a second pattern ten minutes later. She dropped yet a third pattern at 6:54.

Neither vessel displayed navigation lights. They proceeded blacked-out in the utter darkness of night. The *Koiner* stopped her engines and "lowered a motor whale boat to investigate water over dropped charges." Tank tender Ralph Kern remembered being shown an oil-soaked rag that the chief of the boat collected from the attack site.

The surface of the sea was coated with diesel oil. Nonetheless, Lieutenant Commander Judson, captain of the *Koiner* and the senior officer on the scene, declared the contact as "non-sub." He ordered the *Koiner* and the *Howard D. Crow* to return to their stations alongside the convoy.

In a report of the incident, evaluators concurred with the opinion of Lieutenant Commander Judson. "*Koiner's* report of non-sub was made on the basis that there was no movement, that any apparent movement previously was caused probably by current and that repeated attacks on the still target continued to bring oil to the surface, indicating the target to be a wreck, submarine or otherwise."

Little did they know!

Counterpoint

Judson's intra-service bias may have been partially responsible for his opinion that the contact was not a submarine. Navy personnel looked down upon Coast Guard crews as second-rate sailors. This rivalry may have led him - perhaps subconsciously - to deny credit to the Coast Guard for sinking a German U-boat. In making his report, he relied upon the fact that the target was not moving at the time the *Koiner* arrived on the scene. He discounted the *Howard D. Crow's* report that the target had been moving prior to her hedgehog attack, and then was moving slowly prior to her first depth-charge attack.

It is possible that the *Howard D. Crow* either disabled the U-boat or depth-charged it to destruction before the arrival of the *Koiner*. In either case, the target did not move after the arrival of the *Koiner* because either the U-boat was incapable of propulsion, or because it was completely flooded and everyone inside was dead.

Judson may very well have acted in good faith. In any case, his primary responsibility was the protection of the convoy, not the destruction of U-boats. He would have been in serious trouble had the convoy been attacked during his absence.

Nonetheless, there were those who disagreed with Judson's hasty assessment. Moyers tracked down Harold Muth, whose qualifications were impeccable. Before transferring to the *Howard D. Crow*, Muth served as quartermaster, signalman, and soundman on the Coast Guard cutter *Triton,* from April 1941 to July 1943. The *Triton* operated out of Key West, Florida with U.S. submarines, training junior Naval officers in anti-submarine operations.

Muth: "We tracked submarines with our sound gear five days a week for thirteen months. I was . . . in front of the soundstack every single one of those days. I was quite familiar with the performance and limitations of the equipment. We never obtained contact with the submarines at a distance over 3000 yards (mile and a half). We knew that was the greatest distance possible with the sound gear that was available and being used by our navy and coast guard vessels."

Muth was the Gunnery Officer on the *Howard D. Crow* at the time of the attack against the *U-869*. "We knew we were chasing a sub. No doubt in our minds whatsoever. The target was moving on a course almost the same as ours."

According to Muth, "One of the most important aspects to this incident is the distance the *Crow* traveled (at least 3 1/2 nm) before it overtook the *U-869*. It was not possible to pick up a sonar contact at that great a distance. . . . We had a moving target. Wrecks are not moving targets, in spite of the contention of the Escort Cdr that the slight movement 'probably was caused by current'."

During Muth's service aboard the *Triton*, the cutter was involved in the destruction of two U-boats: the *U-157* and the *U-576*. (See Appendix Four for details of the loss of both U-boats.) Even though the *Triton* did not make the actual kills, Muth must have gained considerable experience in antisubmarine action.

Muth: "Regarding the non-submission of an ASW report. The CO [Commanding Officer] of the *Koiner*, a

LCDR [Lieutenant Commander], was the SOPA (Senior Officer Present Afloat) when his ship arrived on scene. He sent in the msg [message] categorizing the contact as non-sub. Our CO., a LT [Lieutenant], and a just recent CO, did not want to contradict a superior. I think he should have submitted an ASW-1 Report, regardless, but he didn't. The officers on board that participated in the attacks, as well as the crew members were disappointed about it, but we knew he was between the rock and the hard place, so we didn't press the point. Besides, he was our CO. It was not wise to question your CO's judgement.

"Regarding the lack of debris, etc.: There was diesel oil released and there was a continuation of air bubbles coming to the surface. The amount of oil is questionable. Diesel oil disperses rapidly when reaching the surface, especially if there is any significant wave action at the time. There was enough released to enable us to track it to its source and use that as a reference point to release the depth charges. . . . When we departed the scene of the *869* it was close to nightfall. Not the best of visibility conditions. No lights of any kind could be exhibited. Strictly forbidden."

Gone - and Forgotten

All the elements of convoy CU-58 proceeded unaware of the successful attack which the *Howard D. Crow* and the *Koiner* had prosecuted against the misplaced German U-boat. CU-58 was not again molested. The convoy split in two northeast of the Azores. Five escorts accompanied their charges into the English Channel, while the other four escorts led their charges into the Irish Sea. All cargoes were delivered safely.

The *U-869* failed to reply to messages, leading U-boat Control to suppose that it had been destroyed by Allied forces off Gibraltar.

To Tenth Fleet analysts, the *U-869* simply vanished. No more radio intercepts originated from Neuerburg. The track on the plotting board simply faded to nothing.

Evaluators in the Eastern Sea Frontier believed that the *Howard D. Crow* and the *Koiner* had attacked a stationary object that was probably a shipwreck.

And there matters stood.

In retrospect, we now know that the closest shipwreck lay five miles north of the *U-869*: an unidentified steamship known as the Herbert Parker. The next closest shipwreck lay twenty miles away: the Norwegian freighter *Bidevind*, which was torpedoed on April 30, 1942 by the *U-752*.

Mistaken Assessment

After Germany's capitulation, the Allies organized an Assessment Committee that was charged with the monumental task of culling German U-boat records for the purpose of determining which U-boats were responsible for sinking which Allied vessels, and which warships and aircraft should be given credit for sinking which U-boats.

The assessors learned that U-boat Control had redirected the *U-869* to Gibraltar. U-boat Control "apparently chose 20 February for her loss without any other basis than the fact that *U-869* made no reports while in her operational area and the date therefore would have to be an arbitrary one. It is noted that there were no attacks made on shipping in the Gibraltar Area while *U-869* was there."

The assessors correlated Allied attack reports with U-boat Control's evaluation. They reviewed three attacks that showed promise by dint of their occurrence at the approximate place and date: (1) USS *Atherton* on February 18; (2) USS *O'Toole* on February 26, and (3) USS *Fowler* and F.S. *L'Indiscret* on February 28. "Of these attacks, (3) above appears the most promising, particularly the resulting debris where depth of water was 1256 fathoms [7,536 feet, or nearly a mile and a half]. . . . In event none of the above attacks is acceptable to the Committee, it follows that loss of the *U-869* must be attributed to 'Cause Unknown'."

Cause Unknown meant that no one received credit

for the kill. Coupling this unwelcome situation with the German assumptions of the time and place of the loss, the assessors recommended reassessment. *"Fowler* established sonar contact at 2900 yards. A pattern of magnetic depth charges was dropped and two explosions occurred 12 and 20 seconds later, followed by 3 or 5 explosions 92 to 128 seconds after the dropping of the first charge. 15 minutes later debris was seen rising to the surface at the scene of the attack. Another pattern of magnetic depth charges was dropped in the middle of the debris, which covered an area of approximately 250 yards. Two explosions occurred 100 and 120 seconds after dropping of the first charge, with no further evidence of damage. The debris reported appeared to consist of lumps and balls of heavy oil sludge. No samples were recovered. Depth of water was 1265 fathoms. 8 hours and 15 minutes later the F.S. *L'Indiscret* attacked a sonar contact in the same area, which caused a large black object to break surface and immediately sink. The object was unidentified and no debris was sighted. No action report was received from *L'Indiscret*, the information on her attack being obtained from an intercepted dispatch. Contact was not regained."

According to the Tactical Analysis Officer's Opinion, "It is not possible to differentiate between the relative effectiveness of the two attacks."

With a stroke of the pen, "probably not sunk" was changed to "probably sunk." Credit for sinking the *U-869* was given - somewhat arbitrarily - to the *Fowler* and the *L'Indiscret.*

And history was made! (Or created.)

This was not the last time that history was "made."

The Secret of Secrets

My faithful readers must be wondering why the Assessment Committee did not take into account the decrypted messages and the plotting room analyses of the Submarine Tracking Officer. The answer is simple: the Assessment Committee was not given access to

Ultra.

As noted above, the breaking of the German codes was the most closely guarded secret of the war - and it remained the most closely guarded secret until thirty years *after* the war. In the United States, the Official Secrets Act included provisions for severe penalties for anyone who released information about Ultra decryption.

Only twenty years had passed between the end of the Kaiser's bid for world domination, and the commencement of the Fuhrer's bid to conquer the world. To the average person, it might appear that the cultural imperative of the German people was aberrant: Germans either lacked good conscience or were pathologically unstable. Twice in the span of a single generation, they had been led like sheep to follow brutal and bloodthirsty leaders who convinced them that they had the right to enslave the rest of humanity. Some people were understandably nervous about another display of German might.

If Germany learned that its codes had been broken, it could be presumed that it would develop a new encryption system in contemplation of war. As long as Germany was secure in the wrongful knowledge that its encryption system was secure, it would lack the incentive to develop a new system.

But the real reason for secrecy was far more prescient: the U.S. and England did not trust their temporary ally, and were already anticipating trouble with Russia after the war. The Soviets were unaware of the code-breaking success and Ultra decrypts. Whenever U.S. and British intelligence units forwarded information to their Russian counterparts, the originating source was withheld. This led Russia to believe that the information originated from spies. Russia was primarily concerned with the accuracy of intelligence, not its origin. As long as the Soviets believed that human informers were responsible for intelligence leaks, and accepted the ability of the U.S. and England to plant spies and recruit local agents, their natural paranoia would induce them to look for spies that did not exist. This would cause them to waste precious time and energy in a worthless pursuit, while protecting the secret that gave the Allies a military advantage in gathering intelligence.

The Assessment Committee based its assessments on partial information. By extrapolation, every assessment that the Committee made is suspect. I make this statement without prejudice. The vogue today is to bash the assessors for making the errors that they made. On the contrary, I think they did a remarkable job in consideration of the fact that so much of the truth was withheld from them. By way of comparison, if you were asked to tabulate a column of numbers, and were not given all the numbers, how close do you think you could get to the correct answer?

In England, everyone who worked at Bletchley Park, or who possessed privileged knowledge of Enigma decryption, was prevented by law from releasing information about decoding operations for *fifty* years. Despite this extra security measure, the Ultra secret was exposed when it became publicly available in the U.S. in 1975.

By then, evaluations of the U-boat war were firmly implanted in the historical record. The circumstances surrounding U-boat losses and successes were cast in a substance that was longer lasting than bronze: they were cast in ink. The flaws that were inherent in the assessment system persevered. Assessments became gospel.

Assessment Fallibility and the *U-166*

The *U-869* was not the only U-boat that was found where it was not supposed to be. Nor was it the only U-boat whose loss was miscredited.

The *U-166* is a perfect case in point. Ten years after the discovery of the *U-869*, the identification of the *U-166* created a stir among historians.

According to the records, the *U-166* was supposed to have been sunk off the coast of Louisiana when a

Coast Guard amphibious plane dropped its sole depth charge on a U-boat as it was submerging. This incident occurred in broad daylight on August 1, 1942. The aircraft's radioman reported that he saw the depth charge detonate alongside the hull. The aircraft was credited with the kill, and the pilot was later awarded the Distinguished Flying Cross for his timely action.

The depth of water where the attack was plotted was 120 feet. Search efforts throughout the years failed to find a U-boat at that location.

The wreck was located accidentally in 1986 during a routine oil and gas survey, but it was not correctly identified until 2001. The actual site was located 140 miles east of the aerial attack position, south of the Florida panhandle in 5,000 feet of water.

Modern historians researched the circumstances surrounding the U-boat's loss. They found that the Coast Guard plane probably depth-charged the *U-171*, which escaped undamaged and returned to Germany, where it reported a depth-charge attack by a floatplane at the place and on the date in question.

Historians then re-evaluated the attack report that was filed by the *PC-566*. She was escorting the passenger-freighter *Robert E. Lee* when that vessel was torpedoed and sunk. (See Appendix Four for full details.) The *PC-566* then dropped nine depth charges on a submerged target that was detected by her sonar unit. Due to the lack of convincing evidence, she was not credited with a kill. When the *U-166* was identified in 2001, its wreckage lay only one mile from the site of the *Robert E. Lee*. The depth charges of the *PC-566* must have sent the U-boat to the bottom.

Thus the discovery of the *U-869* was not unique in resulting in a correction to the historical records. Fifty-nine years passed before the true circumstances of the loss of the *U-166* came to light. Undoubtedly, additional corrections will continue to be made as the ocean frontier is more fully explored. The process is ongoing and never-ending.

Travel Time

In order to bolster his claim that the *U-869* was the unsuspecting victim of the *Howard D. Crow* and the *Koiner*, Harold Moyers split the U-boat's journey into two segments: from Norway to its known mid-ocean transmission point, and from its mid-ocean transmission point to its final resting place. He extrapolated the travel time of the second leg from the progress rate of the first leg (60 nautical miles per day, or 69 statute miles).

Since it took thirty days to traverse the first leg (about 2000 miles), it would have taken approximately thirty-five days to traverse the second leg (about 2400 miles). In this scenario, the U-boat would have arrived on the very day that the *Howard D. Crow* and the *Koiner* made their attacks.

Furthermore, in lamenting the time that a U-boat expended to reach its operational area, German records corroborated the average progress rate of 60 nautical miles per day.

After discovering the attack report, Moyers drew a line between New York Harbor and the wreck site. He found that the compass bearing was 143° - the same bearing as the baseline track of the convoy. Thus the error in location lay directly along the course of the convoy, not to either side. In other words, the error was one of distance traveled. A slight misinterpretation of forward progress could easily account for such an error. Such errors were commonplace during zigzag maneuvers.

Both the time and the place coincided.

Other Attacks

From the Tenth Fleet Anti-Submarine Analysis and Statistical Section, I compiled a list of after action reports in the vicinity of the *U-869*, for the time following February 11 to the end of the war. I plotted the positions that were given in these reports on a nautical chart. Of forty-three reported incidents, the closest attack was sixteen miles from the wreck site; that attack took place on April 29, fully two and a half months after the *U-869* arrived in its operational area. The next closest attack occurred twenty miles away, on March 9. Three other attacks occurred at a distance of twenty miles, all between March 12 and March 18. The next closest attack took place at a distance of twenty-five miles, on April 11.

Moyers found three additional incidents that preceded the sinking of the *U-869*: one at a distance of fifteen miles, the other two at a distance of twenty miles. Despite the statement that was attributed to Chatterton on page 185 of *Shadow Divers* - "Not a single thing happened anywhere near our wreck site during the entire war. Nothing." - there was a great deal of U-boat activity in the area during the final months of the U-boat war.

Assessors might overlook or misevaluate the loss of a U-boat, but a dedicated researcher should not have overlooked a single incident report, much less a slew of them.

Positional Accuracy

Nearly all the positional data that was recorded for attacks - both those of Allied warships against sonar contacts, and those of U-boats against merchant vessels - gave the latitude and longitude within a parameter of three to five miles.

In those pre-electronic days, a vessel began a voyage from a point that was known with absolute precision. Inaccuracies were introduced as soon as the vessel got out of sight of land or aids to navigation (buoys and lightships): from the set of the current, and from the direction and intensity of the wind. If the sky was clear, periodic sextant sightings were taken in order to "get a fix" on the vessel's location.

Latitude could be determined by the height of the sun. To obtain the longitude, the navigator had to "shoot" the sun or a star through the lens and mirrors of a sextant, note the precise time from a chronometer, then make complex calculations from an almanac of

algorithmic tables. If five navigators all took their sightings from the bridge of the same vessel, they were likely to obtain five different positions - hopefully within
three to five miles of each other. That was why navigators were especially careful as they approached shore
or shoals in fog.

An overcast sky prevented sightings from being
taken - sometimes for days or weeks on end. In that
case, a vessel was navigated mostly by her estimated
course and speed, with sharp attention being placed on
soundings (depth of water). This system was called
"dead reckoning" - abbreviated from "deduced reckoning," but sometimes a more accurate description, as
reliance upon such a system might cause a vessel to
run aground.

When an escort vessel separated from her convoy to
chase a moving sonar contact, then made radical
course changes during the prosecution of attacks, the
plotting officer used a dead reckoning track computer
to obtain the bearings, speeds, and times, which he
then drew on a chart. The computer calculated the distance from shaft revolutions, but did not take current
or wind into account. Absolute precision could never be
obtained by such a method, especially if the programmed starting point was inaccurate.

The *U-352* serves as a prime example of the inaccu-
racy that was inherent in taking sextant sightings. (See
Appendix Three for details of the loss and discovery of
the *U-352*.) The Navy put divers down on the wreck several days after it was sunk. The location was duly
noted. Even so, the salvage vessel was unable to relocate the wreck after a two-day return to port. The
search continued for four days before the Navy abandoned the search. When wreck-divers located the wreck
thirty-three years later, they found it a mile and a quarter away from the given latitude and longitude. Keep in
mind the fact that the original Navy sightings had been
taken on a wreck that was stationary.

The GPS coordinates of the wreck of the *U-869* are
39-33.949 North, 73-02.436 West. The latitude and

longitude of the attack location, which was estimated by the *Howard D. Crow* - was 39° 31' north, 72° 59' west. These two points are 4.5 nautical miles apart.

This distance falls within the parameters of positional accuracy that could best be expected at the time.

Deck Log Data

Notwithstanding the above, Muth correlated the relative positions of the hunter and the hunted. "The best and probably the only way to determine the *Crow's* correct position is to reference the 2000 position, normally obtained by star sights. The ship's log establishes the 2000 position as 39 28 N. - 72 56 W. That can be considered as a fact.

"The log also indicates that the *Crow* traveled 8.4 nautical miles between 1900 and 2000. That is a fact. If one would backtrack on course 323 (the reciprocal of the *Crow's* actual course of 143 degrees) from the 2000 position 8.4 nautical miles, that arrived-at position would be almost on top of the established position of the *U-869.*"

Coast Guard Affirmation

Harold Moyers submitted his convoy CU-58 data to the U.S. Coast Guard Historians' Office. After examining his evidence, Coast Guard historians did not hesitate to adopt his conclusion that the destroyer escorts *Howard D. Crow* and *Koiner* should be given official credit for sinking the *U-869.*

It is ironic that, while one branch of the Coast Guard lauded Moyers' research efforts, another branch was dispatched to prevent him from attempting to obtain additional proof.

CHAPTER TWO
Identification of the *U-869*

"There are people who really try to control and direct history."

John Chatterton

Lucky Strike

In 1991, Bill Nagle, owner and skipper of the dive boat *Seeker*, obtained a set of loran coordinates from fishing boat captain named Bogan. These numbers indicated a spot some sixty miles from shore. Bogan had fished the site for years, and thought that it might be the wreck of the *Corvallis*, which he had read about in *Shipwrecks of New Jersey*. The *Corvallis* was a wooden-hulled steamship that was scuttled in 1925 during the filming of a silent movie, *The Half-Way Girl*.

Nagle organized a trip to investigate the site. Chatterton was his sole crewmember. The divers on board were Kevin Brennan, Kip Cochran, Steve Feldman, Lloyd Garrick, John Hildeman, Steve Lombardo, Mark McMahon, Ron Ostrowski, Doug Roberts, Dick Shoe, Paul Skibinski, and John Yurga. They located the wreck exactly where Bogan said it would be found. The divers went down expecting to see the wreckage of a broken down tanker or freighter, or possibly a sailing ship of yesteryear. Submarines were so far from their collective minds that at first glance from a distance they thought the wreck was that of a pipe barge. But it took only moments to realize that they were looking at the unmistakable profile of a submarine. Excitement shot up the anchor line like a jolt of electricity charging up a lightning rod. It was an ecstatic event for all. The date was September 2, 1991.

American or German?

By the sheerest coincidence, Yurga had a book about U-boats on the boat.

The trip was originally scheduled to depart the day before it did. It was blown out due to bad weather. With some free time on his hands, Yurga visited the nearby Brielle Maritime Book Store, which was owned and operated by Bill Schmoldt. He purchased a generic book that described U-boats in a very general way. It was strictly leisure reading material which would help to pass the time.

After the dive, he and the other divers compared the pictures in the book with the submarine that they had seen on the bottom. On the spot, although no one could speak with any authority, they formed the consensus that the submarine was not American, but German.

Telephone, Telegraph, Tell-a-Diver

The group conspired to keep the discovery a secret. By excluding other divers from the site, the group hoped to prevent anyone from vying with them for the rich trove of Nazi souvenirs that they wanted to collect for themselves.

The divers grapevine is the only thing in the universe that exceeds the speed of light. Word quickly leaked into the wreck-diving community. As with the discovery of any new wreck, once the secret was revealed, telephone companies experienced overloaded circuits and insulation meltdowns as the transmission wires burned with the newsflash. I was at sea at the time, diving on shipwrecks off the coast of Virginia. Soon afterward, my travels took me to North Carolina, where news of the discovery caught up with me between offshore dive trips. A curious situation occurred upon my return home in October.

Message from the *Twilight Zone*

I received a phone call from a man who spoke with a thick German accent. He did not identify himself. He asked me if I knew about the U-boat that had recently been discovered. I said "Yes" in expectation of a request for an interview, of which I received more than I had time to grant. After a few curt questions concerning what I knew about the U-boat - which was very little - he grew ominous. He spoke as if he were reading from a prepared political speech. I had no opportunity to interrupt. He ranted about the German sailors who had given their lives for the Fatherland, how their bodies were entombed in the submerged iron coffin, and how they were not to be disturbed. He ended by saying, "They are waiting for you. Go see them." Then he disconnected.

The phone call lasted only a minute or so. By the time I realized that he was some kind of a kook, and not a German historian seeking bona fide information, the one-sided conversation was over. I was left with a creepy feeling - as if I had just received a call from the *Twilight Zone*. Did my phone line drape across a Nazi cemetery, to absorb transmissions from the dead? I also wondered why the anonymous harasser picked me to saddle with his philosophical twaddle. I did not find the wreck, I was not on the boat on the day of discovery, and I had yet to dive on the site. My sole involvement so far was that I had heard about it.

At first I thought the call was just a practical joke, played by one of my dive buddies. But no one ever admitted to it; and all were astonished when I spoke about it. I finally concluded that he picked on me because of my book on the U-boat offensive off the U.S. eastern seaboard, *Track of the Gray Wolf* (published in 1989). The volume was dedicated to the men of the merchant marine: those unsung heroes who suffered so much and who died so horribly at the end of German torpedoes. Because the book portrayed these unarmed civilians as victims, Nazi apologizers - those who were sympathetic with the Nazi cause - believed that the book portrayed German U-boat personnel as victimizers. So be it. The many letters of commendation I received from the men and the families of the merchant marine far outweighed the single letter of protest from a group of Nazi sympathizers called Sharkhunters.

Sharkhunters also objected to my accusation that Reinhard Hardegen, skipper of the *U-123*, falsified his log in order to take credit for sinking the *San Jose*, which actually sank as a result of collision with the *Santa Elisa*. Later, in *Operation Drumbeat*, Michael Gannon corroborated my accusation that Hardegen did indeed falsify his log - on more than one occasion.

Cultural Ethics

After news of the discovery hit the newspapers, Chatterton also received a few hostile phone calls. The most vocal was a man from the German embassy in New York. He claimed that divers had no right to dive what he considered to be a war grave, and that to do so constituted desecration of the dead. There are as many viewpoints about the treatment of gravesites as there are people in the world. Arguments are varied and run at various temperatures. Here are a few from each degree.

The bodies of soldiers who were killed in the field of battle are sacrosanct. In giving their lives for their
   country, they earned the inviolable right to conse-
   cration.
There should be no difference in treatment between the
   bodies of soldiers who died in the service of their
   country and the bodies of civilians who died in the
   protection of their country.
All human remains should be treated with utmost
   respect. They should never be moved or touched in
   any way.
Cemeteries no longer receiving bodies can be relocated
   in order to make better use of the land.
If human remains are old enough, they can be
   exhumed, examined, and put on display. (The definition of "old enough" varies.)
Human remains should be cremated and the ashes
   spread by the wind. This obviates dealing with
   remains.

Consider these points and counterpoints. Some Civil War battlefields have been converted to memorial parks, while others have been plowed under so that farmers can grow crops. Some cemeteries have been nationalized and maintained, while others have been paved over for the construction of interstate highways. Some exhumed bodies are relocated and re-interred, while others are destroyed. Some people visit cemeteries on a weekly basis, while others do not dwell on the dead. Some people pay their respects to the dead by placing flowers on graves, while others carry the memories of lost ones in their hearts and find grave visitations unnecessary.

Tomb Raiders?

With regard to U-boats, is a visit to a wreck site less reverential than a visit to a graveyard, such as the National Cemetery in Arlington? Again, arguments are numerous and highly opinionated. Three of the most often visited East Coast wreck sites are World War Two German U-boats: the *U-85* and the *U-352* off North Carolina, and the *U-853* off Rhode Island. (See Appendix Three for details of their losses.) Both the *U-85* and the *U-853* went down with all hands; there were casualties on the *U-352*. Yet no official objections were raised about wreck-divers swimming around or inside *these* sunken tombs, only the newly discovered one.

A U-boat is a machine of war like a German tank or airplane. During World War Two, Germany built some 1,200 U-boats, 20,000 tanks and 120,000 fighter planes and bombers (of which 95,000 were destroyed in action). Yet Panzers and Stukas were never revered. Demolished tanks and crashed aircraft were swept aside like so much trash, without pious veneration. This begs the question: What doctrine dictates the belief that water poured on a war machine converts that machine to a holy receptacle? U-boats are covered with seawater, not holy water.

Even if we grant that the *U-869* is a war grave, the question that is unanswered is: Should it make any difference with respect to anglers fishing on the hull or to divers exploring the interior? Or, for that matter, to commercial fishing vessels that slam their multi-ton dredges against the hull. There is always a bone of contention with regard to the disturbance of human remains. But what constitutes disturbance? Is swimming past a body that is buried under silt any different from walking past a body that is interred in a national cemetery?

Cultural differences abound, and individual outlooks vary from person to person (and often *within* a person during different stages of life). None of these attitudes follow any rhyme or reason, and certainly they have nothing to do with logic. They are all parts of a complicated belief system which, by its very nature, is indefinable and unexplainable.

Interred human remains are often disinterred for a variety of reasons: additional post mortem forensic studies, removal to a more convenient location (or so the original location can be used for other purposes such as shopping malls), and archaeological examination, to name a few. What differentiates "grave robbing" from "exhumation" is pomp and circumstance, ceremonial officiation, or avowal of respect for the dead.

I have seen how archaeologists and politicians claimed "respect" while staring blankly into a television camera. They appeared to be reciting lines that were penned by a scriptwriter. They uttered the politically correct words and phrases, but exhibited none of the pathos that should accompany them. The concept of "respect" has been reduced to a rubber stamp, like a Good Housekeeping Seal of Approval, and the justification for disinterment was qualified by audience appeal. This vociferated respect was patently false and hollow, spoken for appearances and for the sake of imagery, and was easily detectable due to poor acting skills. True respect is a matter of attitude, not recitation.

The U.S. Navy conducted a major dredging operation on the *U-352* in order to make the wreck safer for recreational divers. In the process of removing ordnance and torpedo warheads, Navy divers used an airlift to excavate tons of sand and debris from inside the wreck. How many human bones were sucked up and jetted out through the exhaust tube went unrecorded. The operation was highly publicized, yet no complaints were lodged about desecrating a war grave. (Details of this operation can be found in Appendix Three.)

I have dived on hundreds and hundreds of ship-wrecks over the course of thirty-five years. I have seen human remains on only two of them: the *U-853* and the *Empress of Ireland*. I have never seen bones on the *U-869*.

Taken to Extremes

Just how far is society willing to go in the quest for reverence? Crashed cars and trucks are towed off the nations streets and highways without any thought given to the people who died inside them. Downed commercial and military aircraft are meticulously disassembled, the human body parts are extracted, and the airframe and components are subjected to intense forensic analysis. Ships and boats that sink in navigable waterways are either raised and scrapped, or are demolished in place.

Sixteen sailors lost their lives in the sinking of the Civil War ironclad *Monitor*. Some of the bodies were entombed inside. Yet, in recent years, the U.S. Navy salvaged the wreck piecemeal - taking it apart under water, and recovering discrete pieces for public exhibition.

The Civil War submarine *Hunley* was raised intact, despite the fact that the hull was a vault for eight Confederate sailors. Disarticulated skeletal remains were dug out of the mud with trowels and high-pressure water jets.

The widely scattered pieces of the space shuttle *Challenger* were salvaged. No one complained that the wreckage should be preserved under water as a monument for seven intrepid explorers.

Construction has begun on the site of the Twin Towers, where several thousand citizens died so tragically on September 11, 2001.

One could say that vehicles, planes, spacecraft, ships, boats, and buildings are desecrated all the time. And the statement would be true.

Every museum in the world displays the personal belongings of individuals who died. That is the sole rationale for a museum's existence. Yet no one criticizes museums for procuring the artifacts that they display, nor from profiteering from their exhibits. Every museum piece had to be acquired or recovered from somewhere, whether it was from an auction, an antique dealer, a battlefield, or a shipwreck.

Reverence for the Dead

In parts of Asia, the deceased are decapitated and the heads are reduced to skulls, which are then stacked in piles for exhibition. In this way, reverence for one's ancestors is maintained by visual reference. Such a display might be considered barbaric in modern Germany or America. Elsewhere, the brain and organs are removed and discarded, and the blood is drained and poured into sewers, then replaced with a preserving solution. Yet Asiatics may find autopsies and embalming procedures primitive and disgusting.

Human bodies and body parts are often put on display. In my hometown, the Philadelphia Museum of Art exhibits ancient Egyptian mummies. The Mutter Museum devotes an entire floor to the display of physical abnormalities: a Siamese twin fetus that is preserved in formaldehyde, complete deformed skeletons, skulls that are encrusted with massive calcium deposits, and other specimens of gross mutation. In some civilized countries, historic heads of state are exhibited in glass-topped caskets for public viewing. Some people keep the ashes of their loved ones on the mantelpiece. All of these circumstances are commonly accepted.

So what is the validity of any of these perspectives? I suppose that in a way they are *all* valid - and in a way they are all invalid. Personal values differ as much as cultural values. Yet these differences do not make any set of values right or wrong: they simply form a contrast. Such values can be viewed only relative to each other. The point could be argued that the only wrongs committed are those of intolerance to opposing values, and enforcement of one's values upon those whose values differ. Philosophical musings aside, often what is considered right is merely what is politically correct and currently in vogue.

It should be noted that the complainer from the German embassy was not the ambassador, or even the ambassador's adjutant. His position in the hierarchy was never established. He was an individual who worked at the embassy - in capacity unknown - and happened to have read the newspapers. He was not a spokesperson for the German people. His outspoken opinion was personal, and did not necessarily reflect the majority view in the country of which he was a citizen.

His opinion was diametrically opposed by that of Peter Hess: "In light of the atrocities [committed] by the Nazis, the German government's posturing about the 'desecration' of shipwrecks is, as their Holocaust victims would have declared, chutzpah of the highest order. . . . if a nation wishes to dictate the rules concerning the spoils of war, then it had better win that war."

Gray opinions fall between those of black and white. I have no enlightenment to offer. These ideological issues can be debated endlessly - and futilely. Yet it cannot be denied that present-day Nazi sympathizers hold and express opinions about which they feel very strongly, and that their emotional imperative has the fervor of fanaticism.

U-Who?

In any case, these grumbles from German malcontents were out of place, because at the time these verbal attacks and complaints were made, the nationality of the submarine had not been confirmed as German, and the wreck had not been identified as a victim of war. If it *was* a U-boat, it was possible that the U-boat was one of six that had surrendered to Allied forces after Germany's defeat. These were escorted to U.S. ports, and were later scuttled offshore. Not until the *Seeker* returned to the wreck that autumn did Steve Gatto find the first artifact that was stamped with the eagle and swastika. This was the UZO - unter-wasserziloptic, or torpedo aiming device.

Divers also observed the presence of a few bones inside the pressure hull. At first this fact was kept a closely guarded secret among the patrons of the *Seeker*, so war grave zealots spoke from groundless assumption. In any case, the bones were rare and seldom seen, and were never disturbed.

In light of this new information, the U-boat had to have been sunk during wartime operations. The question now to be reckoned with was: which U-boat was it? Several U-boats are known to have been lost off the eastern seaboard, other than those that are mentioned above. *Track of the Gray Wolf* provided latitude and longitude coordinates for all U-boats that were known to have been lost in the Eastern Sea Frontier (which extended from Maine to Georgia).

The closest - the *U-521* - supposedly lay 110 miles from the site of the wreck. The next closest - the *U-550* - lay 150 miles away. Their locations were established with a fair degree of accuracy, and were corroborated by survivors. Five other U-boats were lost with all hands in the ESF. In each case, an evaluation committee in the Office of Naval Intelligence reviewed the anti-submarine action reports that were submitted by the participants. All five losses were assessed as "probably sunk." These were the *U-215*, *U-576*, *U-857*, *U-879*, and *U-548*. Their locations ranged from the Gulf of Maine to the coast of North Carolina. The closest "probable" lay more than two hundred miles distant. (See Appendix Four for full particulars of all these U-boats.)

It was certainly conceivable that a U-boat that was damaged in action might continue its patrol, only to sink later in another location. But in the present case, Chatterton believed that the severity of the damage precluded any such hypothesis, for the conning tower and its vicinity were almost totally demolished. According to him, the entire tower assembly had been blown off the pressure hull and deposited on the port side of the wreck. The pressure hull at that point was smashed in severely and laid open to the sea. A gaping hole pierced the pressure hull atop the after torpedo room. These holes were large enough to swim through. Such devastation, according to Chatterton, was clearly the result of a direct hit. He envisioned a scenario in which this utter destruction must have occurred so fast that the crew had not had time to close and dog the watertight doors before massive flooding occurred. The U-boat must have gone down like a stone. (However, the reader is directed to Appendix One for a forensic analysis of damage versus deterioration.)

If this were one of the five "probables," the only way to account for its presence was to presume that it had survived an earlier attack in which the assessors determined that it was sunk, when in fact it was lost in a subsequent attack that the assessors failed to credit. (Bear in mind that the assessors did not have access to Ultra, as explained in Chapter One.) My personal library of U-boat books consisted of more than fifty volumes, all of which I had read (except for those that were written in German). I skimmed through the entire collection, but did not find any helpful wisdom.

No identification was made by the time the diving season ended - not even a tentative one. Speculation ran rampant but to no avail. Among the wreck-diving community, the mystery U-boat became known as the U-Who? (question mark included).

Type Cast

There was far more interest in recovering souvenirs than in ascertaining the wreck's name (or number). Divers collected valuable china plates that were stamped with the swastika and German eagle. They also recovered stamped silverware, bottles, brass mechanical parts, and so on. Like any other saltwater wreck, the U-Who? was a grab bag for souvenir hunters.

Some important information was gleaned by continued exploration of the wreck. One of the most telling was the recognition of the U-boat type. The two most common types of U-boats in the German war machine were Type VII and Type IX, each of which was produced with minor variations among the type. Chatterton and Yurga purchased a set of Type IX plans to complement the book that Yurga already had on Type VII U-boats. These plans provided the information that was needed to identify the U-Who?'s type as IX. The obvious characteristics that most distinguished the Type IX from the Type VII were two stern torpedo tubes (the Type VII had one), and the galley location forward of the control room (in the Type VII, the galley was located abaft the control room).

Another clue to the U-boat's identity was a stainless steel dinner knife with a wooden handle, recovered by John Chatterton. Carved in the handle was the name "Horenburg."

The Horenburg Uncertainty

There are two primary methods for identifying a shipwreck: finding an item on which the name of the ship was marked, and through historical research. The first method is preferred because identification is positive. In the second method, inferences can be made and probabilities assigned; and, while one may be certain in one's heart that a wreck has been identified, there is always a shadow of doubt which the purists are quick to note. Wrecks are often identified not by a single datum or item, but by a preponderance of evidence - including exclusionary evidence.

With the diving season over and an engaging puzzle to solve, Chatterton and Yurga delved into the second method. That winter, they spent a week in Germany during which they conducted research in the U-boat archives. They found answers to some of their questions among the records that survived destruction near the end of the war. And, as so often happens in ship-wreck research, some of the answers led to other and more perplexing questions. As this was Chatterton's first foray into the field of shipwreck research, he was understandably baffled.

The only Horenburg in the U-boat service was named Martin. He was a Funkmeister (Radioman 1st Class) who was serving aboard the *U-869* under Kapitanleutnant Helmut Neuerburg when, according to the records, it was sunk with all hands off Casablanca, on February 28, 1945.

So how did a knife with Horenburg's name on it find its way onto the U-Who?? The obvious answer was that Horenburg was on board at the time of the U-boat's loss. So which information was wrong - the loss of the *U-869* off Casablanca, or the muster roll?

Puzzle Pieces

This was only the beginning of a long and round-about trail of detection to unravel the history of the mystery U-boat. Chatterton and Yurga combined their research efforts. Most of the research they conducted consisted of excluding U-boats from the realm of possi-bility. As Yurga phrased it, "We developed multiple the-ories about what boat it was, then tore them down with logical assessment." This laborious process of whittling away contenders is an important part and parcel of shipwreck research that the non-researcher never sees in the finished product.

Another person who involved himself in the identi-fication project was Richie Kohler. After diving on the wreck, he became captivated by the mystery of a real-life naval whodunit. He conducted his own line of research. His major contribution consisted of corre-sponding with German archives and with the relatives of U-boat sailors. Along the way, he decided to write a book about the U-Who?. Eventually, he enticed a pro-duction company to film a television documentary on the discovery and the attempts to identify the wreck. (See Chapter Five for a critique of *Hitler's Lost Sub*.)

Despite these co-operative efforts, the U-Who? remained nameless (or numberless).

Continued exploration divulged new information piecemeal. An aluminum schematic of the trim and ballast system revealed the yard at which the U-boat was built: the Deschimag facility in Bremen. It also revealed the sub-Type as a IX-C-40, of which thirty-five were built at that facility. An escape lung had an aluminum oxygen cylinder that was stamped with a hydrostatic test date of April 15, 1944. The discovery of a snorkel placed the construction time toward the latter part of the war, when snorkels were included in the design. Each clue added a piece to the puzzle by eliminating contenders, and by narrowing the field of possibilities.

Chatterton and Yurga whittled the list of suspects from five to two: the *U-857* and the *U-879.* The *U-857* was reputedly lost off Cape Cod, Massachusetts, on April 7, 1945. The *U-879* was reputedly lost off Cape Cod on April 18, 1945. As there were no survivors from either U-boat, it was conceivable that one of them survived the attack in which it was listed as missing. Despite the best evidence available - the Horenburg knife - they discarded all notions of the *U-869.*

Robert Coppock: U-boat Expert

Chatterton, Yurga, and Kohler shared information not only among themselves, but also with the person who was unquestionably the most knowledgeable U-boat historian in the world: Robert Coppock. Coppock worked for the Ministry of Defence at Great Scotland Yard, in London. He was a specialist in the Foreign Documents Section of the Directorate of Naval Staff Duties. At his fingertips was an immense archive that covered every aspect of World War Two naval operations: printed Allied records as well as microfilms of captured German documents. Whenever possible, he took time from his official obligations to answer inquiries from the public. Correspondence with Coppock indulged in some interesting speculations, because the U-Who?'s very existence contradicted the known documentation.

After Chatterton and Yurga furnished him with their suspicions about the losses of the *U-857* and the *U-879*, Coppock investigated U-boat operational orders during the final stages of the war. He correlated U-boat transmission intercepts with sightings and reports of attacks. He plotted each U-boat's track across the Atlantic Ocean, and he re-assessed the work that was done by the Assessment Committee after the war. The typewritten letter that Coppock wrote upon completing this monumental research project was six single-spaced pages in length.

From the evidence available, he surmised that the mystery U-boat could possibly be either the *U-857* or the *U-879*. He hazarded a guess that Horenburg might have served aboard one of them before being trans-ferred to the *U-869*, and left the knife behind in the rush of transferring to his new assignment.

Coppock calculated that the *U-857* could not have reached its original operational area before March. Tenth Fleet reports of action in the Eastern Sea Fron-tier for the months of March, April, and May (when Ger-many capitulated) contained forty-two separate anti-submarine attacks. The four closest attack positions lay twenty miles away from the wreck of the U-Who?. Five others ranged from twenty-five to sixty miles away. The rest were farther. (Note that Coppock's information differed slightly from mine, which I presented in the previous chapter. I relied upon American archival sources, not British.)

Of the four closest attacks, one was judged to have been made on a wreck, one was considered to have been a non-contact, one was annotated "sinking doubt-ful," and one resulted in dead fish. (Many whales and dense schools of fish and shrimp were depth-charged during the war, because they returned a sonar echo that was suspiciously similar to that of a submerged U-boat.) The attacks that occurred farther away were equally doubtful.

Mark McKellar and the Ultra Secret

Next to enter the picture was Mark McKellar. He was not a diver, but an amateur historian who was researching the last days of the *U-853* for a magazine article. The *U-853* was credited with actions in the Gulf of Maine in April 1945. During the course of his investigations, McKellar began to suspect that the assessors had erred, and that actions that had been ascribed to the *U-853* should properly be ascribed to the *U-857*. His suspicions were based upon newly discovered Ultra decrypts.

As noted in the previous chapter, Ultra was the name of a super secret code-breaking system that the Allies developed during World War Two. It allowed Allied intelligence experts to read a large percentage of intercepted Axis radio transmissions, both army and navy.

Ultra was such a closely guarded secret that even after the war ended, the Allies kept its existence in the strictest confidence. Nothing was written about it, and those who worked with Ultra were not permitted to so much as mention it. Not until thirty years after the end of the war was the Ultra secret declassified, and a new insight into the history of the war made available to the public.

McKellar came across declassified Ultra decrypts that turned the last months of the American U-boat campaign into complete disarray. According to the plotting room, another U-boat - the *U-869* - was working its way across the Atlantic in January 1945. McKellar mentioned this to his friend, Phil McGrath. McGrath was a U-boat aficionado and a long-time dive buddy of mine.

After the U-Who? was discovered, McGrath and I had many long discussions about which U-boat it could be. He told me that McKellar had unearthed some previously unaccessed intelligence records as part of Ultra, but that McKellar would not say exactly what they contained, only that they referred to the existence of another U-boat off the American eastern seaboard. McKellar did not want his article pre-empted, so he kept the particulars to himself. He especially did not want *me* - an established historian and fulltime author - to gain access to his privileged information until after he published.

I felt strongly that McKellar possessed information that Chatterton needed to have. With McGrath acting as our intermediary, I pleaded with McKellar to share his information with Chatterton, even if he would not share it with me. After some urging, McKellar did so. Afterward, during surface interval between dives, I asked Chatterton if he had spoken with McKellar. Chatterton said, "Yes," but did not elaborate.

Documented Verification

At the time, I was deeply involved in researching and writing my Popular Dive Guide Series, which was intended to cover every major shipwreck along the U.S. eastern seaboard. Because I was researching not just one shipwreck but hundreds, I spent a great deal of time at the archival repositories in Washington, DC: the National Archives, the Naval Historical Center, the Library of Congress, the Coast Guard Records Office, the National Records Center, and the Office of the Judge Advocate General. To make efficient use of my time, I generally made weeklong research trips to the nation's capitol. I stayed overnight at the home of my longtime friend, Dave Bluett.

It was a simple matter for me to add the U-Who? to my long list of research topics. To a professional researcher, the mere existence of a document is a step toward its retrieval. Not only had McKellar unknowingly made me aware of the *existence* of relevant records, he had tipped me off about the *kind* of information that he had uncovered: intelligence records. It required very little effort for me to locate the same records, and to confirm that the *U-869* had missed U-boat Command's transmission of orders to alter course for an alternative operational area off Gibraltar.

There was no doubt in my mind that the *U-869* had

continued toward its original operational area in grid square CA 53. This grid square corresponded to an area that lay sixty miles off the New Jersey coast: precisely where the U-Who? was located.

Perhaps McKellar did not positively identify the U-Who? as the *U-869*, but his information was the key to unlocking the mystery of the U-boat's presence in the Eastern Sea Frontier. The Horenburg knife confirmed the U-boat's identity. Chatterton kept his own council, and I kept mine. But by 1993, there was little room for doubt that the U-Who? was indeed the *U-869*.

The identity of the mystery U-boat was thereafter an open secret among wreck-divers.

Coppock Confirms McKellar

McKellar also wrote to Robert Coppock. Now the U-Who? detection team consisted of five confidants: Chatterton, Yurga, Kohler, Coppock, and McKellar. (Out of deference to their priority, I stayed out of the picture except as a facilitator. The American researchers felt that I did not have a "need to know" what they were learning, because they were afraid that I would write about the U-boat.) What they did *not* know was that Coppock was not a participant in their cabal of secrecy. The information that he unearthed was intended for the world, not for a small group of elitists. If another researcher wrote to him to request his expertise on the same subject that a previous researcher had requested, instead of writing another in-depth compilation of his research efforts, he merely sent that researcher copies of prior correspondence that dealt with the matter. This saved Coppock a great deal of time. I obtained the identical information that the other researchers obtained.

(In order to preserve the continuity of the narrative, and to save my faithful readers the trouble of referring to the previous chapter, I will repeat some of the information that was presented in Chapter One. My purpose in this chapter is to demonstrate the investigative procedure the way it occurred, not to present the ultimate truth that Harold Moyers discovered. This process will reveal how wrong conclusions were reached.)

Coppock sent an intelligence summary that was written on January 25, 1945. It stated, "The intentions and location of *U-869* (Neuerburg) who was ordered to the New York area 29 December are obscure since Control sent her a conflicting message 19 January saying that she was expected to arrive in *U-870's* area, off Gibraltar, about 1 February. Based on signals she received it appears likely that *U-869* is continuing toward her original heading off New York."

The Assessors' Handicap

McKellar concluded that the post-war assessors did not have access to Ultra. To my knowledge, he was the first person to do so. Because I had always accepted the assessment reports as gospel, I was sadly disillusioned to learn otherwise.

Without privilege to Ultra, the Assessment Committee made assessments based upon partial information, and assigned locations and credits for losses accordingly. Ultra decrypts revealed a vastly different picture of U-boat activity than was previously held as truth. The overthrow of this accepted dogma cast very strong suspicions on which U-boat was at which location at a particular time, which U-boat attacked which vessel, which Allied command should have received credit for sinking which U-boat, and the time and location of each U-boat loss. The ultimate chapter in the American U-boat campaign needed to be rewritten.

The Coppock Summary

In 1994, I invited Chatterton and Yurga to accompany me on an expedition to dive on the *Lusitania*, off the south coast of Ireland. Our preliminary stay in London afforded the perfect opportunity to visit Coppock in person, in order to share information about the latest underwater discoveries, as well as Coppock's most recent historical research. As a result of this meeting, and despite the exigencies of Coppock's official workload, he engaged the mystery of the mystery U-boat with newfound vigor, and promised to make the time to investigate its disappearance further, and to communicate his findings by mail.

A new picture of Germany's last-ditch U-boat efforts emerged. Coppock summarized the *U-869*'s participation in possible events. The *U-869* departed Kristiansand South on December 8, 1944, and proceeded toward the American continent. On December 25, U-boat Control allotted the *U-869* a patrol area off the New Jersey coast. On January 6, 1945, *U-869* transmitted a position report from mid-Atlantic. Based on the time it took the *U-869* to reach that location, U-boat Control determined that Neuerburg might not have enough fuel remaining to conduct more than a truncated (and probably futile) patrol off the American coast.

Coppock wrote, the *U-869* "was therefore requested to report her fuel state pending a decision on reallocation of patrol area. When no reply was received by Control, *U 869* was on 8 January ordered to proceed to . . . the west of the Gibraltar Strait. On 9 January she was again requested to report her fuel state and responded early the following day from . . . some 200 miles south of her previously reported position. (*U 869* had actually signaled her fuel state on both 8 and 9 January, but it would appear that neither signal had been received by Control. They were, however, intercepted by Allied listening stations.) No further signals were received from *U 869*.

"In view of atmospheric conditions in that area of the Atlantic adversely affecting wireless transmissions, it is certainly possible that Control's signal ordering *U 869* to the Gibraltar area was not received by the boat, although the principal difficulty seems to have been the receipt by Control of *U 869*'s signals rather than the reverse. Following *U 869*'s last signal on 10 January Control appeared convinced the boat was on passage to her new area . . ."

Ironically, Allied intelligence in Washington knew the position of the *U-869* even if U-Boat Control in Germany did not. So confident was Knowles that the *U-869* was still proceeding toward the eastern seaboard, that he convinced the Navy to dispatch a hunter-killer group to a position along the U-boat's predicted track. The baby flattop *Core* and her bevy of escorts failed to make contact.

Because Naval intelligence intercepted no other transmissions from the *U-869*, they fell back on the assumption that it had altered course for Gibraltar, where it was sunk.

Coppock continued, "In the light, therefore, of the absence of any tangible proof that the *U 869* had received Control's signal ordering her to the Gibraltar area . . . the evidence of the knife and the proximity of the wreck's position to the *U 869's* original patrol area . . . I would concede that the possibility the wreck is *U 869* cannot be ignored."

Misassessment

This left unexplained which U-boat - if any - had been sunk by Allied forces off Casablanca on February 28, 1945. At that time, the plotting room staff reviewed three reports of anti-submarine attacks in the Gibraltar area. Since the staff believed that the *U-869* had been diverted to the area, and that nothing further had been heard from it, they concluded that the U-boat must have been lost during one of these attacks. In order to reflect this conclusion, they upgraded one of the original recommendations from "probably not sunk" to "probably sunk."

This reevaluation indicated the precise moment in time at which the historical record of the *U-869* diverged from reality. Because the assessors did not know the original source of their information (the Ultra decrypts), and did not have full or direct access to that source, they reached a conclusion which in this case proved to be wrong.

The Coppock Theory

Barely a shadow of doubt remained as to the identity of the U-Who?. Yet this supposition begged the question: How was the *U-869* lost, and when? Once a U-boat entered its operational area, it ceased transmitting messages to U-boat Control. The Germans feared that a U-boat's transmission point could be triangulated by Allied listening stations. This was true. Thus the *U-869* maintained silence that never ended.

When news of the U-Who?'s discovery first hit the newspapers, veterans recalled that a plane attached to the Civil Air Patrol claimed to have sunk a U-boat with depth charges. But that incident occurred on July 11, 1942 - long before the *U-869* was even built, and far from the site of the wreck.

According to Coppock, "the most plausible explanation for the damage to the wreck off Point Pleasant is that it was caused by one of the boat's own acoustic torpedoes reversing course, homing onto her and striking her amidships." It is important to note that Coppock based his conclusion on the information that was provided to him. A torpedo strike could certainly account for a single hole in the control room. But Coppock had been misled. He may have rethought his position had he been informed of the second blast hole atop the after torpedo room.

There is more than one incident on record of a submarine being sunk by its own torpedo - American as well as German. To prevent this, every torpedo was then equipped with a fail-safe device that automatically disarmed the warhead if the torpedo turned more than 180°. German U-boat commanders were instructed to dive to 200 feet as soon as the "fish" were away, in order to duck under a circling torpedo. A submarine that was struck by its own torpedo was sure to be sunk by the sudden and massive breach of its pressure hull. Furthermore, there was little likelihood of anyone escaping from a submarine that was struck while operating at or below its periscope depth, at a time when it was already submerged, had little reserve buoyancy, and time for blowing ballast was insufficient.

The damage to the U-Who? is inconsistent with Coppock's scenario of a circular run torpedo. The pressure hull is intact for its entire length except for two spots: the top of the after torpedo room, and the area beneath the conning tower. At the latter location, the port side of the pressure hull is completely open with no overhead, permitting unrestricted access to the control room, while the starboard side is still standing.

Coppock was led to believe that the force of a single explosion peeled open the pressure hull with such violence that it separated the conning tower from its mounts. Just because the conning tower lay on its side along the port side of the wreck, did not mean that it was literally blown off at the time of the U-boat's destruction. (See Appendix One for more discussion of collapse and deterioration.) According to Coppock, this was the way the U-boat would appear if a torpedo had struck the port side under the conning tower.

Furthermore, there are authenticated cases of German U-boats being struck by their own torpedoes - *not*, however, in the control room by an acoustic torpedo. The theory was advanced that some mechanical components in the hydraulic system attracted the acoustical homing device in the torpedo. As discussed in Appendix One, this theory was untenable for any number of reasons.

Furthermore, the circular run torpedo theory did not account for the damage hole on top of the after torpedo room.

It was accepted by all as a foregone conclusion that the mystery sub was the *U-869*. Chatterton and Kohler also adopted Coppock's conclusion about the reason for its demise: the circular run torpedo.

Still, a great number of divers continued their explorations of the U-boat's interior, determined to recover an item that would provide positive identification - the nail in the iron coffin, so to speak. The nail was finally hammered home on August 31, 1997.

Positive ID
Chatterton descended to the wreck wearing a single tank. He, Yurga, Kohler, and Pat Rooney proceeded in

single file into the diesel engine room, to a point at which farther progress was prevented by an obstruction which blocked the path between the engines. Chatterton doffed his tank, pushed it ahead of him, then crawled through the space between the engine and the curvature of the pressure hull. He donned the tank and continued into the electric motor room. Kohler held a light at the hole - a beacon to show Chatterton the way out of the room. Yurga hovered by Kohler's side, videotaping the operation. Rooney hovered behind Kohler.

In the electric motor room, Chatterton found a wooden spare-parts box to which was fastened a plastic tag. He pulled the box off the shelf, and passed it through the hole to Kohler, who then passed it to Rooney. Rooney carried the box outside and sent it to the surface on a liftbag. Chatterton reversed his entry procedure, doffed the single tank, passed it through the opening ahead of him, squeezed past the engine, and donned the tank. Spare cylinders were available for emergency and for decompression.

Marked on the plastic tag was "U 869."

Historically Speaking

It is almost a shame that the U-Who? turned out to be a Type IX-C-40 U-boat. Of all the U-boats that were ever constructed, only three still exist on the surface of the planet, and two of them are Type IX-C-40's. (The other is a Type VII.) It would have been more historically significant if the U-Who? was a Type that was rare.

The *U-505* was captured on the high seas in a daring maneuver in which U.S. Navy sailors swarmed aboard the damaged and sinking boat after its crew had abandoned ship. Eight men clambered down the conning tower hatch in order to close seacocks and disarm scuttling charges. They succeeded in saving the U-boat from sinking.

The U-boat was then towed from the west coast of Africa to Bermuda. From the time of its capture - June 4, 1944 - until the end of the war, the incident was kept a closely guarded secret. The Allies did not want Germany to know that they now possessed an operational Enigma machine and the secret radio codes.

After the war, the *U-505* was towed up the St. Lawrence River and across the Great Lakes to Chicago, where it was beached and put on display. It is still a popular tourist attraction.

The *U-534* was bombed by a British plane on May 5, 1945, off the Danish island of Anholt. The U-boat sank in 210 feet of water in a location that was fairly well documented. In 1986, Age Jensen became the first person to dive on the U-boat. In 1992, Publisher Karsten Ree funded a commercial salvage operation to raise the boat and place it on display in Denmark. The boat was raised and was put on display (although it has proved to be somewhat of a traveling display, as it has been moved several times throughout the years, and may continue to move.)

The *U-995* was a Type VII that survived the war. It was turned over to the British. The British scuttled more than two hundred fifty surrendered U-boats, but saved the *U-995* from destruction. It was later returned to Germany and converted to a museum.

Statistics vary, but it is commonly accepted that Germany built more than twelve hundred U-boats during World War Two - and this number does not include nearly fifty U-boats that had been constructed before the invasion of Poland. The most common model was the Type VII (more than seven hundred). Some two hundred Type IX's were built, of which eighty-seven were Type IX-C-40's.

In World War Two, between 75% and 80% of all operational U-boats were lost in action.

Germany had about three hundred fifty operational U-boats in the Great War. Slightly more than half were lost in combat. By 1921, most of the surviving U-boats had been scuttled, dismantled, or destroyed. France retained ten U-boats to bolster its flagging navy.

CHAPTER THREE
Twisted Tales

"What you have done is not nearly as important as what you can make people believe you have done."
- Gary Gentile

The Plot Thickens

On page 255 of *Shadow Divers*, it was written that Chatterton took Barb Lander to the National Archives in February 1994, to help him search through the Tenth Fleet intelligence summaries. According to the book, it was on this occasion that he first sighted the Ultra decrypts, first learned that the *U-869* had missed the signal from U-boat Control with orders to divert to Gibraltar, and first found that the Tenth Fleet was tracking the U-boat across the Atlantic Ocean, which then issued orders for a hunter-killer group that was led by the aircraft carrier *Core* to intercept the U-boat along its projected track.

As noted in Chapter Two of the present volume, Mark McKellar gave this information to Chatterton in 1993. Not only was McKellar not given credit for his contribution, but his name was not even mentioned in *Shadow Divers*. This gave me cause to wonder: Did Chatterton *not* talk with McKellar, even though I remember Chatterton telling me that he had? Did Chatterton, who was depicted throughout the book as a relentless researcher who left no stone unturned, ignore McKellar's information? Did Chatterton, for reasons of his own, not wish to give credit to McKellar for unearthing facts that Chatterton claimed to have found? Or was my memory flawed?

Fortunately I keep good records, and I had copies of McKellar's correspondence in my possession. According to his own words, he did indeed share the results of his research endeavors with Chatterton in 1993. McKellar and Chatterton not only spoke on the phone, they even met! McKellar wrote: "I have spoken to John Chatterton several times and have viewed about 30 minutes of video he shot of the wreck."

Apparently, McKellar was written out of the story so that the part that he played in being the first to obtain the Ultra decrypts could be given to Chatterton at a later date for greater dramatic effect, and to portray Chatterton as a tireless researcher who eventually "discovered" the decrypts by means of his own endeavors when he dragged Lander with him to the National Archives.

On pages 253 and 254, *Shadow Divers* quoted extracts from a letter that Chatterton purportedly received from Robert Coppock in "late February" 1994. (The reader will recall from Chapter Two that Robert Coppock was the renowned British U-boat authority who was Kohler's and Chatterton's primary source of information.) This was the letter in which Coppock informed the dynamic duo of the possibility that the *U-869* must have missed the transmission from U-boat Control in which Neuerberg was redirected to Gibraltar.

While it may be true that Chatterton received such a letter, *Shadow Divers* neglected to mention that *Coppock's letter was addressed to McKellar*, not to Chatterton! Coppock's letter (which was dated February 17, 1994) was written in response to McKellar's query of November 24, 1993. If Chatterton truly received such a letter instead of a phone call from McKellar, either McKellar or Coppock sent a copy of the letter to him after the fact.

No matter how you slice it, McKellar was ahead of the game. The delayed revelation of Chatterton's "discovery" of the Ultra decrypts put the cart before the horse.

In any event, it was *not possible* to access the Ultra decrypts at the National Archives in 1994, as *Shadow Divers* claimed. At that time, the files of the Tenth Fleet - which included the Ultra decrypts, convoy and routing instructions, and antisubmarine warfare reports - were archived at the Naval Historical Center, which was located in Building 57 at the Washington Navy Yard. The Tenth Fleet files were not transferred to the National Archives until April 1996. Chatterton would have known this had he done the research himself.

Unpardonable Oversight

On page 181 of *Shadow Divers*, it was written that Chatterton spent three days combing through antisubmarine warfare incident reports and the war diaries of the Eastern Sea Frontier. Supposedly, he skimmed through more than a thousand incidents - covering the entire war off the U.S. eastern seaboard - without finding a single instance of submarine activity within a 15-mile radius of the *U-869*. According to the book, not even an oil slick was reported in the area.

This litany was repeated on page 185. Then, on page 187, he supposedly spent four *more* days on research (through records whose designations were not disclosed in the book). This time he expanded his search to a radius of 30 miles, then to 60 miles. *Shadow Divers* emphasized these research trips as if they were incredible feats of endurance that were unequalled.

Chatterton was quoted as saying, "Not a single thing happened anywhere near our wreck site during the entire war. Nothing."

This statement ignored the well-known fact that, on April 30, 1942, the *U-752* torpedoed and sank the Norwegian freighter *Bidevind* only 20 miles from the site of the *U-869*. Seven months later - on December 1, 1942 - the blimp *K-7* dropped depth charges on the slick of oil that was still leaking from the sunken freighter's fuel tanks. Experienced local deep wreck-divers were well aware of the *Bidevind's* location.

Furthermore, within a radius of sixty miles, German U-boats sank ten other vessels during the first six months of 1942. The *R.P. Resor* lies at a distance of 22 miles from the *U-869*; the *Rio Tercero*, 30 miles; the *Coimbra*, 39 miles; the *Gulftrade*, 40 miles; the *Tolten*, 41 miles; the *Arundo*, 47 miles; the *Persephone*, 48 miles; the *Lemuel Burrows*, 56 miles; the *Cayru*, 59 miles; and the *Varanger*, 59 miles. All this information was readily available in *Track of the Gray Wolf*, *Shipwrecks of New Jersey*, and other books and articles.

And this short list comprises only the ships that were sunk. Others were attacked, and antisubmarine incidents too numerous to mention occurred in the vicinity in 1943 and 1944.

As I noted in the Prologue, Harold Moyers located the depth-charge incident of the *Howard D. Crow* and the *Koiner* in ten minutes, by combing through the after war assessments for the period between January 1 and April 1, 1945. That incident occurred at a distance that was estimated to be 4.5 miles from the site of the *U-869*. I then noted in Chapter One that three additional incidents occurred in the month *before* the sinking of the *U-869*: one within 15 miles, and two at 20 miles. Five additional incidents occurred *after* the sinking of the *U-869* within a 20-mile radius of the wreck, and one at 25 miles. Two more incidents occurred at a distance of 40 miles, and one at 60 miles.

All these incidents occurred within a three-month period that was contemporaneous with the demise of the *U-869*. This cursory tabulation ignores any number of incidents that may have occurred during the previous three *years*.

The paragraphs above beg the question: How did Chatterton succeed in missing all these crucial incident reports from 1945, and at least twelve reports from 1942, to say nothing of all the incident reports from the intervening years?

These gross oversights were not in accordance with the statement that is quoted above, and which was attributed to Chatterton in *Shadow Divers*. Nor do these oversights fairly depict a researcher who was unflagging in his devotion to research, the way *Shadow Divers* portrayed Chatterton. The uninformed readers of *Shadow Divers* may find the true explanation for these deficits a little less than astonishing.

The Uncredited Researcher

Here is the research chronology as I know it to have occurred from contemporary events in which I was involved, and as Barb Lander and John Yurga told me.

In January 1994, I was hired to lecture at a technical diving conference in New Orleans, Louisiana. The sponsor and organizer of the show was Mike Menduno. His brainchild was *AquaCorps*, the first technical diving magazine in the world. Because *AquaCorps* was paying my expenses, I had a hotel room all to myself.

At this time, Polly Tapson was organizing a major mixed-gas diving expedition to the *Lusitania*. She invited me to participate. Afterward, three spots became available. Due to the dearth of suitable mixed-gas divers in the United Kingdom, she asked me to find divers in the United States to fill the spots. For a number of reasons, the most experienced technical divers I knew were unable to go. Eventually I extended invitations to wreck-divers who, at that time, had lesser experience: Barb Lander, John Chatterton, and John Yurga.

Polly Tapson attended the conference, not only for what it had to offer, but to meet the American contingent of the *Lusitania* expedition, which was scheduled for the first two weeks in June. She flew to New Orleans from her home London. Lander drove to New Orleans from her home in Pennsylvania (a distance of about one thousand miles). Yurga flew from his home in New Jersey. Chatterton did not attend.

Room rates at hotels that were located near the convention center were expensive. I invited Tapson, Lander, and Yurga to share my room. This not only saved them money, but it provided a convenient venue for us to discuss the complex plans for the forthcoming expedition.

Yurga, Lander, and I also discussed the *U-869*. Lander was particularly interested in getting involved with the research group. I gave her some pointers on how to deal with the people at the Naval Historical Center, and which record groups to access at the textual reference branch of the National Archives: those sources that I had used in my research for *Track of the Gray Wolf.*

Although the emphasis of my book was on the merchant marine, and was told from the Allied perspective, I had done some research on U-boat activity, and knew where to look for additional information. I told her to look in the armed guard engagement reports and logs, the war diary of the Eastern Sea Frontier, after action reports, and antisubmarine warfare records.

I encouraged Lander because I had my hands full in researching hundreds of other shipwrecks for my Popular Dive Guide Series. I was glad that there was at least one other diver in the wreck-diving community who was willing to dedicate herself to conducting primary research. Since we already knew (or strongly suspected) the identity of the U-boat, she concentrated her efforts on determining the reason for its loss.

After the conference she drove straight to Washington, where she had arranged to meet Kohler at a hotel. They spent a day together at the National Archives. (Kohler confirmed this with me shortly afterward.) Later, Lander returned by herself to the National Archives, and visited the Naval Historical Center as well. Because she was a housewife and had flexible free time, and because she lived in York, Pennsylvania (about an hour and a half from Washington), she could drive to these archival facilities in the morning, do a day's research, and return home that evening. She followed this routine for a number of days during the next several months - and made some extraordinary discoveries.

As a starting point, Lander used the hydrostatic test date that was stamped on the recovered escape lung cylinder. This enabled her to concentrate her efforts between July 20, 1944 and March 17, 1945. It was her research that uncovered the *Harper's Ferry* incident that is recounted in Appendix One. She pursued this incident as a way of lending credence to the circular run torpedo theory.

Lander was also intrigued by the reported loss of

the *U-869* off Gibraltar. In March, she sent copies of the *Fowler* and *L'Indiscret* attack reports to Coppock. After investigating the British reports of these actions, Coppock wrote to Lander and proffered his opinion that the nature of the contact "was manifestly not a submarine."

More important, Lander made a list of antisubmarine incidents that occurred in the vicinity of the *U-869*.

The Silver Platter

Lander summarized the results of her research data on a typewritten sheet, added annotations, and sent photocopies to Chatterton and Yurga. She went so far as to highlight six reports in yellow because of their proximity to the wreck site. Of the six that she highlighted, the farthest from the wreck site was 37 nautical miles, the next closest was 36 miles, the next closest was 20 miles, the next closest was 18 miles, the next closest was 10 miles, and the closest of all was 4.5 miles.

Lander's research contradicted the statement on page 187 of *Shadow Divers*, where it was written that Chatterton "found nothing. Not a single event or observation had been recorded within sixty miles of the wreck site."

The attack at 4.5 nautical miles from the wreck referred to the *Howard D. Crow* and *Koiner* incident. Lander mentioned the vessels by name, indicated that contact was made by sound, and noted that attacks were made with both hedgehogs and depth charges. This is the same attack report that Moyers found ten years later in the after war assessments.

Amazingly, not only did Chatterton have the *Howard D. Crow* and *Koiner* attack report handed to him, but the incident was highlighted in yellow - and he did nothing about it!

I asked Yurga how they could have missed such an obvious clue. He explained that by 1994, Chatterton was touting himself as the principle investigator, while Yurga took a back seat in the research department. Although Yurga noticed the *Howard D. Crow* and *Koin-*

er attacks on the photocopies that Lander gave him, he was not privy to the coordinates of the *U-869*. He knew that the attack was close, but not *how* close.

Yurga: "I relied on JC to determine whether any of these attacks were close to the sub's resting place."

Yurga was still actively diving on the wreck. He was principally involved in documenting the activities on the site. He also assumed the primary responsibility of studying U-boat design, which was crucial to exploring the interior. On page 154 of *Shadow Divers*, this role was given to Kohler, who allegedly "studied U-boats like an undergraduate before a final exam. He dedicated every free moment to understanding the U-boat - its construction, its evolution, its command chain, its lore." This description fitted Yurga, not Kohler. Most of Yurga's contributions were written out of the book and ascribed to Kohler (as they were in the television production, *Hitler's Lost Sub*. See Chapter Five for details).

Chatterton did not pursue Lander's highlighted attack reports, nor did he ask her to investigate them further. He clearly missed the boat.

A great opportunity was ignored.

When Moyers obtained this same information, he began to call surviving crewmembers of the *Howard D. Crow* and the *Koiner*, including the *Koiner's* skipper: the person who was responsible for reporting the target as a non-submarine contact.

On page 286 of *Shadow Divers*, it was written that Chatterton lived "according to a single set of principles, that hard work, perseverance, thoroughness, preparation, creativity, and vision made the diver and the man." On a number of pages it was claimed that Chatterton left no stone unturned in his research. He allegedly investigated every crank theory and listened to every nut case that came his way. Yet he disregarded the wealth of information that was put in front of his nose.

Chatterton could have ascertained the facts if he had followed up the attack report the way Moyers did.

Shadow Divers cast Lander in the light of a lackey:

one whose presence on the research team was merely tolerated as an unfledged adjunct. In reality, she became the principal investigator. She discovered valuable information that Chatterton totally disregarded.

Death on the *Texas Tower*

Shadow Divers presented two versions of a fatality that occurred on the *Texas Tower*, each version differing from the other. On page 18, it was written that an anonymous diver died on the wreck in 1984. On page 90, it was written that this anonymous diver died in 1986. In both versions, the only names that were provided were those of Chatterton and Nagle.

In the page 18 version, it was the first trip that Chatterton ever made on the *Seeker* - one that he made only because he wanted to meet his idol. In the page 90 version, this trip was made after an unspecified number of weekend trips on the *Seeker*. Which version was correct - or which version was written for the most dramatic appeal - the reader must decide for himself.

Shadow Divers claimed that the anonymous victim was a "hotshot" who got "cocky," and who spent so much time in trying to remove a brass window that he ran out of air on the bottom. The book also claimed that Nagle and his anonymous crewmembers had just completed their own dives, and could not dive again because of the nitrogen in their bodies. Chatterton then volunteered to dive alone, a task that "no other *Tower* virgin would have considered." He found the body and sent it to the surface on a liftbag, but the liftbag broached in rough seas and the body sank to the bottom. Because of approaching nightfall, it was not safe for anyone else to dive again. Chatterton volunteered to retrieve the body in the morning. Chatterton dived alone the next day, and sent the body to the surface again. Either crabs or fish had eaten parts of the exposed flesh, converting the corpse to what divers called a "creature feature" (as it was written on page 18 of *Shadow Divers*).

The only named witness to these events was Nagle.

With him conveniently deceased, the book offered no way for its readers to verify the account. Giving different dates that were two years apart only added to the confusion.

Down with Anonymity

The account that was related in *Shadow Divers* holds water only as long as no other witnesses exist to deny it. I found four: Gail Amarino, Kevin England, Chris Jazmin, and John Moyer. Here is their account, which is given with the disclaimer that it records events to the best of their recollection after the passage of twenty years.

In 1986, the *Seeker* left the dock some time after midnight for a trip to the *Texas Tower*. The average depth around the *Texas Tower* was 185 feet; the structure rose to within 65 feet of the surface. The *Texas Tower* offered the best visibility of any wreck off the New Jersey coast. Nagle was the skipper; Moyer was his only crewmember. Both Nagle and Moyer were Coast Guard certified ocean operators. Nagle and Moyer took turns at the wheel throughout the night.

Shortly after sunrise, the *Seeker* dropped a grapnel into the wreck. As the divers rigged their gear, Chris Jazmin and Dennis Ziemba discussed their dive plan. Jazmin wanted to touch the bottom because he had never been that deep before, but Ziemba did not want to go deeper than 130 feet. Mark Ruggiero asked if he could accompany Jazmin on his bounce dive to the bottom. Although Jazmin did not know Ruggiero, he agreed.

All three descended the anchor line together. Ziemba halted on the wreck at 130 feet. Jazmin and Ruggiero continued downward as planned. They settled in a washout in which Jazmin recorded a depth of 191 feet. He and Ruggiero exchanged signals, after which they proceeded to ascend to the place where Ziemba was waiting for them.

Jazmin discovered a porthole at 150 feet. He grabbed the dogs but was unable to pull the porthole free. Ruggiero then grabbed the dogs, and tugged hard. After one to two minutes, Jazmin signaled that he wanted to ascend, in order to meet Ziemba at the pre-arranged time. Ruggiero shook his head, signaling that he was going to stay for a while.

Jazmin picked up Ziemba at 130 feet. They ascended and conducted their decompression. Using gestures and hand signals, Ziemba asked Jazmin about Ruggiero. Jazmin shrugged his shoulders, indicating that he did not know what had happened to him. After Jazmin surfaced from the dive, he asked if anyone had seen Ruggiero. He told those on board that he had last seen Ruggiero on the wreck. By this time, all the divers were back on the boat except for Ruggiero.

Nagle and Moyer commenced a visual search of the surface for a diver whom they hoped was drifting down-current. To make matters worse, the grapnel pulled out of the wreck. After a fruitless surface search, Nagle maneuvered the boat over the *Texas Tower* and, with Moyer's assistance, rehooked the wreck.

Nagle notified the Coast Guard of the missing diver. Nagle did not operate on the assumption that the diver was dead, but that he had surfaced at a distance from the anchor line and had been unable to swim against the current to the boat. The Coast Guard dispatched a jet to search the area. The results of the surface search were negative.

The Acceptance of Death

Nagle complained to Moyer that he could not dive because of the gout that pained his leg. Moyer: "I don't remember Bill asking me to search or volunteering. It was just understood that I would do it because I was crew and the most experienced diver there. Also, I had not dove yet and had the time." (By this he meant bottom time, without residual nitrogen from a previous dive.)

Moyer had never dived on the *Texas Tower*. "Bill drew a sketch of the wreck for me, with where he thought we were hooked in and where he thought I might find the body. Around mid-afternoon, Kevin and I made our dive. I don't remember how he was my buddy, but he must have volunteered. He had never been to 180 feet before. Vis was good on the wreck. I dropped down near the sand and searched, Kevin hovered above me at around 140-150 feet. At the very end of the dive, I spotted the body lying in the sand, next to the wreck. I did not have time to send it up or even put a liftbag on it."

After boarding the boat, Moyer described the location of the body to Nagle.

Moyer: "I don't know how it was decided that Chatterton would dive for the body or who dove with Chatterton." No one was positive who dived with Chatterton, but it may have been Glen Plokhoy. "The body was sent up on a liftbag, tied to the wreck with sisal upline. It surfaced about 100 feet off the port side of the *Seeker.* Kevin swam out to the bag, but before he could cut the upline, the bag dumped and the body sank.

"Again, it was just assumed that I would dive the next morning to send up the body. I don't remember how Chatterton became my buddy for that dive. We dove early the next morning. It was black, like a night dive because it was so early in the morning. I think the upline was draped over some of the wreck, not lying 180 feet straight out, flat in the sand. We followed the upline out, away from the wreck, in the sand. It was not very far. I stopped, because I was concerned that once we sent the body up, we would not have the upline to follow back to the wreck. Chatterton went just a little further to the body and put some air in the bag and it went up." Moyer served as a beacon to mark the way back to the anchor line. "We turned and he followed me back to the wreck. The bag surfaced right in front of the boat."

The body was left hanging until Moyer and Chatterton surfaced. Amarino and Plokhoy towed the body to the boat. After the body was brought on board, Jazmin and someone, whose name he could not recall, dived to release the grapnel. By the time they surfaced, the body was wrapped in an improvised shroud. The *Seeker* returned to her dock, where the Coast Guard and police were awaiting her arrival.

The coroner's report was inconclusive, citing the catchall cause of death as carbon dioxide blackout, but mentioned a dose of antihistamines that was unusually high.

None of my witnesses had ever met Ruggiero before; they knew nothing about him. Apparently, Chatterton did not even remember his name. *Shadow Divers* provided no basis for calling him "cocky" or a "hot shot."

The vulgar phrase "creature feature" was a gratuitous invention of *Shadow Divers*. Not only has the phrase never been used by any wreck-diver of my acquaintance, but a survey of experienced wreck-divers failed to find anyone who had ever heard the phrase. *Shadow Divers* implied that the recovery of a decomposed body was such a common occurrence that wreck-divers had created a name to describe it. This was definitely not the case.

Shadow Divers degraded the tragic death of Mark Ruggiero in order to glorify a voluntary solo body recovery that cannot be corroborated by reliable witnesses. Those witnesses concurred that the body search and recovery was very much a group effort.

The Feldman Body Recovery Effort

Shadow Divers went to great lengths to castigate Steve Bielenda as a "pirate," a word that was ascribed to him more than once in the text. I cannot honestly defend Bielenda against a diatribe that was not necessarily undeserved. He and his dive boat *Wahoo* had an unsavory reputation that was not unfounded. My point is that unsupported allegations are inappropriate. *Shadow Divers* should have provided concrete examples of piracy instead of resorting to juvenile name-calling.

Two examples of Bielenda's character were given in *Shadow Divers*. One - the bitter silliness of the *Andrea Doria*'s Third Class Kitchen escapade - was inaccurately presented. (See Chapter Four for details.) The other involved the circumstances that followed the death of Steve Feldman on the *U-869*. The *Shadow Divers* version was distorted and couched in anonymity, and was related in such a way as to make Bielenda appear to be a diving Machiavelli whose dire machinations tricked Nagle into giving him the location of the wreck.

In reality, Bielenda had nothing to do with providing the incentive to search for Feldman's body, with obtaining the wreck's location, or in initiating the search trip. He was not even an accomplice. Howard Klein, Dennis Kessler, and John Lachenmeyer told me the whole story.

To recapitulate, the first dive on the *U-869* took place on September 2, 1991. The second trip took place on September 21. Feldman was on both trips; he died on the second.

Feldman was an occasional customer on Klein's charter vessel, the *Eagle's Nest*, which operated out of Freeport, New York.

On September 29, the *Seeker* returned once again to the *U-869*. On page 108 of *Shadow Divers*, it was written that Kohler took Feldman's place on the boat, and that this trip provided the instance of Kohler's first confrontation with Chatterton. In fact, on board were *four* divers who were making their first trip to the U-boat: Steve Gatto, Richie Kohler, Steve McDougall, and Tom Packer. None of them knew or had ever met Feldman.

The repeat divers - those who had been on the trip on which Feldman had died - made no attempt to search for his body. When Chatterton was questioned about conducting a search, he insisted that they had no chance of finding it because Feldman had been halfway up the anchor line when he let go and dropped to the bottom. His body could not possibly have come to rest on the wreck, and must therefore have been swept away.

Chatterton did not suggest the possibility that the current could have changed and swept the body *against* the wreck, in which case the repeat divers might have felt honor bound to search for their lost comrade, and would have expected Chatterton to do likewise instead of to hunt for artifacts - which he did. According to McDougall's log, Chatterton "found china with the WWII German logo."

By way of comparison, on November 4, 1973, I found the body of Gary Ford pinned against the wreck of the *Cherokee*. He had gone missing the week before. The current had not swept the body away, but instead had held it firmly in place. Frank Messina and I sent the body to the surface on a liftbag. We did not learn of the fatality until the morning of departure, when Tom McIlwee and a buddy arrived at the dock and asked to accompany our club (Aquarama Dive Club) to the wreck so that they could conduct a search in the hope that the current had not carried away the body: a positive attitude that proved to be correct in its assumption.

When Feldman's buddies took no affirmative action, Feldman's sister called Klein and asked for his help in recovering the body of her brother. Klein agreed to do so.

Klein called George Hoffman, a long-time dive boat skipper who ran the *Sea Lion* out of Brielle, New Jersey. Hoffman had been diving since the 1960's. He was a close friend of the Bogans. The Bogans had given the loran numbers of the *U-869* to Hoffman, but he was not interested in running offshore trips any more. Hoffman was the person who gave the numbers to Klein. Bielenda had nothing to do with the transaction. (Nagle did not receive a call from "another dive boat captain" and, as it was written on page 156 of *Shadow Divers*, let the numbers be wrung from him because he was in a drunken stupor.)

Klein was the vice president of the Eastern Dive Boat Association. Bielenda was the president. Klein called Bielenda and asked him to gather some deep wreck-divers who were capable of conducting a body search in 230 feet of water. Bielenda solicited some of the Atlantic Wreck Divers. They agreed to donate their time for the search effort. Klein not only furnished his boat for the trip, but he paid for the fuel and all incidental expenses out of his own pocket.

After hearing through the grapevine that a search trip was being organized, Chatterton called Bielenda and tried to convince him that Feldman's family members did *not* want his body recovered: that they were satisfied that Feldman had been suitably buried at sea. (Much to Chatterton's annoyance, Bielenda recorded the conversation.)

Nagle called Klein to warn him that "no artifacts better come up."

The *Eagle's Nest* search trip took place on October 24 - more than a month after the fatality. Divers included Hank Garvin and Rob Stevenson, Pete Guglieri and John Lachenmeyer, Gene Howley and Dennis Kessler. Bobby Raimo was an emergency medical technician who went as a safety diver. Joel Silverstein went so he could write an article for his magazine, *New York Sub Aqua Journal.*

Bielenda was on board. He did not dive; he logged divers in and out of the water. Despite the best efforts of the divers in conducting searches around the hull, they did not find the body. It had already drifted away from the wreck. Kessler told me that he hardly saw the wreck because he spent all of his time in the sand.

Perhaps if a concerted effort had been made when the *Seeker* returned the week after Feldman's death, a body search might have been successful.

On page 157 of *Shadow Divers*, it was written that Chatterton and Kohler "suspected that Bielenda would be coming back. . . . the pirate flag of Bielenda's intention would fly at full mast." Their suspicions and Nagle's fears proved groundless. Bielenda never took the *Wahoo* to the *U-869*. None of the divers who searched for Feldman's body ever returned to the wreck.

The Rouse Incident

In *Shadow Divers*, the Rouse incident was portrayed in the same manner in which the *Texas Tower* incident was portrayed. The book focused attention on two stage performers who immediately took charge of the situation. The uninformed readers were led to believe that only Chatterton and Kohler took strong affirmative action, that the contributions of Lander and Crowell were merely incidental, and that everyone else cowered in the cabin instead of helping to rescue and to provide life-support for their friends. Indeed, the story was told as if only four people were on the boat that day.

The recapitulate preceding events, shortly after midnight on October 11, 1992, the *Seeker* embarked on a two-day trip to the *U-869*. On the first day, the sea was calm and the weather was mild. Overnight the weather turned a little snotty. Dan Crowell, who was acting as skipper in Nagle's absence, decided to head for home after the divers completed their morning dive, in case the weather worsened.

Chris Rouse and his son Chrissy were the last to hit the water. On the bottom, Chris acted as safety while Chrissy went inside the officers' quarters. Chrissy became either trapped by a fallen object or entangled. It took so long for Chrissy to break free that they overstayed their bottom time. They then went looking for their stage bottles, which were filled with decompression gas. They could not find the bottles, so they made a less-than-controlled ascent to the surface, skipping all their decompression in the process. They swam or drifted to the stern of the boat.

The Myth

According to *Shadow Divers*, Chatterton then tossed two lines to the Rouses as they drifted alongside the hull. The splash rail crashed down on Chrissy's tanks and cracked the manifold, allowing air to escape with a raucous hiss. Each Rouse grabbed a line. Chatterton, Kohler, and "other divers" towed the Rouses to the back of the boat. Chatterton and Kohler grabbed Chrissy and hauled him on board while Chrissy screamed in pain. Kohler "and others" dragged Chrissy to the dressing table, where Lander gave him oxygen, water, and aspirin.

Chatterton and Kohler leaped overboard to help Chris. Chatterton cut Chris's harness straps so that the tanks and other equipment fell away from him. While treading water, Chatterton picked up Chris and slung his limp form over his shoulder. In six-foot seas, the boat "heaved and exploded" in the ocean "with nature's onrushing tantrum." Chatterton climbed up the ladder unassisted, with Chris on his shoulder in a fireman's carry.

Chatterton commenced CPR, alternating positions for heart massage and rescue breathing. He ordered Kohler to get pencil and paper, and to write down everything that Chrissy was saying. Kohler took notes while Chatterton continued CPR for the next hour and a half.

When the Coast Guard helicopter arrived, Crowell ordered that all loose items on the deck be secured, so that the helicopter's prop wash did not suck up a sleeping bag into the rotors and cause the helicopter to crash, or turn dive masks into deadly missiles. All but Chatterton, Kohler, and Lander "ran into the salon." The rescue swimmer jumped from the chopper into the sea alongside the boat. He wore gloves, hood, goggles, mask, and fins. He tossed a medical bag onto the deck, then climbed aboard.

Chatterton was still doing CPR. The rescue swimmer told him to increase the speed of the chest compressions. Chatterton told the rescue swimmer in no uncertain terms that Chris was dead, and that there was no need to waste time in evacuating his body when it would prove more expedient to transport Chrissy to a recompression chamber. A heated argument ensued, in which Chatterton *begged* the rescue swimmer to "forget the father" because the delay in the commencement of recompression treatment on Chrissy might result in his death.

The rescue swimmer radioed the chopper to drop a basket. He warned those who were not afraid to be on deck to avoid touching it because the static charge "can blow you off your feet." The basket "pendulumed in the howling winds before touching a rail and "exploding with the discharge of static electricity."

The rescue swimmer dragged the basket to Chrissy, who was screaming in agony. He placed Chrissy inside the basket. The chopper lowered a cable. Chatterton, Kohler, and the rescue swimmer lifted the basket onto the gunwale and attached the cable, after which the chopper lifted Chrissy and hoisted him into the side door.

Chatterton got into another shouting match with the rescue swimmer, imploring him again to leave the dead father behind. When the rescue swimmer resisted, Chatterton ordered Kohler to get the Rouse's wallets, and the notes of Chrissy's dive profile and vital signs, and put them in a plastic bag for the rescue swimmer to take with him. Kohler tore the boat apart looking for the wallets.

The chopper returned and evacuated Chris in a basket. Twenty minutes later, the chopper lowered the basket for the third time, in order to recover the rescue swimmer. Only then did the other divers step sheepishly out of the salon. They all thanked Chatterton and hugged him.

Chris was pronounced dead on arrival at the hospital. Chrissy died several hours later in the recompression chamber.

Conscientious Critics

Shadow Divers cast Chatterton and Kohler as indefatigable heroes, and everyone else as slinking cowards who ran away and hid when they were needed the most.

Not only was the *Shadow Divers* exercise in imagination not substantiated by reliable witnesses, but those "other divers" were appalled at what they called "a largely fictitious and grossly exaggerated" account of the rescue of the Rouses. Comments such as "Didn't happen" and "Completely fabricated" were the mildest rebukes that I heard from "the others" who were involved. Among those who knew the truth firsthand, the adulterated story - which was combined with a plethora of impossible embellishments in the same vein as other embellishments that appear throughout the text of the book - earned the vanity volume the title of *Shady Divers*.

Despite the intention of *Shadow Divers* to bury "the others" in anonymity, the names of the "other divers" are well known and respected members of the wreck-diving community. I had no trouble in obtaining their accounts of events as they actually occurred.

There were so many inaccuracies and inconsistencies in the *Shadow Divers* fairytale of the Rouse incident that I hardly know how or where to begin to dispute them. To relate the true turn of events in a straightforward chronological manner would fail to accentuate the radical differences between the myth and the reality.

I will first parse the *Shadow Divers* version in order to emphasize some of the inanities. I can then provide the true account as corroborated by attendant witnesses, without having to interrupt the flow. Relevant *Shadow Diver* disparities will be noted in parentheses.

Absurdities

A splash rail is a strip of wood that deflects water away from the boat as the hull cleaves down through the surface of the sea. This length of wood cannot (and did not) damage Chrissy's tank manifold.

Sleeping bags could not be sucked up into the rotors of the chopper because they were kept on the bunks in the cabin, not outside on the open deck where they were exposed to water and weather.

No helicopter has ever crashed as a result of sucking flying objects up from the ground and snapping off the rotors. In Vietnam, I flew in Hueys that landed in jungles and rice paddies under the worst conditions imaginable. The downdraft disturbed the dirt and dust, but no objects of any mass were lifted far off the ground. Objects that were propelled by the downdraft did not have enough mass to become deadly if they struck anyone. Rotors commonly clipped off treetops during troop insertions into hot landing zones, without damaging the blades.

A helicopter may accumulate a static charge on a flight of long duration. The longer the flight, the larger may be the charge. The discharge is invisible: it consists of electricity that goes to ground. In none of the helicopter evacuations in which I have participated have I ever seen an explosive discharge of electricity; nor has any other wreck-diver of my acquaintance. I interviewed Bob Waters about this phenomenon. Waters flew Coast Guard rescue helicopters and made airlifts over water. He never observed an explosive discharge, and he never heard his fellow helicopter pilots mention an explosive discharge.

This discharge, if any, occurs only on the first contact. A hovering helicopter does not have time to accumulate another perceptible charge. In any case, a basket or stretcher would not discharge on contact with the metal rail of the *Seeker*, because the rail was not grounded - it was secured to a wooden bulwark which in turn was secured to a wooden hull. Wood is a dielectric, or insulator; it is not a conductor of electricity.

Furthermore, the deadly static discharge caution is a hoax that is exaggerated way out of proportion to reality. In Vietnam, I jumped into and out of Hueys all the time. I was never warned about the possibility of deadly static discharge, and I never saw or experienced any static discharge. Anyone with helicopter experience can bear out the fallacy of deadly static discharge.

The basket or stretcher could not have been placed on the gunwale because the *Seeker's* gunwale was topped by a short-legged pipe railing. Even so, *Shadow Divers* would have its uninformed readers believe that the basket in which Chrissy was placed was delicately balanced on the narrow highpoint of a wildly rolling boat until the retrieval cable was attached. The rescue swimmer would not have permitted such a precarious situation. An unanticipated lurch could have knocked the basket overboard. Chrissy would have drowned because he could not have released the straps.

According to *Shadow Divers*, Chatterton initiated CPR without first ascertaining if Chris's heart had stopped beating. Anyone who has ever taken CPR training knows that doing chest compressions on a still-beating heart will at the very least be counterproductive, and may very well cause the heart to stop.

In *Shadow Divers*, it was written that Chatterton performed solo CPR for an hour and a half nonstop. Then, as soon as the rescue swimmer arrived, Chatterton pronounced Chris dead and implored the rescue swimmer to leave his body behind. This begs the question: If Chatterton knew that Chris was dead, why did he continue to perform CPR until the very moment of the rescue swimmer's arrival? These opposing actions and mindsets betray a lack of consistency.

Explanations

Cardiopulmonary resuscitation (CPR) is a two-part procedure. One part requires the lifesaver to orally inject air into the victim's lungs, in a process that is known as mouth-to-mouth resuscitation, or rescue breathing. The lifesaver exhales hard enough into the victim's mouth to force air into the lungs. Atmospheric air contains 21% oxygen; exhaled air contains about 15% oxygen, plus carbon dioxide.

Artificial respiration can also be effected by means of a manual resuscitator, or a bag valve mask. The most widely used manual resuscitator is the Ambu-Bag. The Ambu-Bag is a proprietary device that consists of a flexible squeeze bag that is attached to a disposable face mask that is designed to cover the victim's nose and mouth. When the lifesaver squeezes the bag by hand, air is forced into the victim's lungs. The clear plastic bag can be held easily in one hand, and it can be squeezed effortlessly for long periods of time without hand fatigue. (During one rescue operation, I squeezed an Ambu-Bag for more than an hour. It was no more arduous than squeezing a partially inflated balloon which deflated with every squeeze.)

The second part of CPR consists of heart massage, or chest compressions. In order for rescue breathing to have any affect, the heart must pump the oxygenated blood through the arteries to the cells, tissues, and organs. Pressing a heart that has stopped beating simulates the muscular action that makes the blood circulate.

For a victim who is not breathing and whose heart has stopped beating, ventilation is useless without heart compressions, and vice versa. A lifesaver who must perform both functions alone is severely task loaded. He must do thirty heart compressions, reposition himself, then give two breaths: alternating constantly and without relief. With two lifesavers, one can do the heart compressions and the other can do the rescue breathing.

A stretcher is a wire-framed litter in which a person can be airlifted in the supine position. A basket is a wire-framed gondola in which a person sits with his knees bent close to his chin.

The Reality

For the true and tragic account of the Rouse incident, I interviewed Steve Gatto, Steve McDougall, Tom Packer, and John Yurga: all of whom took active parts in the rescue operation.

McDougall told me, "While decompressing on oxygen I saw Chris and Chrissy go down the anchor line. They did not come back up in a reasonable time and I got that 'something could be really wrong' feeling in the pit of my stomach. I remember hoping they had sent up an up line and that they were decompressing on it out of my range of vision, which was the only possible way they weren't in serious trouble."

Chris and Chrissy surfaced forward of the anchor line, then drifted back over top of McDougall but unseen by him. As they passed along the port side of the boat, Gatto (not Chatterton) tossed a line to them (one line, not two) from the wheelhouse deck. Both Rouses grabbed the line, talking excitedly as they did so. When Lander stepped out of the cabin on the deck below, she grabbed hold of the line and helped Gatto to pull it in. Packer, Yurga, Kohler, and Chatterton then grabbed the line. Gatto let go of the line, climbed down the ladder to the main deck, and ran to the ladder at the stern of the boat.

The boat was rolling from side to side, and the stern was pitching up and down. As Chrissy rounded the corner of the port stern, a wave shoved him partially under the hull as it was on a rise. The chine of the hull (not the splash rail) crashed down on Chrissy's tanks, cracking the manifold valve in the process. Air commenced to hiss from the rupture. The escaping air did not materially affect the rescue operation, although the loud hissing sound added to the stress of the situation. (The incessant hissing meant that Chrissy could not have been totally out of air, and that he could have conducted some decompression had he chosen to do so.)

Chris drifted back on the trail line and told people on the boat to take Chrissy first. Chrissy grabbed hold of a rung. He climbed about halfway up the ladder under his own power, but could not make it all the way to the top. In a concentrated group effort, Gatto, Packer, Yurga, Lander, Brad Henderson, Kohler, and Chatterton (not Kohler and Chatterton alone) all reached over the stern rail or through the ladder opening, gripped him by the arms and harness straps, and pulled him through the ladder opening onto the deck.

Packer, Lander, Henderson, and Kohler dragged Chrissy away from the ladder, in order to make room for his father. All together (not just Kohler and Chatterton) they stripped off his tanks and accessory equipment, then lifted him onto the dressing table and laid him on his back. Chrissy was in pain (but he was not screaming epithets). His voice was so soft that Lander had to put her ear close to his mouth in order to hear him speak.

Gatto, Packer, Yurga, and Chatterton leaned over the rail at the back of the boat as Chris climbed partway up the ladder. He stared ahead blankly, and said, "I'm not gonna make it."

Gatto took this to mean that he could not physically climb the rest of the way up the ladder, not that he was going to die. Gatto took an equipment line that happened to be stowed nearby, wrapped it around the crossbar of Chris's tanks, snapped the hook on the line, and said, "I've got you. You're not gonna go anywhere, even if we have to drag your ass up here."

Still staring forward at no one in particular, Chris said, "Tell Sue I love her," and passed out. Chris's last conscious thought was of his wife. He fell back into the water, but did not drift away because Gatto maintained his grip on the rope.

As Gatto held the line, Packer, Yurga, and Chatterton climbed partway down the ladder. Yurga climbed down so far that his chest got wet. Chris's head submerged and slipped under the ladder. The bottom rung pummeled the back of his head.

Gatto yelled, "Get his head out of the water."

Chatterton pulled Chris's knife from its sheath, and used it to slice through the harness straps. The tanks and auxiliary equipment came off Chris's body, but were still secured to the boat by the line in Gatto's hands. Chatterton disconnected Chris's drysuit inflator hose (he did not cut the hose with the knife).

McDougall completed his decompression and swam to the stern of the boat. He saw Gatto, Packer, Chatterton, and Yurga trying to get Chris up and over the ladder. Chris was limp. Someone waved him off (unnecessarily). He "gave them the space they needed to get him up."

Working together, Yurga, Gatto, Packer, and Chatterton hauled Chris up the ladder and onto the deck. (Chatterton did not do a fireman's carry.) Chris was not breathing and did not have a pulse. McDougall climbed up the ladder. When he saw the divers cutting off

Chris's thousand-dollar drysuit, he had no doubt that the situation was serious.

Gatto started chest compressions; Chatterton started rescue breathing.

In the wheelhouse, Dan Crowell called the Coast Guard. (He did not yell "May Day.")

Lander put an oxygen regulator in Chrissy's mouth. She got a cup of water for him. She (not Kohler) wrote down that the Rouse's bottom time was forty-one minutes.

As soon as McDougall doffed his tanks, he relieved Gatto on chest compressions.

Someone (none of the witnesses remembered who) deployed an Ambu-Bag. Packer and Chatterton placed the mask over Chris's nose and mouth, and started squeezing the bag.

There was nothing else to be done for Chrissy except to continue to give him oxygen and water. Packer was so upset that he desperately felt the need to do something more to help. He took over the chest compressions from McDougall. Chatterton continued to squeeze the Ambu-bag.

Packer continued to do the chest compressions, by himself and without relief. Not that relief was not offered; rather, he felt the need to be intensely involved in the lifesaving efforts.

Gatto took station in the wheelhouse in order to assist Crowell in transmitting messages between the Coast Guard (on the radio) and the divers (on the deck) who were assisting in lifesaving operations.

An hour and a half passed between the surfacing of the Rouses and the arrival of the helicopter. Crowell ordered the divers on deck to lash down or remove any loose items; otherwise they might be blown overboard and lost. (Loose items could not get sucked up into the chopper's rotating airfoils. Nor could objects be turned into deadly missiles.) Everyone on deck donned a life vest. That was standard operating procedure for rescue operations, and one that was ordered by the Coast Guard (in case anyone fell or was knocked overboard).

An airlift is a dramatic scene, but it is not life threatening to the participants, as *Shadow Divers* would have its ingenuous readers believe.

The Coast Guard rescue swimmer was lowered to the boat in a basket. (He did not leap into the sea, then toss a medical kit over the rail and climb aboard. The boat was underway and heading into the wind, which was standard operating procedure for a helicopter evacuation.) He wore a survival suit and helmet. (He did not wear gloves, hood, goggles, mask, or fins. There was no explosive discharge of electricity.) He immediately took command of the situation.

The rescue swimmer said to Packer (not to Chatterton), "You're a little slow on the compressions."

Packer knew that it was true. He told me that, after spending more than an hour crouched over Chris and doing chest compressions at the rate of one hundred compressions per minute, he was exhausted. "My knees were killing me." He forced himself to pick up the pace, and he continued to do chest compressions unassisted throughout the airlift operation.

The rescue swimmer said nothing to Chatterton. Chatterton said nothing to the rescue swimmer. Never at any time was there any conversation between them. No "long-atrophied triage instincts flared to life." Chatterton was not doing solo CPR. He was sprawled comfortably on the deck, simply squeezing an Ambu-Bag; he continued to do so throughout the process of airlifting Chrissy, and he interacted in no way with the rescue swimmer or with the airlift of Chrissy.

The rescue swimmer instructed the divers on how the stricken pair were to be lifted to the helicopter. He called all the shots: a task for which he was suitably trained. No bystanders interfered with what were standard operating procedures.

After examining Chrissy, the rescue swimmer called the helicopter on a hand-held radio and issued instructions to lower a stretcher (not a basket). The chopper veered away from the boat after the stretcher was lowered to the deck. The stretcher was placed on the dressing station next to Chrissy. Yurga, Lander, Henderson, and Kohler all helped to lift Chrissy into the stretcher. (Kohler and Chatterton did not do it alone, while the others cowered in the cabin.) The chopper returned and hovered overhead while the cable was lowered. All four divers held onto the stretcher and its four lifting cables: one cable in each corner. One by one, the rescue swimmer motioned for the lifting cables. He snapped each lifting line to the clip at the end of the cable. The helpers continued to hold onto the stretcher until enough slack was taken in the cable to create tension on the lifting line.

The rescue swimmer pulled the line taut above the stretcher, so that there would be no abrupt jerk on the line when it was drawn up to the chopper. He signaled to the crew chief with his upturned thumb. The crew chief retracted the cable by engaging the winch. The stretcher was lifted off the dressing station (not off the gunwale). The rescue swimmer held onto a trailing guideline once the stretcher was lifted into the air, in order to maintain tension so that the stretcher would not swing like a pendulum.

Once the line was taut, the chopper veered away from the boat. A helicopter never hovers over top of a vessel unnecessarily, because a downdraft might force it down, or a loss in engine power might cause it to lose altitude. The stretcher was winched up into the chopper's cargo bay.

Gatto was standing at the wheelhouse door as Chrissy was lifted past him. Chrissy was calm (he was not screaming). Gatto gave him one thumb up, to indicate, "Hang in there. You're going to make it." Tragically, Chrissy did not make it. He died several hours later in the recompression chamber.

The rescue swimmer removed his helmet so he could communicate with the crew chief of the helicopter over his hand-held radio. They discussed the quickest way to effect the airlift of Chris.

The rescue swimmer knelt in front of Chris. Packer was still doing chest compressions nonstop. Chatterton was still squeezing the Ambu-Bag.

McDougall asked, "You guys have oxygen on that chopper for him?"

The rescue swimmer said, "Sure do." He then knelt at Chris's feet. "Listen up. This is what we're going to do. There's no reason why you can't keep doing chest compressions to the last second."

(Chatterton did not reply. He did not speak. He did not argue. He did not shout that Chris was dead and should be left behind. He did as he was told.)

Packer continued the chest compressions. Wordlessly, Chatterton squeezed the Ambu-Bag. (He did not do chest compressions or solo CPR.)

The rescue swimmer informed them that, instead of lowering the stretcher again, Chris was going to be airlifted in the basket that had landed him on the boat. He dragged the basket to Chris's feet. Chris was lifted into the basket. The chopper returned and lowered the cable. The rescue swimmer snapped the hook onto the pad eye of the basket. The basket was lifted off the deck. The chopper veered away as the winch hauled the basket up to the chopper. Chris was pronounced dead on arrival at the hospital.

The chopper returned for the rescue swimmer. It lowered a cable with a snap hook on the end (not a basket). The rescue swimmer snapped the hook onto his harness. From a standing position, he was lifted off the deck of the boat and up to the hovering helicopter, which veered away during the retrieval procedure. After the rescue swimmer was safely pulled into the cabin, the chopper proceeded directly to the hospital.

(The "other divers" did not slink sheepishly out of the cabin, because they were already standing on the open deck. No one thanked Chatterton. No one hugged him.)

There were no slackers in the group. Despite the emotional turmoil, everyone contributed to the rescue operation to the fullest extent of his or her ability.

Gatto recalled how quiet it became after the helicopter departed. The raucous wind and prop wash yielded to a hush of introspection. Emotions were in turmoil. He heard "just a slight murmur of crying from some. Most were just stunned at what happened." In the aftermath of frenzy, the awful truth filled a vacuum that grew in each and every heart.

McDougall told me, "I recall how everyone was calm and professional while at the same time dealing with the sadness and grief of comrades in imminent peril. No panic. Everything went like it was planned and rehearsed: Coast Guard notification, cutting loose of the wreck, gear getting stowed for getting under way, Barb getting info on what happened during the dive from Chrissy, first aid procedures, communicating with everyone on board from the bridge and back through relayed voice communications, coordinating with the CG rescue, clearing the deck of everything and every-one for protection from prop wash, getting into the wind, reminders about the static charge from anything attached to the helicopter."

Both Packer and McDougall told me that they knew that Chris was dead. He turned purple long before the helicopter arrived. But no one gave up hope that, by some miracle of modern medical science, his unrespon-sive body could be brought back to life.

A Mything Link

Shadow Divers exploited the deaths of the Rouses in order to glamorize the mythic qualities of two chosen heroes at the expense of the other lifesavers, whose more important contributions were paramount toward making a successful airlift.

To make matters even more incomprehensible to the uninformed readers of *Shadow Divers*, Chatterton allegedly gave a substantially different version of events to Bernie Chowdhury for *The Last Dive* (2000). For example, in that version, Chatterton thought about intubating Chris instead of breathing mouth to mouth. Such a possibility was absurd under the circum-stances, not only because the *Seeker* carried no intuba-tion equipment, but because intubation could be effected only by someone with special training: an anesthesiologist, an anesthetist, or in some cases an emergency medical technician; not an ex-Army medic with a nine-week course in first aid, and who had not been a medic for a couple of decades.

Betsy Llewellyn, a registered nurse and anesthetist with more than thirty years of practice, told me that even anesthesiologists sometimes had difficulty in intubating patients prior to surgery on a steady operating table, much less on a boat that was rolling and pitching violently. She intubated patients on a daily basis, and sometimes *she* had trouble with the procedure.

In *The Last Dive* version, Chatterton prevented Kohler from performing CPR on Chris because, after asking Kohler when he took his CPR course, Chatterton informed him that his certification had expired.

In times of emergency, it is unlikely that the first thought to come to a lifesaver's mind is a volunteer's CPR certification date. It is also unlikely that anyone will remember the expiration date of his certification. In either case, a person whose CPR certification has expired is no less qualified to perform CPR than a motorist is unqualified to operate a motor vehicle after forgetting to pay the renewal for his driver's license.

The uninformed readers of *Shadow Divers* should note that Kurson had to have been aware of these dissimilarities, because he cited *The Last Dive* as one of his primary sources. Yet Chowdhury did not interview Gatto, McDougall, Packer, or Yurga about this incident. *The Last Dive* did not mention Brad Henderson's name. All the information that Chowdhury obtained was strictly one-sided.

Ignoring additional differences between the two texts, let us jump to the one that is the most glaring. In *The Last Dive*, Chatterton's sentiments are reversed with respect to airlifting Chris. Instead of begging the rescue diver to leave Chris behind because he was dead, as it was written in *Shadow Divers*, in *The Last Dive* it was written that Chatterton pleaded with the rescue swimmer to *please* airlift Chris - this because the rescue swimmer pronounced Chris dead, and refused to take the risk of making an airlift for a body. In *The Last Dive* version, Chatterton had to convince the rescue swimmer to make another airlift for Chris, which he did only reluctantly and only after conceding a long and loud argument with Chatterton.

It should be noted that there is no uncommon risk in airlifting a victim from a boat. Coast Guard personnel are trained professionals who are specialists in airlifting operations. While an airlift may appear risky to the layperson, any inherent risk is mitigated by training and experience with the equipment and procedures.

The confused reader should now be asking, Is *The Last Dive* any more reliable for accuracy than *Shadow Divers*? To help answer that question, I interviewed Bob Burns about an incident that was covered in *The Last Dive*, and in which he was directly involved.

Nitrox Fatality

Burns was the skipper and co-owner of the dive boat *Dina Dee II*. He related the following story to me the way it actually happened. On July 5, 1992, Burns took a charter to the *Arundo*, a Dutch freighter that was torpedoed by the *U-136* on April 28, 1942. The wreck lay at a depth of 130 feet.

On the bottom, Bob Crook chanced across the body of Ed Sollner lying on top of the wreck. Sollner's regulator was dangling uselessly beneath him. Crook tried to tow Sollner to the anchor line, but had difficulty in manhandling the body. Gary Matz, mate of the *Dina Dee II*, came along and took over from Crook. Matz towed the body to the anchor line and ascended to his 20-foot decompression stop, at which point he let the body go to the surface on its own buoyancy.

Someone on the boat spotted the apparently unconscious diver on the surface, and shouted an alarm. Tim Stumpf jumped into the water and starting doing mouth-to-mouth resuscitation. He towed the body to the boat between breaths. Stumpf removed Sollner's tanks. Several people dragged Sollner onto the back of the boat, and immediately commenced CPR.

Burns called the Coast Guard and requested heli-copter evacuation. The divers continued CPR for an hour and a half, until Sollner was airlifted off the deck. Sollner was pronounced dead on arrival at the Jersey Shore Memorial Hospital.

Chowdhury interviewed Burns about the incident. Burns told the same story to him that he told to me. Yet in *The Last Dive*, it was written, "The dive boat chugged solemnly back to port with Ed's stiffening corpse lying on the deck, covered with a tarp and lashed down to prevent it from rolling about the deck. . . . At the dock, an ambulance met the dive boat."

Although this single instance may not necessarily set the tenor for *The Last Dive*, it certainly casts suspi-cion on its credibility.

Conundrum

With respect to the argument between Chatterton and the rescue swimmer, Chowdhury supposedly sent his manuscript to Chatterton for approval. Chatterton purportedly approved it, or at the very least let it stand. In a similar fashion, on page 337 of *Shadow Divers* it was written, "Upon completing the book, I asked Chat-terton and Kohler to review the manuscript for accura-cy." Thus both authors claimed that Chatterton verified the story that he related to them.

On an Internet forum, Chatterton repudiated *The Last Dive* version and confirmed the *Shadow Divers* version.

Which version should the uninformed reader believe? Did Chatterton argue to have Chris left behind, or argue to have him taken away?

As it happens, these contrary accounts are irrele-vant, because neither version is substantiated by the testimony of reliable witnesses.

The Most Objective Witness of All

None of the witnesses I interviewed remembered *any* discussion between Chatterton and the rescue swimmer. None of the witnesses recalled that they even spoke to each other until the rescue swimmer said, "Listen up," at which point Chatterton listened.

But the best witness of all was a video camera. As a New Jersey state trooper, Steve McDougall understood better than most the importance of recording evidence for posterity. When the helicopter arrived, Steve McDougall grabbed his video camera and taped the rescue operation. He held the camera discretely at his side under his arm, where its presence was for the most part imperceptible.

The videotape showed events that differed radically from what was written in *Shadow Divers*. The videotape confirmed the airlift version that is given in the section above entitled "The Reality," and which was corroborated by all four witnesses I interviewed. Throughout the airlift operation, the videotape showed Chatterton sitting on the deck, leaning against a cooler with his legs extended in front of him, perfunctorily squeezing the Ambu-Bag. I do not mean to imply that his was not an important role. But the videotape clearly showed that Chatterton was *not* an active participant in the airlift. The videotape clearly showed the rescue swimmer taking charge of the situation and giving instructions. The videotape did *not* show Chatterton speaking to the rescue swimmer, arguing with him, or communicating with him in any way. The videotape did *not* show Chatterton giving instructions to Kohler. The videotape clearly showed that Chatterton stayed silent and out of the way until Chris was placed in the basket and airlifted off the deck.

When the rescue swimmer said, "Listen up," those words and the following dialogue were audible on the videotape, as was McDougall's question about oxygen - because at that time McDougall was holding the camera over Chatterton's right shoulder next to his head. The audio track contained *no* dialogue from Chatterton.

Witnesses may forget a few minor details, or be confused about chronology, but video cameras record events in sequence as they actually occurred.

The Fatality Fallacy

Diving is many things to many people: challenge, excitement, beauty, wonder, marine life encounters, and uncommon experiences.

It is important to reassure my faithful readers that diving fatalities are few and far between. I have often quipped that the most dangerous part of a dive trip was the drive on the highway to and from the boat.

Shadow Divers went to great lengths to exaggerate the dangers of diving. On page 4, the book went as far as to state that diving is "a sport that regularly kills its young." From this kind of base overstatement, the book's uninformed readers might infer that divers do not reach middle age.

It is estimated that several *million* Americans are certified to dive. To insinuate that all these people confront the extreme risk of not living long enough to raise their children, become grandparents, and collect Social Security, is excessive inflation even by the standards of yellow journalism.

Shadow Divers dwelt on fatalism and fake near-death scenes as mechanisms to achieve a background of spectacular melodrama against which the book's diving prodigies could be conspicuous in brave ostentation. Mature, safe, and responsible divers do not engage in pretentious displays of courage.

The Great Escape

Perhaps the most sensational scene in *Shadow Divers* was recounted on page 323: a breathtaking finale that represented climax in its purest theatrical form. According to the book, Chatterton doffed his tank and shoved it through a restriction in the diesel engine room, donned his tank, proceeded into the electric motor room, found a spare parts box, and passed the box through the restriction to Kohler. Kohler handed the box to an anonymous diver to take to the surface and inspect it for tags that might have the U-boat's number stamped on it.

Chatterton returned for a second box, but got

strangled in cables. Kohler waited on the other side of the restriction, noting by his watch that Chatterton was "crazy late." Chatterton disentangled himself but ran out of gas in the process. He removed his tank in order to swim through the restriction, and - even though the tank was empty - he shoved it through the restriction in front of him. He then spit out the regulator. Holding his very last breath, he passed Kohler in the diesel engine room without stopping to breathe from Kohler's spare regulator, swam fifty feet through the wreck and over the top of the hull to reach "the stage bottles." He opened a valve, stuck a regulator in his mouth - and breathed.

It was a hairbreadth escape if ever there was one.

Der Tag

I was on the boat that day. After completing my photographic survey, I waited on the surface for the tag recovery team to return. When the liftbag popped to the surface, Will McBeth swam to the liftbag with a safety line, which he secured to the mesh bag. Affixed to the spare parts box was a plastic tag. He rubbed the tag through the mesh of the bag in order to clean it. The tag was marked "U 869". He towed bag to the boat.

Harold Moyers wrote congratulations and the U-boat's number on a slate. McBeth secured the slate to a lead ankle weight, and allowed it to slide down the anchor line to the decompressing divers. The number came as no surprise to anyone on the boat, for we had all known for years that the U-Who? was the *U-869*. Identification was therefore somewhat anticlimactic.

The tag recovery divers completed their decompression. One by one they climbed on board. No one said anything about getting strangled by cables or running out of air. No one said anything about waiting breathlessly for an overdue diver who was trapped inside. According to post-dive conversation, the dive had gone strictly according to plan with nary a hitch.

After reading the account in *Shadow Divers*, I wondered if perhaps, in the intervening years, I had slipped through a warp in space-time and emerged in some alternate universe, where history took a different path and where events occurred otherwise. If any diver had as close a call as *Shadow Divers* claimed that Chatterton had, he would have mentioned it to somebody.

Only an inexperienced or panic-stricken diver would brush past his buddy without taking his spare regulator. That was one of the reasons that wreck-divers carried spares.

Furthermore, the distance from the diesel engine to the top of the wreck was less than twenty feet, not fifty feet.

Kilroy Was Here

Although *Shadow Divers* claimed that Chatterton and Kohler were the only two members of the tag recovery team, they were in fact assisted by John Yurga and Pat Rooney. Yurga was in charge of shooting videotape; Rooney was a safety diver. Despite the fact that the four divers who were involved in the tag recovery yakked volubly about the dive afterward, so that everyone on the boat knew everything that had occurred on the bottom, for the writing of this book I asked Rooney to recount the events that occurred underwater.

After Chatterton staged two sling bottles outside the entry point (a safety measure that *Shadow Divers* neglected to mention), all four divers entered the opening of the control room, and proceeded through the watertight doorway into the diesel engine room.

Chatterton removed his tank and proceeded through the space between the engine and the curvature of the hull. He donned the tank on the other side of the restriction.

He must have been shocked to see a flashing strobe that lighted the way for him! Let me back up . . .

On page 209 of *Shadow Divers*, it was written that Chatterton once dropped through the damage hole that was located immediately behind the after torpedo loading hatch, in order to explore the after torpedo room. On page 199, it was written that Kohler also explored the after torpedo room on another occasion. The after torpedo room is adjacent to the electric motor room. The book made no mention of any attempt to reach the electric motor room from the after torpedo room: a shorter and more direct route that a diligent diver would have explored. On page 312, the book went as far as to claim, "There is no way out the other end of the electric motor room, as its aft end has been crushed downward."

Will McBeth entered the water before the tag recovery team. He swam to the after torpedo loading hatch. Originally, this hatch was angled toward the stern. Due to blast damage and subsequent collapse, the hatch had swung down on rusting metal until it pointed slightly forward, directly at the watertight doorway that led to the electric motor room.

He faced aft as he hovered above the hatch. In one smooth motion, he dropped down through the hatch, bent his knees as he reached the bottom, bent forward at the waist, and pushed backward into the electric motor room. He did not have to remove his double tanks in order to effect this maneuver.

McBeth's method of entering the electric motor room was quicker and safer than Chatterton's laborious and time-consuming route through the control room, the diesel engine room, and the restriction. McBeth easily made the penetration alone and while wearing double tanks. He knew that Chatterton would soon be entering the electric motor room from the other direction, so he left a strobe light as a marker for him. He was like the frogman who sneaked onto a Japanese-held beach the night before an Allied assault, and left a sign on which was written "Kilroy was here."

On the boat after the dive, Chatterton displayed abject annoyance at McBeth for entering the electric motor room ahead of him, and at having his penetration pre-empted. Although McBeth's route was simple and direct, it lacked the staginess and histrionics that Chatterton performed for the camera. Despite this lack of dramatic appeal, McBeth's method of entry and exit provided an excellent emergency escape route.

It is interesting to note that Chatterton was the only one who ever entered the electric motor room via the diesel engine room. Forever afterward, everyone else accessed the electric motor room by means of the route that McBeth pioneered.

The Not So Great Escape

Rooney's account continues. . . .

Chatterton pulled a spare parts box off its shelf. He passed the box through the restriction to Kohler, who turned and handed the box to Rooney. Rooney carried the box out of the diesel engine room into the control room, which, because the overhead had rusted away, was essentially outside the wreck. Yurga videotaped Rooney as he placed the box in a mesh bag, secured a liftbag to the mesh bag, then inflated the liftbag with gas from his regulator. The liftbag rose toward the surface.

Kohler and Chatterton emerged from the wreck. Yurga and Kohler swam toward the anchor line. Still breathing from the regulator that was attached to the tank on his back, Chatterton clipped one of his sling bottles to his harness. He fumbled with the other sling bottle.

Seeing that he was having difficulty in clipping the second sling bottle to his harness, Rooney swam to his side and helped him to secure the tank. They then proceeded together to the anchor line. They ascended the line and conducted their decompression.

Rooney did not observe any unusual activity that would indicate that Chatterton was out of gas, or even low on gas. The dive went according to plan, the way it was intended to appear on television.

While the actual performance lacked theatricality, Rooney's accounts had the advantage of being accurate.

CHAPTER FOUR
Skewed Accounts

*"If you tell the truth, you don't have to remember any-
thing."*

- Mark Twain

Who's on First?

Several years ago, John Chatterton told me that he
had employed someone to write his book for him. Generally, when a ghostwriter produces a work for hire, he
writes what he is told to write. He is not given the onus
of ascertaining or verifying the truth of what he is told.
The employer is accountable for the facts and for their
accurate presentation - as well as for any errors, oversights, inaccuracies, misstatements, and misrepresen-
tations: in other words, for any and all deviations from
the facts.

The authorship of *Shadow Divers* appears to have
been different, and somewhat muddled or convoluted.
Chatterton and Richie Kohler formed a partnership
called the U-869 Partnership. *Shadow Divers* was copy-
righted in the names of Robert Kurson and the U-869
Partnership. This implied that all three - Kurson,
Kohler, and Chatterton - collectively shared the burden
of authorship in one form or another: the research, the
writing, and the presentation.

In the source notes, Kurson called Chatterton and
Kohler his business partners in the writing of the book.
Kurson also stated that Chatterton and Kohler
reviewed the manuscript for accuracy. This may appear
to let Kurson off the hook for any misinterpretations of
events as they were depicted, but in reality it did not,
as portions of *Shadow Divers Exposed* amply demonstrate.

Credit must be shared equally.

The *Andrea Doria* Gate Caper

The Third Class Kitchen was not readily accessible from outside the wreck. No external doorways opened directly into the kitchen or the adjacent dining room. One could *peer* into the adjacent Third Class Dining Room through a grille near the stern of the Foyer Deck. This grille may have provided ventilation for the dining room. The metal bars of which the grille was constructed were spaced too close for a diver to fit through while wearing a standard double-tank rig and pony bottle.

On page 109 of *Shadow Divers*, it was written that, late in 1989, Chatterton "squeezed through a tiny opening." The book was singularly lacking in details, for it failed to mention how he accomplished the squeeze: was he was wearing tanks at the time, or did he doff his tanks and then don them inside the grille?

Shadow Divers gave the impression that Chatterton was alone when he made this penetration. The book neglected to mention that Glen Plokhoy and Bernie Saccarro stayed outside the grille in order to assist him through the bars.

Shadow Divers gave the wrong date. This penetration occurred in 1988, not in 1989.

Carrying the Torch

Bill Nagle and Chatterton spearheaded the effort to burn off one bar of the grille, in order to permit entry to the Third Class Dining Room through the enlarged opening.

Nagle already owned a Broco torch, with all the necessary hoses and fittings. He bought it in preparation for a trip to recover the bell from the *Andrea Doria*, in 1985, because he thought that we might have to burn the bell off its davit. After trials, he and John Moyer used the torch to cut a porthole off the *Great Isaac* and a helm off the *Ioannis P. Goulandris*. Because we recovered the bell by pounding out the drift pin, we did not need the Broco torch to do the job.

Now, three years later, Nagle took the *Seeker* on a special trip to the *Andrea Doria* in order to torch a way through the grille. Nagle's schedule was uncommonly aggressive. On August 21, the *Seeker* departed Brielle to conduct two dives on the *Texas Tower,* which lay seventy miles from the dock. After returning to Brielle, on August 22 the *Seeker* traveled one hundred fifteen miles to Montauk, New York. There Nagle refueled the boat, and departed for the *Andrea Doria,* which lay another hundred miles farther.

The weather forecast for August 24 was bad, so Nagle figured that he might have only one day on site in which to complete the job before having to run for shelter.

Shadow Divers made no mention of anyone helping Chatterton in the operation. The implication was that Chatterton did it all by himself. According to Jon Hulburt, who participated in the venture, "The task of cutting the opening took 2 dives from everyone involved. Some of us reset the tie-in and placed the cutting hoses and cables. Once we had completed setting up the hoses, Chuck Wine and I cut away close-by hazardous netting and moved it aft. Divers were needed to feed the rods to Chatterton and Nagle."

Both Nagle and Chatterton took turns at burning through the grille: first Nagle, then Chatterton, then Nagle again. Glen Plokhoy was Chatterton's assistant.

Hulburt: "Plokhoy videotaped Chatterton cutting as well as helping change over cutting rods, not to mention the safety backup which all excellent wreck divers provide. Chatterton was more proficient than Nagle but without Nagle's two stints of cutting, the job could not have been completed before the weather blew up. Especially critical were Nagle's recommended improvements in the process of removing spent rods and restarting the Broco. By evening, the target bar was cut away."

On page 110 of *Shadow Divers*, it was written, "As the bar fell away and the hole opened up, the video showed a white mountain of dishes inside that looked piled by Walt Disney himself."

Hulburt, who shot the video to which *Shadow Divers* alluded, strongly disputed the sentence that is quoted above. "The facts are that when Nagle finished cutting through the bar, all video cameras were aboard the *Seeker*. Secondly, a diver peering inside the opening could not have seen a single dish. The first ones found were more than 50 feet forward behind a metal bulkhead on the far side of the cavernous Third Class Dining Room. Many were later found in silt more than 40 feet below. These are measured distances, not Kurson distances. Visibility outside was spectacular all day, perhaps more than 50 feet. But inside the *Doria* with a dive light, no dishes were seen from more than 5 feet away. The dark silt absorbed all light and camouflaged the few dishes observed out in the open. Third, the first video taken inside on this last trip of the season revealed an occasional single scattered dish and one pair stacked together, every one of them more than 50 feet from the grille. The sentence is a total fabrication.

"Ed Suarez dived and sent up the torch and hoses. He then entered the newly cut opening and unexpectedly collected a couple dozen dishes from the kitchen. Because Hulburt was shooting video, he was directed to penetrate the grille while the interior visibility was clear, with Wine as his dive buddy. They squeezed one at a time through the horizontal opening now available. Hulburt swam forward, videotaping the Third Class Dining Room as he passed the tables. He penetrated the entire length of the hallway at 205 feet depth, which ran below the kitchen and above the #4 hatch. Hulburt shot video of the kitchen overhead and retrieved a cup and spoon. Also during the dive, he cut away dangling cables to make the area safer for everyone."

Because Chatterton and Plokhoy made only one torching dive (compared to Nagle's two), they had time to make a repetitive dive late that afternoon, after Hulburt, Wine, and Suarez made their dives. Hulburt recalled that Chatterton and Plokhoy recovered three silver trays, but they reported that they had dropped a stack of trays into a corner of the Kitchen in the process.

The *Seeker* stayed hooked into the wreck overnight. The next morning, with the weather worsening, Wine penetrated into the Kitchen and recovered several dozen dishes. The divers had agreed earlier to split the artifacts equally among themselves. Sharing artifacts was a typical wreck-diving procedure whenever a team effort was required in the recovery process.

Hulburt: "Each diver received 5 dishes from Wine and 3 dishes from Suarez. Plokhoy and Hulburt made copies of their underwater footage and shared them with the other wreck divers who had helped make this lightning expedition a success."

Chatterton and Plokhoy went down to release the tie-in line, but first they made another penetration into the Kitchen. Those who were forced to remain topside expected Chatterton and Plokhoy to retrieve the silver trays that they had dropped the day before. That way, everyone on board could go home with a unique memento of this special trip. Instead, Chatterton and Plokhoy reconnoitered the Kitchen to their own advantage, not only gaining knowledge of the interior layout that they could exploit on another trip, but leaving behind the silver trays which they would have had to share with the other divers if they had recovered them at that time.

Hulburt recalled that he "and several others were much aware of Chatterton's ploy. They had expected better."

In addition to the six names mentioned above, Mike Boring, Dave Bright, and Clint Zineker played important roles on the grille cutting team.

The grille-cutting episode occurred in August 1988. Yet, as noted above, it was written in *Shadow Divers* that Chatterton squeezed through the grille late in 1989.

The Great Gate Escapade

Once the way was open, Nagle was aware of the possibility that divers from other boats might enter the compartment and recover some of the artifacts that "his" group left behind, before he and his team had another opportunity to reap the rewards of their efforts. His notion was fully justified, for that was precisely why Steve Bielenda moved up the date for his first *Doria* trip the following year - and he sold out the charter on the basis that a new and productive area had been found inside the wreck.

Little did Bielenda know that his claim-jumping tactic was to be pre-empted. The diver's grapevine is more like a multi-media broadcast than a backyard gossip channel. Just as Bielenda heard about the torching of the grille, and the opening of the way to the Third Class Kitchen, Nagle heard about Bielenda's stratagem to clean out the cabinets before the hard-working *Seeker* team had the opportunity to reap the rewards of their own efforts.

Ironically, on page 110 it was written that someone on the *Seeker's* grille-cutting trip "turned traitor" by informing the Atlantic Wreck Divers of the torching job, while on page 169 it was written that had it not been for "one honest guy" among the Atlantic Wreck Divers, the *Seeker* clique would not have learned about the pre-emptive trip. Which cliché is more appropriate: "A rose by any other name . . . " or "What's good for the goose . . . "?

In the event, neither a traitor nor an honest guy existed outside the imagination of the author. As noted above, Jon Hulburt explored the kitchen after the grille was cut away, and shot videotape of artifacts as he plucked them out of the silt. Because the grille removal operation was not intended to be a secret, he had no compunction against showing the videotape to his fellow divers (including this author). The job was common knowledge.

Hulburt: "Nagle explicitly expected that other boats and divers would respect the work that the *Seeker* had put into opening the Third Class Dining Room. Bill expected they would allow the *Seeker* to be the first charter to return in 1989 as scheduled. After that, Bill really did not care who entered the new opening. He knew there was plenty for all."

The *Wahoo's* dive schedule was printed on fliers that were disseminated throughout the diving community in order to attract business. During the winter of 1988-1989, Hulburt received a *Wahoo* flier in the mail. The June trip to the *Andrea Doria* was openly publicized. Hulburt mentioned the trip to Nagle.

In one sense - because Hulburt showed his videotape to me and other divers, then told Nagle about the *Wahoo* flier - he was both the "traitor" and the "one honest guy." In another sense, the "one honest guy" was Bielenda, for printing and distributing the flier. It should be noted that Hulburt was not a member of the Atlantic Wreck Divers, although he frequently enjoyed diving with them. The *Shadow Divers* version of events violated the truth of the situation, and spun a yarn that catered to dramatic entertainment.

Although the *Wahoo* schedule was given to prospective customers at dive conferences over the winter, and was posted openly on the boat's bulletin board, the primary purpose of the trip was known to only a few. Nagle presumed that Bielenda's purpose was to take advantage of the open way to the kitchen. In this case, his presumption was correct.

Shadow Divers led its uninformed readers to believe that the Atlantic Wreck Divers chartered the *Wahoo* for the pre-emptive trip. In actuality, it was a captain's charter. This meant that the *Wahoo* was not chartered to any specific group or individual, but that it was open to anyone who wanted to go. Five Atlantic Wreck Divers signed up for the trip: Pete Guglieri, Gene Howley, Dennis Kessler, Richie Kohler, and Brad Sheard. Nine other divers included Mark Hill, Pete Manchee, Jack Moulliet, Ed Sollner, Ed Suarez, and four who are pictured in my group photo, but who I do not recognize.

It should be remembered that Suarez participated in the *Seeker's* grille cutting trip. He was instrumental in hauling cables, and had recovered a number of items from the kitchen.

After hearing about Bielenda's June trip, Chatterton and Plokhoy decided to reclose the opening, but in such a fashion that those who went to the *Doria* aboard the *Seeker* could reopen it. They did this by having a sophisticated stainless steel gate constructed. The measurements were calculated from Plokhoy's video footage of the opening. A welding fabricator built the gate to their specifications. Crosshatched bar stock and flat iron created a mechanism that looked like a miniature jail cell door, complete with sliding dowels and matched holes for a lock. The gate was so heavy that it had to be lowered to the wreck on a liftbag, and maneuvered into place.

After the vertical slides were extended inside the opening, the gate was secured with a chain and lock mechanism which was brainstormed by Hulburt and Nagle. Hulburt: "The end result was a specially hardened chain of square links, which could not be cut by either bolt cutters or by metal saws, and fastened by an eccentric recessed bolt. The head of the bolt had a peculiar Allen-wrench-like head that took an equally peculiar Allen wrench to turn." Then a well-oiled brass lock was clamped in place as a decoy.

The gate was installed during a "sneak" trip to the wreck that took place only a week before the *Wahoo's* scheduled departure. The entire operation was such a closely guarded secret that even the Russians did not know about it. That in itself was a monumental achievement, considering how much divers like to prattle about their exploits.

As a finishing touch, Chatterton cable-tied a white plastic sign to the gate. It read:

CLOSED FOR INVENTORY
PLEASE USE ALTERNATE
ENTRANCE
THANK YOU
CREW AND PATRONS OF
SEEKER

Death by Laughter

The *Wahoo's* opportunistic trip to the *Doria* was
scheduled for late June 1989. In addition to the fourteen divers who are noted above, six crewmembers were
on board: Cathie Cush, Hank Garvin, Gary Gilligan,
Don Schnell, Sally Wahrman, and this author. As
usual, Gilligan and I had the job of tying in.

Bielenda showed us on the plans where he wanted
the anchor line shackled: in the stern, just abaft the
enclosed promenade deck. Gilligan and I were not privy
to any ulterior motives for such a placement - we were
innocent dupes - but I noted right away that the spot
was near a number of places that I had "worked" in the
past, and near others that I suspected had the potential to yield unique artifacts. I also knew that the spot
was near the place where the *Seeker's* divers had forced
an entry to the Third Class Kitchen the previous year.

The grapnel snagged about fifty feet abaft the optimum tie-in position, and two decks lower. When we
settled down onto the hull, Gilligan and I recognized the
landmarks, and knew exactly where we were. We
dragged the downline only a few feet against an ener-
getic current before we were forced to acknowledge that
nature was stronger than we were. We slung the chain
around a stanchion in order to take off the strain and
to catch our breath. Then I unscrewed the bolt from the
shackle - and dropped it!

I felt like such a fumble thumb. The bolt fell fifteen
feet and vanished into the silt on the horizontal bulkhead of the walk-around deck. I left Gilligan holding the
chain while I descended slowly into the open corridor.
Luck was with me that day: there was a perfect imprint
of the bolt in the top layer of silt. I stuck my hand into
the thick mud and wrapped my fingers around the bolt.
I carried it up triumphantly to Gilligan. He was as
astonished as I about my luck in recovering the bolt.
Now we would not have to tie the chain in a knot
around the stanchion.

We released a couple of Styrofoam cups to let the
topside crew know that the tie-in was successful, so

they could slack off the anchor line and let the boat ride on the downline.

We had some bottom time remaining, so we went exploring. Together we dropped into the walk-around and looked forward into the alcove - and that was when Chatterton's bizarre sense of humor nearly caused me to drown. I went into such paroxysms of laughter that I spat out my regulator, and even after I found the mouthpiece and put it back between my teeth, I could not stop laughing. Gilligan suffered just as badly. After recovering from our laughing fit at 190 feet, we broke off the plastic sign and carried it up with us. All during the decompression, we kept exchanging looks and breaking out into guffaws that again and again nearly resulted in our demise.

Alternate Entrance

What Gilligan and I treated as comic relief was met with shock and indignation aboard the *Wahoo*, as though it were Grand Guignol. If we had not brought back the plastic sign, no one may have believed our story. No one else saw the irony or the exquisite black comedy of the plotters being outfoxed by their intended victims. Perhaps instead of dogging the footsteps of others, they should have been making their own path. Be that as it may, it did not make for a happy lot who signed up for easy pickings and wound up empty-handed. Those divers were overcome with gloom and anger. But the majority of divers had come simply to dive on the *Andrea Doria*, not to take advantage of the *Seeker's* forced entry to the Third Class Dining Room and Kitchen.

To me the sign presented a challenge. I studied the plans with the idea of trying one of the alternative routes that circumvented the gate. On our next dive, Gilligan and I swam to the aft end of the foyer deck and entered a doorway into a tiny cubicle at a depth of 200 feet. The corridor that led forward to the rear wall of the dining area was blocked, but a transverse passageway that went down appeared to be free of obstruction.

Because this was a service area that was not intended for passengers, the passageway that connected the two parallel lengthwise corridors was narrow: only slightly wider than a person's shoulders. It was also dark and foreboding.

Gilligan maintained station as I descended into the shaft. It was like falling into a surrealistic and incredibly deep grave. My arms scraped both sides. When I reached the end of the vertical passageway, I found myself at the junction of a horizontal corridor that extended fore and aft like an inverted tee. The way forward appeared to be open, if no wider. Before proceeding out of Gilligan's line of sight, I rolled over and shone a steady beam upward - our pre-arranged signal that all was well - then checked my gauges perfunctorily. The depth was 220 feet.

I surveyed my surroundings carefully for snags and possible entanglements. The corridor was clear. With only three feet of clearance, anti-silting propulsion techniques were useless. I swam little more than a body-length when the "floor" beneath me - actually a horizontal partition - fell away to reveal a closet. The closet was empty, but the next one forward gleamed of shimmering white porcelain through an irregular rusted opening: from side to side and top to bottom it was filled with cups and saucers. I stared in disbelief. All thoughts of going any farther were abandoned, even though the way to the Dining Room was unobstructed ahead of me.

I backtracked. Rolling over to look up, I found myself staring at receding steps in an enclosed stairway. After my heart stopped pounding like a trip hammer, I realized that I had not gone far enough. A few more feet brought me to the vertical entrance corridor, where Gilligan's light shone down like a friendly beacon. I shook my light as a signal for him to come down (it also could have meant that I was in trouble). He was by my side in an instant. I waved for him to follow me. A few feet away, I aimed my light into the closet below. His reaction mirrored my own.

He and I required no more communication. We had dived together often enough to know exactly what roles to take. I squirmed down into the closet while he unleashed his goodie bag and held it over the lip. He illuminated the rim of the bag with his light. I reached into the muck, grabbed a handful of china, ascended to the "top" of the closet, and dropped the items into the bag. After a couple of grabs I was blinded by agitated sediment, but it did not matter: wherever I put my hand I touched unbroken cups and saucers. I did not need to see. Time and again I rose up out of the black obscuring cloud, spotted the dim glow of Gilligan's light on the mesh bag's metal hoop, made my deposit, then plunged back down for more. In short order we accumulated forty-two cups and saucers. There was no end in sight - or in feel. Gilligan kept an eye on his timer and let me know when we had to go.

We retreated in reverse order. Passing under the stairwell, I waited at the bottom of the vertical shaft until Gilligan reached the top before making my ascent. We exited the cubicle without difficulty, then made our way to the anchor line. Gilligan clipped the mesh bag to his harness, and for an hour he had to bear the weight of our haul. Our return to the boat was met with jubilation. The somber atmosphere dissolved at once and an air of hope prevailed.

Inventory Taken

Meanwhile, Pete Manchee took a different tack, and made a spectacular penetration into the Third Class Kitchen by way of the grille in the Third Class Dining Room. His feat is not to be underrated for audacity or achievement. Manchee had worked for years as a commercial diver before moving on to other occupations. He thought that he could fit through the grating if he doffed his double tanks.

He asked Mark Hill and Hank Garvin to be his safeties. The three of them descended to the alcove at the bottom of the anchor line. Manchee carried a single tank in addition to the doubles that he wore on his back. He doffed his doubles in the alcove, donned the single tank, and squeezed through the bars of the grille.

Manchee angled down past table pedestals that were secured to the deck of the Dining Room. Fifty feet from the grille, at a depth of 205 feet, he encountered a horizontal partition that was the starboard sidewall of the port hallway between the Kitchen and Hold #4. He proceeded forward beneath a vertical partition into kitchen area. He was not disappointed. He found a cache of china that had never before been seen. He grabbed a few items, then made a hasty retreat to the grille.

What's on Second

Our entire collection was laid out on the deck: the cups and saucers that Gilligan and I recovered, and the plates that Manchee recovered.

The now-exuberant *Wahoo* patrons photographed the lot. Excelsior and packing straw, surviving these many years, and the lack of shelving in the closet, suggested that the ware that Gilligan and I found was packed in boxes to replace broken china. We posed for pictures, grinning with our booty. We held between us the *Seeker's* "Closed for Inventory" sign as an additional note of sarcasm.

Manchee was photographed with his plates. High-spirited comments of derision ensued from those who felt that they been cheated by the *Seeker's* counterplot.

Fellow wreck-divers thrust deck plans beneath our noses. They wanted to know where Gilligan and I had gone. We pointed out the compartment that was the storage closet. More important than its location was the convoluted way of reaching it, and the extreme working depth of 223 feet. Without exception, none of them had ever been that deep before. This posed serious problems with respect to individual tolerances to nitrogen narcosis: an unknown quantity whose effects were likely to be exacerbated by confinement and by the length of the penetration. The consequences of these psychological factors were not to be pooh-poohed.

Gilligan and I were careful not to underrate the difficulty of the dive. We described in exacting detail every reference point along the way, in particular the overhead stairwell that initially might go unnoticed. Upon return, a narked diver who turned upward too soon, and entered the stairwell instead of the adjacent shaft, could not be expected to overcome the resulting disorientation.

In the event, most of them could not find the doorway to the cubicle, while others found a doorway whose interior layout did not match our description. After post-dive debriefings, I determined that they had gone to the wrong deck: an easy error to make under low-light conditions where the decks looked so much alike, and where lack of familiarity with the wreck and the plans led to confusion.

More Inventory Taken

Manchee returned to the Third Class Kitchen on his next dive. This time his safeties were Ed Suarez and Sally Wahrmann. I carried down the single tank that Manchee planned to use, left it with Suarez and Wahrmann by the grille, then proceeded on my own dive of exploration with Gilligan. We did not return to what had already been dubbed the "Cup Hole." We left that for the patrons. Instead, we explored the Third Class Gift Shop and Bar.

Manchee did an instant replay of his first penetration. This time, he filled his mesh bag with such a huge stack of dinner plates that he could not obtain enough buoyancy to keep from sinking toward the bottom of the hull with all the weight. He had to hop from table to table like a frog leaping on lily pads to cross a pond. He made a tremendous jump from the sixth table aft, which was located almost directly beneath the grille. By kicking as hard as he could, he barely managed to catch the bottom bar of the grille with his fingertips. He hauled himself up by pulling and kicking.

He handed the mesh bag through the grating to Suarez. Then he swam to the top of the grille and squeezed through the grating to the outside of the wreck. All three ascended for a lengthy decompression.

Manchee's notes on that dive indicated that Wahrmann ran out of air and missed the oxygen hose that hung in the water off the bow of the boat. His notes also indicated that I took a spare bottle to her, and stayed with her throughout her decompression. Oddly, I had forgotten this incident.

The Final Irony

Needless to say, the *Wahoo's* patrons were ecstatic over these two incredible finds.

We returned to the Cup Hole on the next trip several weeks later. This time the patrons were more successful, some choosing to dive in teams of three, with one safety diver stationed at the top of the shaft, and another at the bottom, while the third moved laterally to reach the closet. A guideline down the shaft would only have created an entanglement.

After a couple of dives, performance increased so dramatically that repeat divers recovered several hundred cups and saucers. Even first-timers went home with souvenirs that were donated by those who were more fortunate.

This episode was not without its irony. The *Seeker* arrived on site about a week after the *Wahoo's* first departure. Chatterton unlocked the gate to enable the divers to work in the kitchen.

Hulburt noted, "We all 'squeezed' through the grating after the one bar had been cut, throughout 1989 and later. Even with the bar cut, the space between bars was not large. It wasn't difficult because one could do so with tanks on but it was snug enough to make one a little apprehensive, especially hanging over into so much space."

When the *Seeker* departed, the gate was left lying on the bulkhead, so that entry was unopposed - as Nagle had intended. Yet on the *Wahoo's* second trip, although we moored within a few feet of the opening, *no one went there.*

I Don't Know is on Third

It was written in *Shadow Divers* that two anonymous crew members splashed to set the hook, that Bielenda drew straws to determine which of the Atlantic Wreck Divers would have the first opportunity to enter the dining room and kitchen, that Kohler and Pete Guglieri won the draw, that they discovered the gate, that Kohler nearly lost consciousness from anger, that Kohler beat against the gate until his air supply was depleted, that Kohler cut off the sign and brought it to the surface, and that Kohler was the one who brought word of the gate to the rest of the *Wahoo's* patrons.

It should be obvious to my faithful readers that the account that was written in *Shadow Divers* was an outright lie.

I am not a doctor, but I do not believe that it is possible for a person to lose consciousness from anger, especially one as daring and driven as Kohler was depicted in *Shadow Divers.*

As a somewhat experienced diver, however, I *can* state categorically that if a diver stayed on the bottom at a depth of 190 feet until his air supply was depleted, he would have no air remaining for the ascent and decompression.

None of the other *Wahoo* divers entered the water until *after* Gilligan and I returned from the tie-in dive. That was standard operating procedure on every *Andrea Doria* trip on the *Wahoo.*

I witnessed no drawing of straws. Guglieri did not remember any such drawing.

Conspiracy Theory

Kohler was one of the divers on the trip that is described above. It goes without saying that he was fully aware of the facts as they actually occurred. Yet the uninformed readers of *Shadow Divers* were led to believe that *he* discovered the gate and recovered the sign. This rendition constituted not just clever deception, but pure fabrication.

Kohler wrote an article about the events that are

described above. The article was published in the November 1991 issue of the *New York Sub Aqua Journal*. In the article he made no mention of the sign that *Shadow Divers* claimed he recovered. He also deigned not to credit Gilligan and me with our discovery of the Cup Hole: "Another team of divers surfaced with third class cups and saucers, the likes of which had never been recovered before!"

Chatterton knew all the details of the trip. He and I often joked about it. For years afterward, I jestingly berated him for playing a practical joke that nearly caused my death by laughter. Harold Moyers fondly remembered one such conversation, as Chatterton and I reminisced about the event in which we both played crucial roles. Moyers also remembered that, at a party at the home of Tom and Joanne Surowiec, Chatterton said, "I knew those guys were going to get in there, but they weren't going to do it my way."

After writing the rough draft of the story of the gate for my book on the history of wreck-diving, I sent a copy to Chatterton for suggestions, additions, and corrections. He offered a few extraneous details, and suggested some minor changes. I incorporated his suggestions and comments in the text. I then sent the revised draft to him for approval. He approved it.

Kurson should have known the truth for two reasons. I wrote a detailed account of the event in *The Lusitania Controversies*, which he cited as one of his primary sources. He also interviewed Guglieri about the circumstances. I asked Guglieri why - or if - he told the story that was related in *Shadow Divers*, and if he uttered the words that were attributed to him.

Guglieri replied, "I told him exactly what I knew, and then he went ahead and printed whatever the hell he wanted." Guglieri was emphatic in stating that the quoted dialogue was not spoken by him, and that he never said any such words to Kurson or to anyone else.

All three contributors to *Shadow Divers* knew the truth without a doubt. Yet the book was contrived in such a way as to give Chatterton and Kohler sole credit for the achievements of those they desired to keep anonymous. What was once a funny story that both sides relished in the telling, became a lopsided victory for the two stage players in *Shadow Divers*.

Mixed-Gas Initiative

As noted in Appendix Two, after breathing air while diving to a depth of 290 feet on the battleship *Washington*, I knew that breathing mixed gas was the only way to proceed to wrecks like the *Ostfriesland* (which lay at a depth of 380 feet).

In order to spread the word on what I already believed would be the next major development in deep wreck-diving, and to promote mixed gas as a means of reaching deeper wrecks, in 1989 I coordinated a mixed-gas diving initiative. It began with a meeting at Bart Malone's house. I chose his home instead of mine because he was more centrally located in Bellmawr, New Jersey: closer than Philadelphia to where most deep divers lived.

Malone was particularly interested in the concept of mixed-gas diving because of his low tolerance to narcosis. I should emphasize that an individual's threshold or response to nitrogen narcosis has little to do with ability or experience, any more than the way one is affected by, say, an analgesic determines intellect or skill. Codeine reduces the severity of a headache for some, and puts others out like a light. The depth at which narcosis becomes an impediment is determined by innate and so far unexplained physical phenomena. Only the psychological effects can be overcome by training.

The meeting was an informal gathering. We swapped stories and traded anecdotes, but my discourse on mixed gas went over like a balloon filled with lead instead of with helium. People listened but were unimpressed - or were scared off by the exceptional depth of the proposed dive to the *Ostfriesland*. I stressed the value of breathing mixed gas at intermediate depths, where replacing some (but not all) of the nitrogen with helium could reduce the debilitating narcotic effect. Instead of extending the depth range of working dives, mixed gas could permit all divers to perform at their full potential, unaffected by narcosis. In that sense, helium could be viewed as an equalizing agent.

These ideas were too far ahead of their time. The seeds were planted, but the germinating process was slow. The time for conceptual breakthrough had not yet arrived.

Mixed-Gas Initiative - Take Two

The publicity that resulted from the first *Ostfriesland* dive fired the imagination of the wreck-diving community. The possibilities that were offered by adding helium to a breathing gas were almost limitless. Not that everyone wanted to dive on scuba to 380 feet, but for wreck-divers who possessed an unusually low tolerance to narcosis, replacing nitrogen with non-narcotic helium enabled them to achieve a potential that was commensurate with their skill and experience. Mixed-gas diving was a Pandora's box, but one that was slow to open and reveal its many treasured contents.

The mixed-gas diving initiative that I had slapped together prior to the *Ostfriesland* trip met with little more than a yawn, tempered perhaps by a pinch of awe, or worse, by a dash of lunacy. At that time the concept was unproven: a mere flight of fancy from an overactive imagination. Attitudes changed after the successful performance of the dive in 1990.

That autumn, Steve Gatto arranged a second get-together, one that was attended by more open minds. The gathering was held in the recreation room of his home in Atco, New Jersey - as before, a central location. This time the yawns were stifled by enthusiasm and an eager desire to learn. All but one changed his attitude.

What was a one-hour drive for me was a three-hour trip for Ken Clayton. Other attendees included Kevin Brennan, Kevin England, Mary Grace Garcia, Jon Hulburt, Rick Jaszyn, Dennis Kessler, Bart Malone, John

Moyer, Tom Packer, Jeff Pagano, Gene Peterson, Glen Plokhoy, Pat Rooney, Lou Sarlo, Brad Sheard, John Yurga, and John Chatterton.

Gatto called the meeting to order with a preamble about the purpose of the gathering, then introduced Clayton. Because Clayton was primarily a cave diver, and relatively new to wreck-diving, he was unknown to the attendees. (Everyone else knew everyone except for Clayton). Clayton and I described our dive on the *Ostfriesland*, paying particular attention to the gases we breathed, to decompression protocols, to auxiliary tank transportation methods, and to back-up procedures. Helium - a gas that was discovered by studying Fraunhofer lines in the Sun - was definitely heaven sent.

Very quickly the exchange of views became a heady free-for-all. Clayton and I were inundated with questions that were wonderfully upbeat and hopeful. Instead of having to plead a case on the defensive, as I had at the previous meeting, I found myself speaking to willing ears.

The only dissident in the crowd was Chatterton. His skepticism arose from his experience as a commercial diver. He was used to the security of hoses that connected a diver to the surface like an unborn baby to its mother: an umbilical through which a continuous supply of air was pumped to the diver.

Gatto recalled that Chatterton argued vehemently against breathing mixed gas, and about the inherent danger of diving to extreme depths on untested helium mixes. He was interested to hear about it, but was dead set against it. Both Gatto and Packer distinctly remember Chatterton stating, "You wouldn't be the first person to die on mix."

Chatterton was the only attendee who voiced opposition.

Overshadowed

On page 194 in *Shadow Divers*, it was written that an anonymous "group of cutting-edge warm-water divers" introduced trimix to Chatterton. This so-called group espoused the advantages of trimix over air on deep dives, such as "widened peripheral vision, sharpened motor skills and coordination, longer bottom times, shorter decompression times, reduced risk of oxygen toxicity and deep-water blackout, elimination of narcosis."

The first quote in the previous paragraph concealed the truth of the matter. The second quote demonstrated lack of understanding of the effects of trimix. Trimix does not permit longer bottom times. Bottom time is predicated upon the amount of breathing gas that a diver carries, not on the type of gas. Decompression times are not made shorter by breathing trimix, but longer. Breathing various blends of nitrox during the stages of ascent is responsible for reducing the decompression requirement, independent of whether one breathed air or mixed-gas on the bottom.

Chatterton obviously knew that he attended the meeting at Steve Gatto's house, at which Clayton and I introduced him to the possibilities of helium mixes. Although he may not have known the advantages of mixed gas at the time of the meeting, he should have known them by the time *Shadow Divers* was written. Chatterton breathed air on the discovery dive of the *U-869*, which occurred a year after the second meeting. (He did not attend the first meeting.)

Kurson should have known that Chatterton attended the meeting, and should have been aware of the true effects of mixed gas, because I gave full accounts of both in *The Lusitania Controversies*, which he cited as one of his primary sources.

Seven members of the Atlantic Wreck Divers attended the meeting: Gatto, Jaszyn, Kessler, Packer, Pagano, Rooney, and Sheard. Kohler did not attend.

Poky Pioneer

Mike Menduno, the publisher of the first technical diving magazine, *AquaCorps*, once wrote, "You can always tell a pioneer by the arrows in his back." On page 196 of *Shadow Divers*, Chatterton was classified as a pioneer mixed-gas diver. Yet, even after the second mixed-gas initiative, he did not embrace the use of helium for a year and a half (as related on page 197).

It was written on page 196, "There were no technical diving classes or certification agencies." This statement contradicted the previous paragraph on the same page, which stated that Chatterton attended a mixed-gas workshop. How could he attend a workshop if none was available? As a point of fact, he took his introductory trimix course on April 18, 1992, along with twenty-one other students. Billy Deans flew from Florida to New Jersey to teach the course.

Deans stayed at Gatto's house for a week. In Gatto's basement, he taught a certified nitrox course and a non-certified trimix course. The latter course was for those who did not care to earn a certification and who were not planning to attend a formal class, but who wanted to know about trimix and who wanted to dive while breathing it.

Some of the divers attended the April 18 class at the Gas Station: a new dive shop that Bart Malone and Lou Sarlo opened specifically to serve the technical diving community by dispensing nitrox and trimix.

On page 196, in reference to mixed gas, Deans was quoted as saying, "We don't know exactly how this works in cold water." Deans made no such statement. I kept him fully informed of the experimental dives on the Billy Mitchell wrecks.

CHAPTER FIVE
Television Static

"You may deceive all the people part of the time, and part of the people all the time, but not all the people all the time."

- Abraham Lincoln

Foreshadow Divers

Since the day of its discovery, stories relating to the *U-869* have existed in a constant state of flux. Published and broadcast accounts differed radically, despite the unity of source. What was quoted or stated in one account was contradicted in another, or altered, or embellished, or exaggerated. The culmination of this divergence from the facts appeared in *Shadow Divers*. And there is no guarantee that the variations will stop even there.

Steve Gatto noted wryly that in *Shadow Divers*, the first deviation from veracity appeared on the front cover, where the fourth word was "true." However, it is my belief that the deception began long before the publication of *Shadow Divers*.

I do not know when and where the first distortions appeared. Likely they began orally, then moved into print and made their way onto television, before being assembled in *Shadow Divers* for the most heightened dramatic effect. The earliest published account of tortured facts that I can find was published in the May 1994 issue of *Philadelphia*, a local city magazine, although there may be newspaper items that can claim priority.

In an article that was entitled "Voyage to the Bottom of the Sea," bylined by Pamela Miller, Chatterton took credit for discovering the *U-869*. By that time, Nagle was dead and could not dispute the charge. (Nagle passed away on November 15, 1993.) Chatterton had no more claim of discovery than the other twelve divers who made the discovery trip. Yet ever since Nagle's death, Chatterton has claimed to be the sole discoverer of the *U-869*.

According to the article, Chatterton wrote in his dive log on the night of the discovery, "Much research indicates this is the *550*." This quotation contradicted the quotation on page 66 of *Shadow Divers*, in which Chatterton allegedly said, "I know nothing about U-boats."

With respect to research, Chatterton was quoted in the article as saying, "At the Navy we went through everybody from the coffee boy up to the director." My faithful readers must decide for themselves if this statement was simple truth or grand hyperbole.

Chatterton was quoted as saying, "I did CPR on Chris Sr., while one diver worked the radio with the Coast Guard and another stayed with Chrissie." In this truncated version, even Crowell, Kohler, and Lander are not given credit for their support, as they were in *Shadow Divers*, much less the other divers on the boat.

According to the article, "By the time the rescue helicopter came, Chatterton had been breathing air into the elder Rouse's lungs and pumping his heart for two hours straight." The time was exaggerated, and there was no mention of Gatto and Packer doing chest compressions, or McDougall doing rescue breathing, or the Ambu-Bag. Or, for that matter, any fierce argument with the Coast Guard rescue swimmer about airlifting the elder Rouse.

The article described as "useless trash" a "size 43 military boot disintegrated halfway up the calf," which Chatterton recovered. There was no mention of foot bones that may have been inside the boot.

Misdirection had begun.

Docudrama

In May 2002, I gave a series of slide presentations at a technical diving conference in Fort William, Scotland. Chatterton gave a presentation after one of mine, in the same room. I decided to sit through his presentation. Because he was not a photographer, he showed excerpts from the cable broadcast, *Hitler's Lost Sub*.

I had not seen the broadcast. I did not watch television and did not have cable connection. My television had been unplugged for more than a decade, except on rare occasions when I used it to watch a movie on videotape or DVD. I preferred to read books in my limited leisure time.

Chatterton's show ended with footage of divers gathered around the spare parts box that had been recovered from the electric motor room. The camera zoomed in on the tag that was stamped with the U-boat's designation, as eager fingers wiped the tag clean. Chatterton asked for questions at the end of the presentation.

I raised my hand. "John, I was on the boat the day the box came up. I don't remember there being a film crew on board."

Chatterton laughed off my question for the audience. "That Gary Gentile. He's like Forrest Gump. He's in the background of everything." He then admitted that the final scene had been faked. Eventually, this led me to wonder how much of the rest of the show had been faked.

Hitler's Lost Sub

I viewed a videotape of the television broadcast for the purpose of writing this book. I also interviewed Will McBeth, Pat Rooney, and John Yurga about their participation in the production.

The full broadcast version differed from reality in a number of instances. It neglected to address the issue of the damage hole abaft the after torpedo loading hatch, and it failed to mention people whose research was crucial to establishing the history of the *U-869*. For example, Mark McKellar and Barb Lander conducted much of the original research. Not only did they not receive credit for their valuable contributions, but their names were not even mentioned.

Shadow Divers went to great lengths to reiterate the

respect that Chatterton and Kohler held for the souls of the German dead. This so-called "respect" was poured into the book as thick as molasses; it came off so sickly sweet that it could hardly be consumed without gagging. On page 165 of *Shadow Divers*, Chatterton was quoted as saying, "I didn't videotape any of the bones." On page 166, he was quoted as saying, "I deliberately did not video them. It's a matter of respect."

Kohler patted a skull with reverence and - if you can believe what was written on page 207 - he spoke to it: "I'm going to do my best to figure out your name."

Despite this so-called reverence for the dead, the camera highlighted a skull and a femur within the first minute of *Hitler's Lost Sub*, and dwelt on them again later in the film. These scenes contradicted the quotes in the previous two paragraphs.

Respect appears to have been a later invention, conceived to adopt a posture that was more politically correct, and to create a more wholesome image for promotional purposes.

Tom Packer noted with evident fidelity, "Respect and identification were smokescreens for artifact collection." Steve Gatto added, "How many dishes do you need? Dishes won't identify the wreck." Yet Chatterton and Kohler continued to add china and broken shards to their collection.

In *Hitler's Lost Sub*, it was wrongly claimed that some divers quit diving as a result of Steve Feldman's death.

In *Hitler's Lost Sub*, it was claimed that helium blends were untried at the time that Chatterton began to breathe trimix on the *U-869*. In fact, the U.S. Navy had been using mixed gases since the 1930's, commercial divers since the 1960's, cave divers since the 1980's, and wreck-divers since 1990. (See Appendix Two for details.) *Ultimate Wreck Diving Guide* - the first book ever published on technical diving and mixed-gas gear configurations - was already in print by that time. The statement that trimix was still in the experimental stages was patently false.

The recoveries of the Horenburg knife and the spare parts box were faked. They were filmed on a tug in 60 feet of water.

Of all the falsifications, the second most glaring showed Kohler accompanying Chatterton to Germany for the initial meeting with Horst Bredow, in 1991. In fact, it was Yurga who went to Germany with Chatterton. Much of Yurga's participation on the *U-869* venture was written out of the script in favor of Kohler.

Yurga told me that Kohler had so little interest in U-boats that he could not even keep his mind on research when Yurga first took him to the Naval Historical Center. Kohler spent most of the day browsing through the museum. In both the book and the television show, most of Yurga's research efforts was given to either Chatterton or Kohler. Yurga definitely got the short end of the stick.

The astute viewer will notice that, when Chatterton and Kohler "returned" to Germany after the recovery of the tag that identified the U-boat, Chatterton, Kohler, and Bredow were all wearing the same clothes that they wore in 1991: identical shirts, ties, jackets, and pants. What are the chances of that happening in real life?

The most glaring falsification was the penetration into the electric motor room. This penetration could have been made easily through the after torpedo loading hatch, as Will McBeth amply demonstrated. As I watched this sequence in *Hitler's Lost Sub*, I realized that the scene was nothing more than a stunt that was performed for the camera, and that the sequence had been stitched together from footage that was shot on different dives.

The film made no mention of Chatterton getting strangled by a cable, of running out of gas inside the wreck, or of his breathtaking escape: invented incidents that were later glamorized in *Shadow Divers*. There was no mention of Kohler single-handedly moving a fallen escape trunk in the diesel electric room, as depicted in *Shadow Divers* on page 303. Not one of my acquaintances ever heard of the escape trunk escapade until it appeared in the book.

It was anticlimactic that another scene that was faked for the camera was the one in which the identification tag was cleaned to show the U-boat's number, while the stars of the show stood around the box in eager anticipation. As noted in Chapter Three, McBeth cleaned the tag through the mesh of the bag as the spare parts box still hung in the water.

The astute viewer can see that, when the camera panned the deck from the flying bridge, it showed four divers wearing drysuits - but only one set of doubles on the boat! Everyone's hair was dry. This scene was faked at a later date by taking the boat a couple of miles from shore, and pointing the camera away from the beach.

Hitler's Lost Sub was promoted as a documentary. By definition, documentary means "presenting facts objectively without editorializing or inserting fictional matter."

Complicity in Crime

Once the tradition of distortion and embellishment was established in *Hitler's Lost Sub*, television carried the tradition to extremes in *Deep Sea Detectives*. I experienced this firsthand when I was hired to appear in an episode. I wrote the book on diving on the *Andrea Doria* (now two books), and had made more than 170 dives on the wreck (now more than 180).

Jennifer Lorenz, the onsite director, told me that before commencing work on *any* episode of *Deep Sea Detectives*, she first referred to my books for background material. I never received credit as an historical consultant. As it developed, I am glad that I did not. Here is the reason why.

I was dozing in my bunk between dives when Chatterton woke me to ask how many women had dived on the *Andrea Doria*. Half asleep, I thought for a moment before replying, "At least a dozen or two." That was all that Chatterton wanted to hear. He left in a hurry.

As I lay there thinking, I mentally pictured women I knew who had dived on the wreck. I passed the dozen mark quickly. Then I passed the two dozen mark. I was on my way to the third dozen when I heard the actors and film crew on the deck overhead.

Suddenly Chatterton exclaimed, "And Carrie Bisetti just became the thirteenth woman to dive on the *Andrea Doria.*"

I leaped out of my bunk and ran out of the cabin to correct him. But I was too late. The shot was already in the can, and they had no intention of reshooting the scene. Chatterton should have known that more than twelve women had dived on the wreck. Kohler should have known it, too. But no one cared about historical accuracy. They could have made the change in postproduction, because they did not even use the scene that they filmed. Instead they used a voice-over - *twice* - and perpetuated their error!

This was the kind of mock research that went into the episode, and, by extrapolation, other episodes too.

I suppose it would not have been as sensational to state that Bisetti was the thirty-seventh woman to dive on the *Andrea Doria*, but it would have been closer to the truth.

Breathless Hams

Being on the boat during the film shoot enabled me to see how the fieldwork was accomplished. After each dive, as soon as Chatterton or Kohler climbed up the ladder and sat on the bench, the camera operator shoved a lens in his face. They both gasped for air as if they had just run the Preakness on foot, instead of having decompressed in calm seas with no current.

I was shocked that they were in such poor physical condition that they were completely out of breath after doing nothing more than hanging onto the anchor line for three-quarters of an hour. Anyone so out of shape should not have been diving. I was concerned for their health, lest they keel over and die from exhaustion.

Bisetti climbed up the ladder and sat on the bench as quietly as if she had stepped out of the powder room. She ignored the lens and calmly doffed her equipment.

Footage of debriefing her after her "record-breaking" dive lasted only long enough for her to exclaim, "I did it." Perhaps heavy breathing would have earned her more screen time.

If Chatterton's and Kohler's dialogue had been printed, many of their sentences would have ended in exclamation marks as they hammed it up for the camera.

Historical Inaccuracies

Lorenz promised to send me a videotape of the completed production, but she never did. I did not see the *Andrea Doria* episode until Harold Moyers showed it to me as research material for the present volume. I was shocked at the glaring errors and stupid narrative that permeated the broadcast.

The mistakes began with the claim that the collision occurred fifty years earlier. This claim was then repeated later in the broadcast. The collision occurred on July 25, 1956. The dialogue was filmed on a three-day trip between July 15 and July 17, 2003, and the film was aired that autumn. Simple subtraction yields forty-seven years. Could all of those who were involved with the production of the show have been such poor mathematicians, or was this another example of disregard for accuracy that was based upon the premise of "Who cares?"

They claimed that the *Stockholm* and the *Andrea Doria* were locked together for "several minutes." In fact, the two ships were never locked together, not even for a moment. As the *Andrea Doria* sped past the *Stockholm*, the bow of the *Stockholm* penetrated the *Andrea Doria's* hull and was instantly sheered off. The *Andrea Doria* continued forward at nearly full speed.

They claimed that the *Stockholm* did not return to New York until days after the sinking of the *Andrea Doria*. In fact, she limped into port the following day.

They claimed that Johan-Ernst Carstens-Johannsen was the helmsman on the *Stockholm*. In fact, he was the third officer, and was in command of the bridge at the time of the collision. The helmsman was Peder Larsen.

They claimed that they had never heard that the collision resulted from the misinterpretation of radar. This fact has never been disputed; it was publicized in newspapers immediately following the collision. It has been repeated in nearly every book and article that has ever been written about the loss of the *Andrea Doria.*

They claimed that both ships were enshrouded in fog as they approached each other. In fact, only the *Andrea Doria* was enveloped in a fogbank. The *Stockholm* enjoyed a clear sky and good visibility.

The broadcast lacked self-consistency, for the graphic representation of the two ships approaching on a collision course contradicted the dialogue. In the animated reconstruction, the *Stockholm* was shown proceeding through a fogless sea.

Perhaps a minor mistake (but obnoxious to a purist) was the narrator's frequent mispronunciation of the name: *Dory* (two syllables) instead of *Doria* (three syllables).

Onsite Omissions

The stated premise of the show was to obtain new evidence to determine the reason why the *Andrea Doria* sank. This premise was absurd on at least two counts.

It was the height of vanity to expect that, on three twenty-five-minute dives, they could learn more than hundreds of others had already learned after spending thousands of hours on the wreck. Furthermore, the premise totally ignored the fact that Peter Gimbel had already made that determination a generation earlier, during two lengthy commercial diving expeditions: one in 1975, and another in 1981.

Gimbel was more qualified and better equipped to study the wreck than the deep-sea "detectives." In 1975, Gimbel and other divers on his team made hour-long dives while breathing helium mixes through umbilical hoses. Over a two-week period, they made extensive penetrations into the hull. On the seabed, at the bottom of the hull, Gimbel discovered a crack that measured two and a half feet in width. This crack was caused by the *Stockholm's* steel stem. Gimbel swam through the crack into the dark interior.

Gimbel returned to the *Andrea Doria* in 1981. This time he employed a saturation system that permitted him and his team members to stay on the bottom for days at a time. He remained on site for several weeks. He penetrated completely through the wreck and emerged on the seabed from the crack. This penetration clearly established that the damage to the hull was more extensive than anyone had previously speculated.

By omitting all mention of Gimbel's large-scale expeditions, *Deep Sea Detectives* must have made a conscious decision not to tell its uninformed viewers that anything that they hoped to accomplish on their three-day trip had already been accomplished more than two decades earlier. All this information was readily available in *Dive to an Era*, the book that Lorenz claimed to have used as her primary source. Chatterton and Kohler had access to the book more than ten years before. (It was published in 1989.)

Underwater Stupidities

At the beginning of the episode, I used the deck plans to demonstrate to Chatterton and Kohler how the hull and superstructure had deteriorated over the years. This educated the audience (and should have educated Chatterton and Kohler) about the present condition of the wreck. For all practical purposes, my account of the state of collapse was an up-to-the-minute report. After Dan Bartone and I made the tie-in dive, and placed the grapnel where the film crew could make the most effective use of their bottom time, we explored enough of the wreck to describe its current condition.

In clear and certain terms, I explained for the camera how the superstructure decks had sloughed off the hull to create a broad debris field on the bottom, and how the two upper decks within the hull had hinged down like a folding knife so that their passageways no longer existed.

Nonetheless, the narrator ignored my observations and stated that the divers intended to explore decks that I had gone to great lengths to explain were long since gone: "We're gonna drop down into the Promenade, swim down to a doorway, drop through the doorway, over to a stairwell, down two decks through the stairwell, come out to the Foyer, cross the Foyer, through another doorway, across the dining room, down to a corridor at 230 feet, at the end of that corridor, that's where we wanted to be."

This moronic Rube Goldberg route was wrong on any number of pathways. It was equivalent to stating that, in order to go from the bedroom to the bathroom, one had to climb out the window, scamper down the drain spout, crawl across the grass to the basement window, squeeze through the window, traverse the cement floor in the dark, climb the steps to the kitchen, exit the house through the back doorway, sneak around the house, enter through the front doorway, ascend the stairs to the hallway, and walk along the hallway to the bathroom.

One might reach the bathroom by such a complicated and circuitous route, but it was easier to walk directly through the bathroom doorway. (By the way, Reuben Goldberg was a cartoonist who was noted for drawing intricate diagrams of complicated, impractical contraptions that were designed to effect comparatively simple results.)

To reach the collision crack, all they had to do was to drop straight down to the seabed adjacent to the hull: the way Gimbel did twenty-eight years earlier.

To make matters worse, the described route started abaft (behind) the point of collision, went around in circles, then led *away* from the collision point, not toward it. This demonstrated flagrant lack of understanding of the layout of the wreck, because that was most definitely *not* where they wanted to be.

As the penultimate blunder, I explained to Chatterton and Kohler on camera that the Promenade Deck fell down to the seabed in 2000. The stairwell through the Upper Deck to the Foyer was crushed flat, then shredded apart like cheese on a grater. The Foyer no longer existed because the upper hull that comprised its outer bulkhead now lay flat against the vertical deck - like the wall of a house that had fallen onto the floor. In short, no part of the described route existed. They used the footage of me describing the present state of deterioration, but ignored my advice when they explored the wreck and edited the film!

Finally, they hired maritime artist Ken Marschall to update the 1991 painting of the *Andrea Doria* on which he and I had collaborated. He had painted the wreck the way I had described its condition. Although Chatterton and Kohler are shown on camera discussing interim changes with Marschall, they were with him only as window-dressing. Marschall actually used my new descriptions to make the revision. We discussed the alterations mostly over the Internet. The updated painting was shown in the broadcast. Yet the graphic representation that was also used in the same broadcast showed the wreck the way it appeared forty years earlier!

It was never explained to the viewer that Billy Deans shot his footage of the Promenade Deck in the early 1990's. The broadcast was edited in such a way as to imply that this footage represented the current condition of the wreck.

To add inconsistency, the graphic reconstruction that was shown after the verbal description did not match the route that was depicted. Furthermore, the computer generated layout of the wreck showed the collision point in the wrong place: in cargo hold number two (forward of the bridge). The actual point of collision was *fifty feet* farther aft. As a point of interest, when Gimbel explored this hold in 1975, he established with certainty that no connection existed between the hold and the area of the collision hole.

The various pictorial images that were used to give

visual references to the audience, about the layout of the wreck, were not only contradicted by reality (and by my physical description), but they conflicted with each other. I had the feeling that different people produced various scenes for the episode without communicating with each other about what they were producing; then someone entirely different mixed the scenes as if he were shuffling a deck of cards. After the film was edited, they either did not bother to correct the gross inconsistencies, or they failed to notice them. Either case smacks of clumsy and inept production.

Viewers must have been truly befuddled by seeing three different versions of the wreck's appearance - the graphic art view that was forty years out of date, the Deans footage that was more than a decade old, and the updated Marschall painting that was accurately based on my descriptions - none of which correlated with the narration.

Under water, the "detectives" and the film crew never even entered the wreck. They swam along the debris field toward cargo hold number two, filmed the underside of a collapsed hull plate, and turned around without ever entering the hold. Thus they did not even follow the directions that the narrator exaggerated for the audience.

According to the broadcast, the underwater "detectives" planned to start from a place that no longer existed, follow an imaginary route in the wrong direction, to a spot that they could not reach from the way they were going, and whose connection with the collision hole had already been disproven.

That's All, Folks!

According to the broadcast, the film crew was unable to complete the search for the collision hole via cargo hold number two because of strong current that they encountered on their third and final dive. Beside the fact that they were searching in the wrong place, the current was not as bad as they would have its uninformed viewers believe.

The film crew made three dives during the course of three days (one dive each day). Bartone and I made five dives (two on the first day, two on the second day, and one on the third day). On the last day, we entered the water before the film crew, and did not experience any current that was extraordinary for the *Andrea Doria*. Perhaps they used strong current as an excuse for their failure to locate the collision hole. In any event, if they intended to make a bona fide attempt to "solve" a mystery that was the premise of the show, they should have stayed on site instead of returning to shore after making only three dives.

After showing the final dive, the narrator stated that it was likely that the point of impact might never have been seen by human eyes. In fact, they could have seen it if they had looked in the right place, as Gimbel did in 1975 and again in 1981. They also could have seen the point of impact if they had looked at the two television specials that resulted from those expeditions: *The Mystery of the Andrea Doria* and *Andrea Doria: the Final Chapter*.

Finally, in reconstructing the state of collapse as it existed in 2003, they claimed that the wreck had compressed five feet. In fact, the wreck had compressed *twenty* feet.

My faithful readers can now understand why I am glad that I received no screen credit as a consultant. I would have looked stupid for overlooking such blatant errors. Had I known that the episode was going to be so hokey and contrived, I would not have agreed to appear in it.

What was the point of hiring an expert if they did not intend to utilize my expertise? They never asked me to review the episode for historical or underwater accuracy. They used me only to lend credibility to an incredibly clumsy production.

Deep Sea Detectives must bear all the blame for the errors - of commission as well as of omission - and for foisting such vacuous and insipid programming upon viewers who were kept in ignorance of real events.

Guilty Again!

On the *Andrea Doria* film shoot, Lorenz and Chatterton devoured my coffee table photo album, *Great Lakes Shipwrecks: a Photographic Odyssey*. The book was the result of fifteen years of photographing shipwrecks in all five Great Lakes. I cannot state too often that the Great Lakes possess the greatest shipwrecks in the world. Of the fifty-odd wrecks that I covered in the book, they chose one of the least interesting for a future episode.

The *Regina* was a freighter that sank with all hands in the notorious Great Lakes Storm of November 1913. The wreck was discovered in the early 1980's, and was subsequently salvaged by a commercial outfit. The 80-foot depth encouraged a steady stream of wreck-divers to visit the site. It was one of the best-known and most dived wrecks in Lake Huron.

I did not see the episode, but when I gave a presentation in Ohio at the annual dinner of Bay Area Divers, many of the three hundred attendees complained bitterly about the broadcast. Supposedly, after spending only one day on the wreck, the film crew "discovered" the reason why the freighter sank: a dent in the hull that must have been caused by collision, and that had been overlooked by thousands of divers over a period of twenty years.

Throughout the Great Lakes, the series has ever since been called *Deep Sea Defectives* (spelled with an "f" instead of a "t".)

Triple Play

Moyers chose three other episodes for me to view. He knew that my books must have provided the background material for the wrecks that they covered: the *San Diego*, *S-5*, and *Marine Electric*. I wrote a book on the *San Diego*, and wrote extensive chapters on the *S-5* and *Marine Electric*. I found historical inaccuracies in all three episodes. I also found that, as in the *Andrea Doria* episode, they neglected to mention that none of their solutions were new or revelatory: the "detectives" merely retread ground that had been covered exhaustively by contemporary investigative agencies.

There is no need to dissect these episodes in as much detail as I did with the *Andrea Doria*. A few annotations will serve to make the points that I want to make.

In the *San Diego* episode, Jon Hulburt was the tour guide, and John Chatterton and Melanie Paul were the so-called detectves. Paul co-hosted the episode but did not participate in the underwater "detective" work, such as it was. Chatterton purported to look at the remnants of the same explosion hole that Navy and salvage divers examined when they surveyed the wreck in 1918, at a time when the hull plating was not rusted away by more than eighty years of deterioration.

The "detectives" planned only one day of diving in which to "discover" the cause of the sinking. They acquired very little footage because, after entering the cool water, the lens or dome port fogged as a result of water vapor condensing inside the housing.

Hulburt: "They hadn't planned to even dive a second day; observations made the first day caused them to elect to spend the money to dive a second day."

The second day's diving was terminated prematurely when the video light failed. They never returned. The "detectives" could not have seen evidence of damage that had not already been observed over *tens of thousands* of recreational dives since the wreck was first visited in the 1960's.

In fact, Chatterton saw very little of the *San Diego* because his rebreather malfunctioned on all three of his dives. With respect to the bilge keel, Hulburt noted, "Chatterton may have gotten within a few feet of it, but he did not see the relevant damage because his rebreather was not scrubbing properly. We were told later that Chatterton put a rag or sponge in the absorbing canister to help pick up moisture. This caused the absorbent to malfunction and pass CO_2."

Hulburt also told me that the detectives "failed to see anything else related to the sinking but the bent keel, and its meaning had already been explained to them" by him and Brad Sheard.

In order to wow the viewers of the dangers of penetration, they described a convoluted Rube Goldberg route like the one that they described in the *Andrea Doria* episode. Once again, they did not follow the route that they described: they simply entered a compartment through a rust hole that flooded the interior with outside light. The macho but phony penetration that was portrayed may have enhanced the "detectives' " image, but it had nothing to do with their exploration of the wreck.

On the *S-5* episode, the "detectives" neglected to mention that the Navy conducted 477 dives on the wreck. After a thorough investigation, there was never any doubt that the submarine sank as the result of a malfunction of the main air induction valve. In addition to instituting changes in the design of this essentially important valve, the Navy installed indicating lights in the control rooms of other submarines, to show when the valve was open or closed.

According to the narration, the "detectives" entered the control room and filmed an object that they identified as the main air induction valve. They exclaimed that they saw nothing wrong with the valve. First of all, the main air induction valve was not located in the control room, but in the engine room. The valve that was shown in the broadcast was some other valve. Secondly, they should have known that the component that failed was the gate inside the valve, and that this mechanism could not be seen by looking at the outer casing. Their remarks were as stupid as those of an auto mechanic who looked at a car and, without lifting the hood, exclaimed that he did not see anything wrong with the engine.

In actual fact, Kohler did not enter the control room at all. He was filmed entering the electric motor room with a video camera in his hand. At that point, Steve Gatto's footage was spliced in to make it seem as though Kohler went forward into the control room, when it was Gatto who entered the control room.

They claimed that the rudders were set to hard rise. In fact, the rudders could be turned only left or right, in order to steer the sub. If anything was set to hard rise, it was the hydroplanes.

They claimed that all the pumps failed when the submarine hit the bottom. In fact, only the high-pressure pump failed, after blowing a gasket. The regulating pumps continued to operate.

They neglected to mention that, before using a brace and bit to drill through the pressure hull, the trapped men used an electric drill until a fault developed in the electrical system and the men started getting shocks.

They failed to mention that, although the sub initially sank in 180 feet of water, the battleship *Ohio* towed the sub to shallower water. When the towing cable snapped, the *S-5* settled to her final resting place at a depth of 160 feet.

Underwater, they claimed to have touched the glass in the portholes on the conning tower. In fact, Navy divers removed the glass in 1920. According to the salvage report in my possession, the eye-port glasses "were replaced by steel and oak disks, held in place against rubber gaskets by the usual eye-port keeper rings."

On page 87 of *Shadow Divers*, it was written, "he needed only brush an ankle or a weight belt against an object to deduce that object's identity and condition." It was odd that he could not distinguish glass from steel and oak after touching it. Other divers had determined that there was no glass in the ports simply by looking at them.

Once again, a minor equipment failure terminated the underwater examination. In order to pad the story to reach the desired length, some scenes were repeated as many as half a dozen times.

In another episode, they claimed that the *Marine Electric* was constructed as a T-2 tanker. In fact, she was constructed as a T-3 tanker, and was later lengthened by 101 feet. (A T-2 was a tanker of any design whose length measured between 450 and 499 feet; a T-3 measured between 500 and 549 feet in length.) The original length of the *Marine Electric* was 504 feet; the replacement of her midship cargo body increased her length to 605 feet.

Although it is petty, cargo is stowed, not stored.

On the wreck, the metal that they claimed was paper thin, or wafer thin, was not metal from the middle of a hull plate, but metal along the edges where the plates were broken. Broken metal edges deteriorate more rapidly than metal in the middle of a plate. Razor sharp metal edges are common features of metal-hulled shipwrecks.

The "detectives" never learned anything new about the wreck. They merely rehashed the conclusions that were reached by the Coast Guard Marine Board of Investigation and the National Transportation Safety Board. This constitutes reporting, not detecting.

Innocent at Last

The historical inaccuracies that are noted in the previous section could have been avoided if the "detectives" had copied the information correctly. Instead, they made mistakes that demonstrated sloppy research, inattention to detail, and intentional alterations. Other errors were matters of omission or general ignorance of shipwrecks, all of which was on par with *Shadow Divers*.

The underwater "investigations" lasted no longer than a couple of days. In reality, they were nothing more than one-day or two-day film shoots that contained little or no true investigative value. A bona fide investigation would not have been abandoned after only a cursory look at a wreck, or terminated prematurely after a minor mechanical malfunction.

It seemed to me that budget restraints limited the production of anything worthwhile. But a low budget had nothing to do with historical accuracy: that was a function of dishonest endeavor.

I began to see a pattern in the series. After making a token trip to a selected shipwreck, the "detectives" miraculously "solved" a "mystery" that thousands of divers had supposedly been unable to solve over a span of many decades.

In reality, the "detectives" either created a mystery where none existed, or they took credit for solving a mystery that had already been solved years before by real investigators. Some so-called "mysteries" appeared to have been fabricated, then solved in post-production after a storyline was created around the meager underwater footage.

These deceptive techniques served to create mindless entertainment of dubious quality and doubtful educational value. Presenting such dross as true history is an insult to the intelligence of the viewing public.

A *Titanic* Mistake

Wreck-divers who live in the Great Lakes region, and those who reside along the eastern seaboard, were affronted by the chaff that *Deep Sea Detectives* presented. Although they number in the tens of thousands, they have a small voice: their collective protest against inaccuracies was overshadowed by the awe of the uninformed masses.

Another group is small in number but has a louder and more prominent voice: the *Titanic* enthusiasts. These dedicated people know everything there is to know about the White Star liner, and then some. They were not about to remain silent about a passionate subject that was so close to their hearts. They had their own publications, and they had good connections with the media.

The flak hit *Deep Sea Detectives* even before their *Titanic* episode was aired. This resulted from advertisements that announced new "discoveries" in order to hype and promote the show. The "detectives" made only three dives, yet they claimed to have discovered a new section of the wreck - a section that fully explained how and why the *Titanic* sank.

Charles Haas was a leading expert on the *Titanic*, co-founder of the Titanic International Society, and co-author of several books on the history of the ship. In response to a query from Steve Gatto, he wrote, "You may be right about new Ballards, especially in the 'Let's Claim Credit for What Others Did' and the 'Let's Rewrite History' Departments." ("Ballards" referred to Bob Ballard, who had a known reputation for taking credit for the accomplishments of others while expunging all mention of their names.)

Haas: "During the 1998 expedition, a very full mapping of the wreck site was done by Paul Matthias of Polaris Imaging using special sonar and digital photography. It showed the piece in question.

"The pieces of the double bottom were known to the RMS/IFREMER expedition of 1993, and were fully explored via the Magellan ROV [remotely operated vehicle] in 1996 and 1998. I clearly recall standing with Bill Garzke at my side looking at the high-res. images of the bilge keel on one of the pieces during the 1998 expedition."

Garzke was the chairperson of the Society of Naval Architects and Marine Engineers. Wreck-divers who belonged to Forensic Panel of SNAME and who attended the quarterly meetings were Steve Gatto, Jon Hulburt, John Moyer, Harold Moyers, and Tom Packer.

After seeing a preview of the episode, Haas informed the History Channel of the true history of the double bottom hull section, but they proceeded with the broadcast anyway.

Paul-Henri Nargeolet confirmed Haas's statement. He was co-leader of the *Titanic* Research and Recovery Expeditions of 1987, 1993, 1994, 1996, and 1998. In an article that was featured on the website of the Titanic International Society, Nargeolet confirmed everything that Haas wrote. He added that all the expeditions were well aware of this third piece: a fifty-foot section of bottom plating that lay upside down on the seabed, and that stretched the full width of the hull from one bilge keel to the other. He even stated that the paint was still visible and in good condition on the bilge keels.

When the episode was aired, it showed exactly what Nargeolet described.

The "detectives" claimed that, as a result of what they learned by observing this "new" or "previously undiscovered" section of the hull, the *Titanic* sank sooner than expected. In fact, after calculating the rate of flooding, Harlan and Wolf engineer Thomas Andrews reported to Captain Edward Smith that, in his estimation, the *Titanic* would sink in one hour to one and a half hours (after his thirty minute inspection). In the event, she managed to stay afloat for two hours and forty minutes after the collision. This was longer than Andrews' prediction, not shorter.

Fully half of the show was a poor rehash of material that had been presented ad nauseam throughout the years. The episode was merely another commercial attempt to cash in on the *Titanic's* established renown. The "new" evidence and subsequent "deduction" were merely gambits to justify another moneymaking broadcast.

The "gosh wow" dialogue that was common to the series fell as flat in this episode as it did in the others.

One anonymous correspondent on the *Deep Sea Detectives* forum summarized his opinion succinctly when he wrote, "Seems every year some rivet counters head to the *Titanic* to try to beat a new trick out of an old dog."

The Histrionic Channel

I viewed five episodes of *Deep Sea Detectives*. I found inaccuracies, misstatements, and factual errors in every one. A statistician might claim that my sampling was too small to extrapolate any meaningful critique about the series as a whole. Mathematical equations aside, I am still left with the incontestable fact that five out of five episodes failed to conform to elementary documentary standards for the presentation of facts.

This experience led me to wonder about the integrity of the series. I have firsthand knowledge of the subject matter of the episodes that I watched. How much faith can I have in the truthfulness of other episodes, which covered subject matter of which I do not have personal knowledge?

By extension, if *Deep Sea Detectives* was an example of the kind of shows that the History Channel presented to the public as history, how accurate was the rest of the programming?

L'envoi

A year and a half after the *Andrea Doria* film shoot, I saw Chatterton at the Florida Dive Show, on December 3, 2005.

I spotted him when he was engaged in an intense conversation with someone. I approached from the side, stuck my hand into Chatterton's, and said, "Hi." When he glanced aside and saw who was shaking his hand, he yanked his hand out of mine as if my hand were molten steel. He continued to maintain his ardent conversation without verbally acknowledging my presence. Rather than interrupt, I thought that it would be more gracious to talk with him later, when I could have his full attention.

Twice I approached him as he was walking through the crowd. On both occasions, as soon as we made eye contact, he turned his back on me and walked away. We never talked. I did not understand his conduct until I read *Shadow Divers* the following month. He might have thought that I had already read the book, and that I wanted to confront him about some of its horrific lies, ridiculous embellishments, and blatant inaccuracies. I just wanted to say hello to someone I had known (or thought I had known) for nearly two decades.

CHAPTER SIX
A Horse of a Different Color

"Oh, what a tangled web we weave, when first we practice to deceive."

- Walter Scott

First Contact

In the autumn of 1986, I invited some fellow *Andrea Doria* divers to come to my house on the following Saturday. Our purpose was to view pictures of the summer's trips, to chat about the penetrations that we had made into the Grand Dame of the Sea, and to study deck plans in preparation for the following year's explorations.

What started as a simple get-together with two or three divers became an impromptu party that grew to include more than twenty people. Once word got around, divers from all over the tri-state area called to ask if they could attend, or if they could bring a friend.

Bill Nagle wanted to know if he could bring an *Andrea Doria* wannabe. Although the wannabe was a novice wreck-diver with only a few months experience, Nagle told me that he and I had something in common: we had both served in Vietnam. I said that it would be okay to bring him: not because of his status as a veteran, but because of his interest in the *Andrea Doria*.

The person was John Chatterton.

Chatterton was enthralled by the display of artifacts that I had recovered from the First Class Dining Room, the First Class Gift Shop, and other areas of the *Andrea Doria*, both inside and outside. He listened intently as I showed him on the deck plans how to reach those places. He soaked in every word of every story that everyone had to tell.

Vietnam Syndrome

Over the years, Chatterton and I spoke often about

our experiences in Vietnam. I was a infantryman in the 25th Infantry Division. He was a medic in the Americal Division. I showed him the inch-long scar on the inside of my right elbow. That scar was a very important scar: it represented the difference between my writing these words today, and having my name engraved on a wall in Washington, DC.

I was severely wounded in a firefight. A medevac Huey flew me to a forward fire base. I was about to expire from loss of blood when a medic saved my life by performing a cut-down: a delicate procedure that medics were not trained to do. In this procedure, the flesh on the inside of the elbow was sliced and separated in order to expose the vein that lay underneath. The danger was in nicking the shallow vein, which could cause uncontrollable bleeding and death. With nothing to lose, the medic sliced through the skin, felt inside the cut with his finger, pulled out the vein, and inserted a needle for a blood transfusion. The transfusion kept me alive until a C-130 cargo plane airlifted me to a base medical unit that had surgeons on standby.

Chatterton agreed that my information was correct: that he had not been trained to perform such a procedure. In all the experiences that we shared about Vietnam - as one veteran to another - Chatterton never said anything about being in combat. When I spoke about my combat experiences, he never reciprocated with any combat experiences of his own. He told me that he was a base medic, not a field medic. He always recalled laughingly that Vietnam had been largely a great party experience: he spent most of his tour high on marijuana.

Chatterton had a cushy job in an Army hospital in Japan. After one hallucinatory episode, when he and some of his buddies got high on LSD, someone fell asleep with a lighted cigarette between his fingers. The cigarette started a fire. In their drug-induced stupor, no one could figure out how to operate the fire extinguisher. They ran for their lives, and the barracks burned to the ground.

The men concocted a story to account for the blaze. When the commanding officer interrogated the men one at a time, one of them broke down and told the horrible truth. The CO could have court-martialed the lot of them. Instead, he decided upon a worse punishment for the druggies: he sent them to Vietnam.

Throughout the years, Chatterton repeated this story to me and to many of his fellow divers. He regaled us with similar depictions of his "service" in Vietnam. His stories were always offbeat, and replete with drugs and sex. I will not repeat any of his other accounts because of their blatant licentious nature.

Imagine my shock when I read in *Shadow Divers* that Chatterton volunteered to give up his job in Japan, and demanded a transfer to Vietnam out of some pious sense of idealism.

A Different Vietnam

Shadow Divers depicted Chatterton as the stereotypic Hollywood champion: the medic who swatted bird-sized insects, who slogged through alligator-infested rivers, who crossed rice paddies near the Laotian border, who started on patrol with a .45 pistol, who walked point, who dodged a hail of bullets in order to reach a wounded comrade, and who volunteered for a six-month extension which was to commence after a two-week return to the States.

Chatterton never talked about any of these things. At first I questioned my sanity, or my memory. Then, as a science fiction author, I imagined that I had somehow been teleported to a different universe or an alternate dimension, in which history had taken another course. Chatterton's Vietnam was different from mine.

My Vietnam did not have bird-sized insects. My Vietnam did not have alligator-infested rivers in the highlands (although some alligators inhabited the lowlands as they do in Florida). My Vietnam did not have rice paddies in the mountains that approached the Laotian border; rice was grown in the lowlands along the coast.

In my Vietnam, a medic carried an M-16 for self defense. In my Vietnam, no self-respecting platoon leader would let his medic walk point - *ever*. The medic was almost as valuable as the radiotelephone operator. On patrol, both the RTO and the medic walked in the most protected position possible: in the middle of the platoon. In my Vietnam, a platoon leader who let his medic walk point would have been either fragged or relieved of command.

In my Vietnam, John Wayne heroics occurred only in the movies. In my Vietnam, soldiers on patrol operated as a team, under the coordinated orders of superior officers, not as individual loose cannons who took unwarranted chances that might result in the decimation of the company.

In my Vietnam, a soldier who volunteered for a six-month extension did not go home on two week's leave. The purpose of the extension was to save Uncle Sam the expense of transportation; the soldier benefited by receiving an early discharge after his extension.

True or False?

I was not the only one who was shocked by the revelations in *Shadow Divers*. Those whose memories agreed with mine were Steve Gatto, Will McBeth, Harold Moyers, and John Yurga. We all wondered why we never heard any of these fabulous stories of bravery in conversation with Chatterton on the boat, where divers share their innermost secrets with those who are part of their extended family. None of us could explain it. For more than a decade, Yurga was Chatterton's closest friend; eventually they came to work together. McBeth and Moyers shared crewing duties with Chatterton for weekend after weekend aboard the *Seeker*. Gatto was instrumental in exploring the *U-869* with Chatterton.

I cannot state that the combat stories in *Shadow Divers* were untrue. Every word may be factual. But if the stories were all true, then Chatterton must have been lying to me and many others when he talked about his drug-filled life in Japan and Vietnam. Perhaps he actually performed all the bigger-than-life heroics that were related in *Shadow Divers*. I do not know, because I served in a different Vietnam.

But my faithful readers must understand my quandary. Should I believe the stories that Chatterton reiterated for twenty years - in confidence as well as in the presence of others - or the incredible tales that I and many others heard for the first time in *Shadow Divers*?

Surgical Procedure

Shadow Divers quoted Chatterton's battalion surgeon, Dr. Norman Sakai, in order to lend support to its claim that Chatterton walked point as a medic. I contacted Sakai. He vaguely remembered speaking with someone about four years previous, in a conversation that he described as "brief."

Sakai was quoted on page 81 of *Shadow Divers*: "Even going on patrol was stretching it for a medic. But walking point? You never heard of a medic walking point."

When I presented the quote that was attributed to him, Sakai told me, "I don't think the quote sounds like me."

I told him that in my outfit, "We *never* went on patrol without a medic. A medic was an integral and essential part of small unit operations, and every platoon had one. As a battalion surgeon in Vietnam, I would have thought that you must have known this."

His reply: "Of course I know that medics must go on patrol. I also know they shouldn't walk point, which would be in violation of the Geneva accords."

The Depth of Exaggeration

On page 44 of *Shadow Divers*, it was written, "There were no experienced 230-foot divers in 1991." On page 93, 230 feet was called "crazy deep." On page 157, the wreck was "lunatic dangerous." Uninformed readers were likely to accept these statements as factual, but the massive amount of historical documentation paints a vastly different picture of the state of deep diving in 1991.

In the 1950's, underwater explorer Jacques Cousteau habitually dived to depths that were greater than 230 feet, and so did all his companions. He wrote several books in which he recounted his deep diving excursions.

Scuba came into its own in the 1960's. On July 20, 1960, John Light made the first of many dives to the *Lusitania*, off the south coast of Ireland. On that day he attained a depth of 245 feet. For the next two years, he and a number of his fellow divers made numerous explorations of the wreck to a depth of 275 feet.

Northeast wreck-diver Mike de Camp started organizing deep dive trips in the mid-1960's. He consistently ran trips to the wrecks in the Mud Hole: that extension of the Hudson River which exceeds 200 feet in depth. In 1966 and 1967, he organized the first two recreational dive trips to the *Andrea Doria*, which lay at an average depth of 240 feet (with deeper washouts).

In July 1968, Bruno Vailati and his crew dived on the *Andrea Doria* for three weeks. Their numerous excursions to the seabed around the wreck were shown in the film *Fate of the Andrea Doria.*

In the late 1960's, de Camp's friend Elliot Subervi continued de Camp's tradition by organizing a club whose specific purpose was to dive on deep shipwrecks off the New Jersey coast (including those in the Mud Hole). The Eastern Divers Association quickly gained renown as *the* club for deep divers. Tom Roach assumed the presidency of EDA in 1972. He was even more determined than Subervi on running trips to the Mud Hole and to deep offshore wreck sites. He organized a recreational dive trip to the *Andrea Doria* in 1974.

After EDA dissolved in 1977, Norman Lichtman's Dive Shop of New Jersey ran specialty trips to deep shipwrecks for the shop's more adventurous clientele, and continued to do so for more than a decade.

By 1980, deep wreck-diving was a well established activity. In July of that year, John Lachenmeyer ran the first captain's charter to the *Andrea Doria*, on the *Sea Hunter*. This was the initial step on a treadmill which, after a quarter of a century, has no end in sight. By the middle of the decade, excursions to the low side of the *Andrea Doria* were routine: both inside and outside the hull.

In 1981, Billy Deans started taking divers to the U.S. cruiser *Wilkes-Barre*, which lay in 250 feet of water off Key West, Florida. Over the next fifteen years, he ran hundreds of trips to the wreck site; his customers made thousands of dives. By 1991, he had personally logged several hundred dives on the *Wilkes-Barre*. His clientele included many northeast wreck-divers.

1984 saw the commencement of a six-year legal battle over access to the Civil War ironclad *Monitor*. The wreck lay at a depth of 230 feet off the Diamond Shoals of North Carolina. The government's sole reason for denying access was its claim that diving to such a depth on scuba was not safe. The judge disagreed. He found that "the appellant and other staged decompression divers are not sport or novice divers. Their training, experience and certifications reflect a substantially greater proficiency."

As a result of this landmark decision, deep wreck-divers started to make annual pilgrimages to the *Monitor* in 1990. The extreme significance of the case was common knowledge in the entire diving community. Additionally, nationwide publicity made the general public eminently aware of the results of the lawsuit and the ensuing dives. There were eighteen deep wreck-divers on my first two-week expedition. All this information was readily available in *Ironclad Legacy*.

In the late 1980's, I was privileged to meet a few of the Great Lakes divers who had been diving to 250 feet for more a decade: Paul Ehorn, Tom Farnquist, Ryan LeBlanc, Emmett Moneyhun, Gary Shumbarger, and Charlie Tulip. This handful represents only a fraction of the deep wreck-divers who were active throughout the decade. Many times that number commonly explored the deep-water wrecks in the ice-cold lakes. Because deep water lay close to shore, these wrecks were more accessible than deep-water wrecks off the eastern seaboard.

Hal Watts was the owner of Forty Fathom Grotto, a deep spring that was located near Ocala, Florida. According to his 1989 résumé, he had made 459 dives to depths that ranged between 200 and 240 feet; 54 dives to depths that ranged between 245 and 290 feet; and 31 dives to depths that ranged between 300 and 390 feet. Through his Professional Scuba Association, he had trained *hundreds* of divers to dive to 240 feet. And hundreds of other instructors did deep-water training in the Grotto. The people who have dived in the Grotto number into the thousands. Watts was a prime witness in the *Monitor* case.

As noted in Appendix Two, the opening gambit in a series of extremely deep mixed-gas dives commenced in 1990. The initial dive was made on the German battleship *Ostfriesland*, which lay at a depth of 380 feet. This dive pushed the technical diving snowball down the hill, encouraging and accumulating deep wreck explorers at an ever expanding rate.

All of the above does not take into account the hundreds of Florida cave divers who were exceeding 230 feet on a weekly basis - and who had been doing so for many years. Nor does it take into account the number of deep divers in the rest of the world.

Culpable Negligence

By laying the claim that there were no experienced 230-foot divers in 1991, *Shadow Divers* contrived to make its uninformed readers believe that a dive to such a depth was exceptional. It would be more accurate to state that there were no experienced 230-foot divers on board the *Seeker* in 1991 (except for Nagle). The *Seeker* was a small pond in the huge ocean of deep divers who populated the world.

On page 44 of *Shadow Divers*, Nagle was quoted as

having said, "This is deeper than I was expecting." This statement is absurd. Certainly Bogan knew the depth, as he had fished on the wreck for years before he gave the numbers to Nagle. Nagle had only to chart the numbers to ascertain the depth of the site, and he was smart enough to do so.

Chapter Three in *Shadow Divers* went to great lengths to describe the adverse affect of depth on the divers who made the discovery trip to the *U-869*. It was obvious that they were exceeding their experience level.

Steve Feldman may have been the least experienced of all. On page 96 of *Shadow Divers*, it was written that he rarely ventured deeper than 100 feet. On page 97, it was written that he exceeded 120 feet only once, when he dived to 170 feet. On page 60, it was written that Feldman dived mostly in warm-water resort locations in the search for lobsters.

A diver who was so lacking in deep-water experience should never have been permitted to dive to 230 feet. To invite an inexperienced diver on such a deep dive, in order to fill the charter, was unconscionable. Feldman's death on the following trip was the sad and tragic result of pushing a diver beyond his limits.

As noted in Chapter Three, when the *Seeker's* divers declined to search for Feldman's body, Howard Klein and Steve Bielenda had no difficulty in obtaining a boatload of divers who *were* capable of making such a dive. As Joel Silverstein wrote in *The New York Sub Aqua Journal*, "These would not be simple dives yet among these seasoned divers the depth was just a matter of course." This fact further belies the claim that there were no experienced 230-foot divers in 1991.

In mid-February 1992, Feldman's body was brought to the surface in the net of the offshore dragger *Pina Lin*. The fishing vessel took the fully rigged body to Atlantic City, New Jersey, where the Atlantic County Medical Examiner took charge of it. The body was decomposed after five months on the bottom; it was identified by the dive gear.

Afterward, Will McBeth and Harold Moyers grimly

recalled Chatterton telling them about the accident and Feldman's long soak on the bottom. Chatterton ended his ghoulish story by observing, "He does have the record for bottom time."

The Uninvited

On page 42 of *Shadow Divers*, it was implied that there were no experienced divers who were willing to take a chance on a discovering a new wreck; that deep wreck-divers wanted a sure bet; and that, as a result, the boat was filled with divers who were willing but less experienced. This allegation misrepresented the true state of affairs.

Northeast wreck-divers were actively conducting offshore search and exploration trips, and had been doing so for a number of years. That dedication was constantly paying off in the discovery of deep-water shipwrecks. Most divers were pooling their resources and sharing their information in order to facilitate new discoveries.

When Bogan gave Nagle the location of his uniden-tified wreck, Bogan thought that it might be the *Corvallis* (see Appendix Five for details). Many deep wreck-divers would have jumped at the opportunity to dive on the *Corvallis*, but none of them was invited on the search trip. Because the most well known divers were intentionally excluded, unqualified divers were recruit-ed to fill the boat.

The Starfish Enterprise

As mentioned in Chapter Three, in 1993, Polly Tap-son invited me to dive on the *Lusitania*. Polly and her husband Simon lived in London, England. The *Lusitania* lay in 300 feet of water off the south coast of Ire-land. As a way of organizing the expedition, the Tap-sons and six up-and-coming mixed-gas divers formed a group called the Starfish Enterprise. The other six members were Christina Campbell, Nick Hope, Paul Owen, Jamie Powell, Richard Tulley, and Dave Wilkins. Two other divers tentatively agreed to join.

I was invited to dive with the Starfish Enterprise on the expedition that was scheduled for the first two weeks of June 1994. For logistical reasons, the optimum number of participants was twelve. When the Starfish Enterprise could not find additional suitable mixed-gas divers in the United Kingdom, they asked me if I could find an American diver to fill the gap.

As chance would have it, the eastern seaboard's most experienced deep wreck-divers were not available for a variety of reasons: family responsibilities, work obligations, lack of funds, and so on. After exhausting the list of divers who had the most amount of experience in diving on shipwrecks, I contacted second string divers who showed promising technical expertise. The one who was the most eager to go was Barb Lander.

Lander had dived on a number of my deep search trips and deep exploration dives, including the *Monitor* and the Billy Mitchell submarines (see Appendix Two for details). I had dived with her on a number of occasions, and trusted her ability to dive to 300 feet. She agreed to be my dive buddy.

When the two tentative U.K. divers opted out, I was asked if I could find two more Americans to replace them. When I discussed this latest development with Lander, she said that when she had mentioned to Chatterton that I had invited her, he told her that it was his life's ambition to dive on the *Lusitania*. She suggested that I ask him to participate.

I had invited Chatterton on one of my trips to the Billy Mitchell wrecks. He accepted my invitation, but failed to appear at departure time. We waited for an hour or so. It was imperative that we adhere to our timetable, so we were forced to leave without him. After the trip, he called to tell me that he had decided that he was not ready for the dive. I would rather have someone back out of a deep dive because he recognized his limitations, than to have him go against his better judgment.

Lander told me that by now Chatterton thought that he was ready for such a dive.

One rarely has the opportunity to fulfill a person's lifelong ambition. About ten o'clock at night, I called Chatterton and asked him if he was interested in diving on the *Lusitania*. He was astonished at my offer. He said that he would do *anything* to get on the trip. I laughed, and told him that he did not have to do anything for me. He just had to do his one-twelfth of the work on the expedition. He said that he would have to call his boss in order to obtain permission for two-week's vacation. I also asked him if John Yurga, his number one dive buddy, would want to participate. Chatterton said that most likely he would, but that Chatterton would have to call him. I told him to let me know.

Chatterton called me twenty minutes later. He was going! When I asked him how he had contacted his boss so quickly at that hour of the night, he told me that he had not contacted him, but that he was going on the expedition even if he had to quit his job to do so. In the event, both he and Yurga joined the expedition.

The Tangled Skein of Gratitude

Upon the successful completion of the *Lusitania* expedition, we talked about what to do next that could exceed the *Lusitania* in deep exploration. The *Britannic* was high on the list of unexplored shipwrecks. Only Jacque Cousteau and his dive team had ever dived on the wreck in the Mediterranean Sea. We agreed that if any of us had the opportunity to participate in such an expedition, he would contact the other members of the *Lusitania* expedition.

Several years later, when some Brits organized an expedition to the *Britannic*, Chatterton was asked to participate and to find three additional divers. He purposely did not invite me. Instead, he invited two Americans and one Canadian, and swore them to secrecy, so that I did not learn about the expedition until it was an accomplished fact. On page 91 of *Shadow Divers*, it was written that Chatterton was "capable of intense reactions when his sense of principle was offended."

Misplaced Credit

Although Nagle obtained the location of the *U-869*, then furnished the boat in order to investigate the site, since his death Chatterton has continuously taken credit for its discovery. In actual fact, Chatterton was Nagle's mate on the trip. His job was to help steer the boat and to set and pull the grapnel. This did not make him the "discoverer" any more than anyone else on the boat, and certainly not in place of Nagle.

Shadow Divers also gave Chatterton credit for discovering and/or identifying the *Pan-Pennsylvania* (page 9), the *Norness* (page 291), the *Sebastian* (page 291), the *Carolina* (page 293), and the *Texel* (page 294). Not only were these succinct assertions unsupported in the book, but by their very simplicity they failed to reveal the circumstances that surrounded them. The allusion to truth was illusion: a product of smoke and mirrors.

Brad Sheard provided the loran numbers for the *Norness*. The loran numbers of the *Carolina* were published in *Shipwrecks of New Jersey* (1988).

Pan-Pennsylvania

On July 8, 1994, the *Seeker* departed from Montauk, New York on a three-day trip to investigate hang numbers. The primary goal was the *Pan-Pennsylvania*, a tanker that was torpedoed by the *U-550* on April 16, 1944. One set of hang numbers was extremely close to the latitude and longitude that were given in *Track of the Gray Wolf*.

Twenty-five merchant seamen lost their lives. Notwithstanding a bold tactical maneuver in which the U-boat submerged and tried to evade offensive countermeasures by ducking *under* the slowly settling tanker, the *U-550* was depth-charged nearly to destruction in harsh retaliation, courtesy of three aggressive U.S. Navy destroyer escorts. One DE, the USS *Gandy*, engaged in a running gun battle with the severely damaged U-boat. The *Gandy* got the better of the *U-550*. Thirteen German sailors managed to escape from the U-boat before it took its final plunge. One died later of his wounds. The remainder served out the war as prisoners.

Overshot tracers ignited the spreading pool of gasoline that surrounded the *Pan-Pennsylvania*. The sea and the ship erupted into flames. The tanker capsized and settled by the stern until the fantail came to rest on the bottom with the bow still protruding from the surface. She remained in that unstable condition for more than a day, a definite hazard to navigation whose position was thoroughly documented. A combination of shellfire and aerial bombs was required to complete her submergence.

On the way to the primary goal, we stopped at an alternate set of hang numbers. Lo and behold, the depth recorder spiked a solid target that rose more than 30 feet from the bottom. After making a notation, we continued to the main objective area.

Although the numbers were right on target, the *Pan-Pennsylvania* was a bust. One would have thought that a ship that exceeded five hundred feet in length would have made an awesome wreck to explore. On the contrary, the tanker lay intact and upside down in an expanse of soft mud at a depth of 250 feet. Only the keel and the bottom of the hull were exposed. The "good" part of the wreck - the superstructure - was buried, and there was no way to get inside the unbroken hull. Ten feet of murky visibility curbed the desire to explore very far from the anchor line.

Those who made the discovery dive were John Chatterton, Ken Clayton, Dan Crowell, Tom Hirose, Barb Lander, Brad Sheard, Brian Skerry, Harvey Storck, and this author.

No positive identification was made. I have no doubt, however, that the wreck was that of the *Pan-Pennsylvania*: it was the right size, in the right spot, and no other sizeable wrecks were known to have gone down in the vicinity. After the dive we took a vote. No one was eager to dive on the *Pan-Pennsylvania* again. Instead, we opted to investigate hang numbers that might possibly be the site of the U-boat (whose ultimate position was admittedly problematical). If we did not find the U-boat, we would return to the unknown target that we had spiked on the outgoing passage.

Sebastian

None of the other hang numbers produced any "hits." Plan B went into effect. Chatterton went down first and alone to set the hook. Because the *Pan-Pennsylvania* had been such a dull and uninteresting wreck, enthusiasm waned on the second unknown. Once bitten, as the saying goes. The general consensus was to wait for Chatterton's report before troubling to dive on another potential zero.

I felt otherwise. I was always eager to dive on an unexplored shipwreck, even if it proved to be nothing more than a barge or broken down snag. I was dressed and ready to splash as soon as Chatterton signaled that the grapnel was secure. He did this by releasing a Styrofoam cup from the bottom. I gave him a twenty-minute head start before going over the side.

The water was clear and tinted a somber shade of green. At 205 feet, I alighted on the forecastle of a massive steel-hulled vessel that stood upright and which appeared to be intact. The starboard anchor lay on top of the deck. The port anchor was tucked inside its hawsepipe. There were four double mooring bitts secured to the deck farther aft: two on each side. A large windlass stood on the centerline of the after edge where the forecastle ended and dropped down to the main deck ten feet lower.

I dropped over the starboard rail to the shell hash and dark granular sand that comprised the seabed. The depth was 251 feet. After an examination of the hull, I ascended to the main deck and proceeded aft. The deck was partially collapsed at a spot where two more mooring bitts were secured. A huge winch was mounted on the centerline of the main deck. Abaft the bitts, the hull and deck were intact. I passed two wooden hatch covers that were secured to the coamings. Then I reached an area that was crisscrossed with nets that were festooned with colorful sea anemones. Under the netting I could barely make out another pair of hatch covers.

After glancing at my pressure gauge and decompression computer, I decided that it was wise to work my way back toward the anchor line. I crossed to the port side, then proceeded forward. When the ten-foot rise of the forecastle bulkhead loomed in front of me, I knew that I was only twenty feet away from the grapnel. A doorway opened into the forecastle, and much of the after bulkhead had collapsed, leaving a broad open space that was more than adequate for entry.

I fanned my light left and right before entering. Along the centerline I saw a curious assembly which I recognized at once by the clapper inside the flared bronze bowl: the ship's bell! It was mounted on a gooseneck davit that had fallen backward off the forecastle deck. After a brief examination I determined that the bell was still secured to the davit, but that the davit was free and clear.

I glanced at my gauges. To rig the bell properly and to send it to the surface on a safety line - so as not to lose the artifact in case the liftbag should deflate - would require more time than I thought prudent to spend, in consideration of the amount of air that I had remaining in my tanks. I clipped a 100-pound liftbag to the gooseneck as a territorial marker. I put enough air in the liftbag to hold it upright. Then I skedaddled for the anchor line.

Chatterton was decompressing ahead of me, at a shallower stop. I grabbed his attention by shaking the anchor line, then pantomimed the curvature of the bell with my hands. I was embarrassed when I realized that my impromptu charade could have been easily misinterpreted as the three significant curves of a shapely female form. But Chatterton's present mindset was not oriented pornographically. He understood immediately what I wanted to communicate.

He completed his decompression before I did. By the time I boarded the boat, everyone knew that I had found the key to the wreck's identity. Now there was a mad scramble to explore this extraordinary shipwreck. I asked Chatterton to go with me on the next dive. I did not need help in the recovery operation, but I thought that it would be a noble gesture to let him share the experience of sending the bell to the surface: the bell which he had swum past without recognizing. We planned our steps, then executed the recovery with clockwork precision.

The name engraved in bronze was SEBASTIAN.

After a lifetime of shipwreck research, I prided myself on my encyclopedic knowledge of ships that had been lost off the eastern seaboard. But the name *Sebastian* did not "ring a bell." Five minutes after my return home, however, I ascertained the general circumstances of the *Sebastian's* loss by fire from my extensive files and library. I had even made a notation about the wreck - twenty years earlier in my research career. I had not researched the *Sebastian* further because of the prohibitive depth and the distance from shore.

In the meantime, technique and technology had caught up with wreck-diving.

Carolina Exclusion

On page 294 of *Shadow Divers*, it was written, "There was no greater prize than the *Carolina*." In reality, the *Carolina* was only one of six vessels that were sunk on Black Sunday - June 2, 1918 - by the *U-151*. The other five were the *Edward H. Cole, Isobel B. Wiley, Jacob M. Haskell, Texel*, and *Winneconne*. All six vessels were being sought equally as hard, not just the *Carolina*.

The wrecks were grouped together in deep water off the coast of New Jersey. The latitudes and longitudes were published in *Shipwrecks of New Jersey*, but the positions were approximate interpretations that were made by the Navy. Hang numbers that were circulating throughout the wreck-diving community showed a number of wrecks that lay in the same pattern, but whose positions were offset from the Navy locations: as if a marked sheet of clear plastic were laid over top of a marked chart, but the plastic sheet was displaced so that the positions did not align.

The trick was to find and identify one wreck, which would then serve as the key to unlock the relative positions of the other five. Despite the cooperative effort of certain northeast wreck-divers, the search was hampered by a dearth of skippers who were willing to take their dive boats sixty miles offshore.

In 1992, Gene Peterson organized two search trips that were canceled by bad weather. In 1993, he scheduled two more trips which met with a similar fate. On one trip, we got as far as twenty miles offshore before we were forced by heavy seas to turn back. (By "we" I meant the principal investigators: Steve Gatto, Tom Packer, Peterson, and this author.)

Steve Gatto recalled, "In June 1994, on the way back from the wreck of the U-Who (which we did not dive due to heavy seas) on the dive boat *John Jack*, I mentioned in passing conversation while lying in the bunk above John Chatterton, and staring up at the ceiling, that we really needed to find the *Carolina*, and that Tom Packer (who was on the port side in a bunk) and I are on a trip in August. John leaned out of his bunk and said, 'The *Carolina*? What's that?' From that point on it must have been an obsession of John's, he wanted to get on any trip going to the *Carolina*."

After eight years of wreck-diving, this was Chatterton's first awareness of the existence of the wreck, and the inspiration for his interest.

In August of that year, we made another attempt to locate a Black Sunday wreck. Halfway to the site, one of the *Horizon's* engines broke down, and the trip was terminated.

The first Black Sunday wreck to be found was assumed to be the *Winneconne*, by estimation of the wreck's size and dimensions, although positive identification has never been made. The divers on the discovery trip, on board the *Calypso*, were John Chatterton, John Hulburt, Will McBeth, Innes McCartney, John Yurga, and this author. The date was May 28, 1995.

The *Winneconne* was the key that opened the lock to the locations of the other wrecks. Chatterton announced that he was chartering the *Bounty Hunter* for two weeks hence, in order to search for the *Carolina*. The hang numbers that he intended to investigate were published in *Shipwrecks of New Jersey* as Steamer #2. At that time, we could not be certain that Steamer #2 was the *Carolina*. It could have been Steamer #1 or Steamer #3.

In addition to organizing my own search trips, I signed up for every other search trip for which I was available. I called Chatterton right away to sign up for his trip. He bluntly disinvited me. Although I had given him the opportunity to achieve a lifelong ambition by inviting him to dive on the *Lusitania*, he did not want me on what might prove to be the discovery trip to the *Carolina*. I was excluded in favor of Barb Lander, Brad Sheard, and John Yurga. The date of the discovery trip was June 15, 1995. Also excluded were Steve Gatto, Tom Packer, and Gene Peterson: all of whom had helped to spearhead the years-long search for the Black Sunday wrecks, and one of whom (Gatto) was the first person to inform Chatterton of the wreck's existence.

The wreck was loaded with premier artifacts. Chatterton would not reveal which hang numbers were those of the *Carolina*. Those of us who had initiated the search for the Black Sunday wrecks had to continue the search without his cooperation. Chatterton maintained exclusivity to the wreck for only two months before its location became public knowledge.

When Harold Moyers informed Chatterton that those of us who had been excluded from the discovery trip had organized our own trip, Chatterton told him, "You can forget about ever diving on the *Seeker* again." Chatterton presumption of control over Dan Crowell was groundless, for Crowell told Harold, "Don't worry about Chatterton." Moyers went on many subsequent trips aboard the *Seeker* - even some trips to the *Carolina*.

Texel Identified

Gene Peterson chartered the *Robin II* for July 25, 1995. In addition to Peterson, on board were Steve Gatto, Peter Hess, Ken Mason, John Moyer, Tom Packer, John Yurga, and this author. Chatterton was invited, but failed to appear at the appropriate time. We postponed departure for as long as we could, but the person who was quoted on page 90 of *Shadow Divers* as having said, "Reliability is everything," never appeared.

Our goal was what we hoped would be the Dutch steamship *Texel*, which had been owned and operated by the Holland American Line before she was purchased by the United States Shipping Board for service in the Great War. We found the wreck right on the hang numbers, on the location that conformed to her position in the pattern. We stayed for two days.

On the very first dive, I recovered a porthole that was stamped "Rotterdam," where the *Texel* was constructed. Gatto, Moyer, Packer, and Yurga recovered china plates that were embossed with the monogram of the Holland American Line. These items provided clear proof of the wreck's identity. Chatterton did not find the brass letters until a much later trip.

The Wreck-Divers' Code

Many experienced wreck-divers prefer to dive alone. When they dive as a pair or as part of a team, the reason usually has to do with safety or efficiency. Sometimes four hands are better than two. For example, I have made a number of penetrations into the *Andrea Doria* in order to recover china or other artifacts. Whenever I dived with a buddy, we always split the take fifty-fifty. I have made such splits with Steve Gatto, Gary Gilligan, Ted Green, Matt Heintz, Jon Hulburt, John Lachenmeyer, John Moyer, Bill Nagle, and Bob Raimo. The split was the same on any other wreck. Often, a single item was shared by having one person display it for a while, then letting the other person display it for a while.

When Gatto and I opened the way to the First Class

Dining Room, in 1983, it was my eighth trip to the *Andrea Doria*. I had already done considerable exploration outside the hull, along the Promenade Deck, and inside the Foyer that led to the Dining Room. It was Gatto's first trip to the *Andrea Doria*. Nonetheless, we dived together as partners, each bringing our diverse experiences and backgrounds to the wreck. Our successful penetration and recovery of china was a shared endeavor; we divided equally the rewards of our efforts.

After several years, the route to the Dining Room became well known, but it was risky because of thick electrical cables and telephone wires that hung vertically across the corridor like a bamboo curtain. Some of the divers who ventured into the Dining Room for souvenirs had minimal skill or experience.

Hulburt feared that someone might get tangled in the cables, especially while exiting in reduced visibility after stirring the silt. He brought cable cutters on one trip in order to clear the way and make it safer. He was willing to sacrifice a dive for the good of the cause. We entered the corridor together. I slipped between the hanging cables and proceeded to the Dining Room for chinaware. Hulburt spent his entire dive cutting cables. I gave him half my take.

Carolina Safe

In 1995, Chatterton put dibs on the *Carolina's* safe by obtaining salvage protection in Federal court. For the next three years he did nothing to effect its recovery. In 1998, the year in which his salvage claim was due to expire, he quit recreational diving. He did not renew his claim. According to admiralty law, in order to maintain exclusive salvage rights and to continue to receive the protection of the court, salvage operations must be active and ongoing. By all these criteria, as well as his failure to renew his claim, Chatterton's salvage rights expired.

Chatterton recommenced wreck-diving in the spring of 2000. On June 25 of that year, He and I served as crewmembers on a trip to the *Carolina* aboard the *Seeker*. On the way to the wreck, we discussed the current legal status of the safe. He acknowledged that not only had he let the salvage rights expire, but also that he had lost his special interest in recovering the safe. He just wanted to look around the wreck.

We went down together to tie in the hook. The grapnel landed between the engine and the boilers. The shank lay against a beam that was a perfect spot for tying-in. The topside crew slackened the anchor line only moments after our arrival on the bottom. It took but a couple of seconds to sling the chain around the beam and to hook it around a tine. It was the classic textbook tie-in.

Better yet, the safe lay less than fifty feet away! Ambient light visibility was good enough to see the anchor line from the safe. Chatterton hefted the iron-clad box, which was about the size of a dishwasher. It was unattached. Then we left it to explore the farther reaches of the wreck.

After the dive, I initiated a discussion on recovering the safe. Chatterton continued to profess disinterest. But I was persistent. "The safe is loose! All we have to do is wrap a choker around it and snap on a couple of liftbags." I thought that we should go for it. Chatterton scowled, but evidently he thought hard about it. Fifteen minutes later his enthusiasm resurfaced. He began to gather materials for making a choker.

Then Dan Crowell deflated our newfound hope with bad news. According to the latest weather update, a storm that was brewing would surely catch us offshore if we did not soon head for home. If we waited for the customers to get sufficient surface interval before making their second dive, we were sure to get clobbered during the return to port. Crowell wanted Chatterton and me to pull the hook as soon as the last customer reached the deck.

Normally the conversation would have ended right there. According to policy, the convenience of the paying customers was paramount. Crewmembers were not paid for their services; the primary inducement for crewing was the opportunity to dive. Crewmembers were not supposed to extend the length of a trip unnecessarily.

But the fire that I had sparked exploded in flames too large to extinguish, and the bond between Chatterton and Crowell was open to influence. Chatterton managed to persuade Crowell to allow us a few extra minutes bottom time in which to accomplish our self-appointed task. Chatterton also approached each customer and asked if he or she minded the short extension. Instead of a five-minute bounce dive to pull the hook, I figured that we could do the job in ten. In diving to extreme depths, however, the duration of a dive was not determined as much by the time spent on the bottom as it was by the decompression penalty, which increased geometrically. When no customers complained, Crowell relented, albeit reluctantly.

Now *I* was having second thoughts on the matter - not because I did not want to proceed with the recovery, but because my body did not always tolerate a repetitive deep dive after a short surface interval: I was prone to minor decompression injury. Physiological concerns prompted me to devise an alternative plan.

Chatterton did not need my assistance to sling the choker around the safe. He could do that by himself. What he could *not* do was carry an extra bottle full of air, because his rebreather harness was not equipped with D-rings. My open-circuit harness permitted me to carry two sling tanks conveniently: one filled with decompression gas (nitrox-70) and another filled with air for inflating the liftbag.

In order to reduce my bottom time, I gave Chatterton a three-minute head start before commencing my descent. By the time I reached the grapnel at 230 feet, I could see him snugging the choker in place. My exhaust bubbles alerted him to my approach. He did not look up or acknowledge my presence - he had no need to, for experienced divers working in synchronization can communicate without making eye contact. We utilized hearing and peripheral vision, and took certain actions for granted.

Chatterton secured a 250-pound liftbag to the choker while I unclipped the extra tank and a 500-pound liftbag. I helped him to rig the safe for the lift. Like a well-rehearsed act, we went about our assigned tasks with clocklike precision. There was no wasted effort between us, for we both knew what to do. We attached the 500-pound liftbag, then filled both liftbags with air from the extra tank.

The safe rose off the bottom in extreme slow motion, practically crawling for the surface. As soon as it was out of sight I grabbed the extra tank and, clipping it to my harness on the fly, we both kicked hard toward the grapnel - looking up all the while in case the safe should come down upon our heads. The signal for Crowell to give slack on the anchor line was the appearance of the liftbags on the surface. Chatterton and I reached the grapnel in moments. We positioned ourselves to release the chain, and waited no more than thirty seconds before the anchor line went slack. It took only the barest flip of the wrist for Chatterton to slip the chain off the tine. As the grapnel came free, I grabbed it and foul-hooked it while the anchor line towed us through the water and clear of the wreck.

According to my timer, I left the bottom only eleven minutes after commencing my descent. Chatterton's bottom time was fourteen minutes. My decompression penalty - accelerated by the reduced percentage of nitrogen in the gas that I breathed during the decompression phase of the dive - was barely twenty minutes. I decompressed five minutes longer as an added safety margin. I felt anxiety during the decompression because of my inability to see Chatterton beneath me, as his rebreather did not release bubbles. Since he was breathing different gases than I was breathing - both on the bottom and during decompression - and because his bottom time was three minutes longer than mine, his first stop was deeper than my first stop, and his shallow stops were longer. I went back down the line to make certain that he was okay.

I was first up the ladder, returning - as Christina Young phrased it - from a "safe" dive. By that time the safe was being hauled aboard the boat by means of the jib pole and a block and tackle. Everyone pitched in to handle the lines and take photographs and shoot video-tape. Chatterton soon climbed aboard. Then Bill Cleary started tapping the safe's iron exterior with Enrique Alvarez's famous stainless steel hammer. It required only a couple of hefty taps to shatter the rusting iron sheath, and expose the wooden box of drawers and cabinets within. Then the frenzy began.

The customers fought excitedly and good-naturedly to dig their hands into the black and solidly caked muck in order to unearth the precious contents: gold coins (double eagles, eagles, and fractional eagles), brass and gold pocket watches, gold rings studded with tiny diamonds, brass lockets, leather pocketbooks, sil-ver coins of various denominations, even a double handful of pistol bullets (but no gun).

These items possessed a definite market value in the stream of commerce. The diamond ring appraised at more than $6,000. The gold coins were highly valued by collectors. Chatterton took the safe and its contents home in order to begin the process of cleaning and preservation.

For my inspiration and effort, Chatterton gave me one worn and tarnished silver dollar. Everything else he kept for himself.

On page 113 of *Shadow Divers*, it was written that Chatterton was a "man of honor and principle."

Near-Death Experience

Between pages 200 and 203, *Shadow Divers* went to great lengths to demonstrate how Chatterton took immediate charge of the situation when Lew Kohl sur-faced from the *U-869* after making an uncontrolled ascent without stopping for decompression. Chatterton "shoved aspirins down his throat" and administered oxygen until the Coast Guard helicopter arrived to air-lift Kohl to a recompression chamber.

A similar incident occurred on the *Andrea Doria*. I do not know the precise date or all the details of events that transpired. I was not involved in the incident, and Ed Suarez has since passed away. My recollection is based upon conversations that I had with Suarez and Chatterton shortly afterward.

Suarez was an avid mixed-gas diver who dived on wrecks and in caves. He dived to 380 feet on the *Ostfriesland* on my 1991 trip. (See Appendix Two for details of the *Ostfriesland*.) This was the year before Chatterton took his mixed-gas course (which he took in 1992). Suarez's cave and wreck-diving experience was far beyond Chatterton's.

In the incident that occurred on the *Andrea Doria*, Suarez was diving from the *Sea Hunter* when he ran out of gas and was unable to complete his decompression. He was forced to surface. He drifted away from the *Sea Hunter*. The *Seeker* was approaching the wreck site from the direction in which Suarez was drifting. He waved his hands as a signal for help.

The *Seeker* stopped alongside Suarez and lowered its ladder. He clambered onto the boat and collapsed on the deck, screaming that he had missed an hour of decompression. He was terribly frightened.

Chatterton stooped by his side. Although Suarez was terrified by the onset of the bends, he knew that his only hope for survival lay in immediate oxygen therapy, until he could be airlifted to a recompression chamber. He asked urgently for oxygen.

In the wheelhouse, Crowell called the Coast Guard to request helicopter evacuation. On the deck, Chatterton declined to administer the life-saving oxygen.

Suarez shouted and pleaded frantically for oxygen, but Chatterton steadfastly refused to give it to him. (The reader may recall from Chapter Four that Suarez was instrumental in helping Nagle and Chatterton to cut through the grille into the Third Class Dining Room.) Suarez lay on the deck for more than an hour before the helicopter arrived, during which time he was deprived of oxygen therapy.

Suarez was lucky. He was treated successfully in the chamber, and suffered no lasting aftereffects. But he could have gone the way of the Rouses. Or he could have been paralyzed for life. No one can explain how one person can skip an hour of decompression without sustaining long-lasting injury, while another can skip ten minutes and become paraplegic.

I could hardly believe the story when Suarez told me the particulars. On a subsequent trip, I had a heated argument with Chatterton over his refusal to provide Suarez with oxygen. To me, it did not matter that he was a diver from another boat, or that he may have overstayed his bottom time or mismanaged his gas. In fact, Suarez had a history of running out of gas. But that was not the time to teach him a lesson.

Whatever circumstances contributed to his situation were irrelevant. Suarez was a human being and a fellow diver who deserved better treatment - especially from an ex-medic who, according to page 79 of *Shadow Divers*, once risked his life against a hail of enemy fire to save someone.

My words were heated but Chatterton remained calm. Although I chastised him severely for action (or inaction) that I considered to be negligent and contemptible, he calmly defended his decision to let Suarez take his chances without therapeutic oxygen.

On page 81 of *Shadow Divers*, it was written that Chatterton believed, "It is easiest to live with a decision if it is based on an earnest sense of right and wrong."

Murphy's Law

On August 26, 2000, the dive boat *Seeker* took a group of divers to an offshore hang that was the forward section of a wreck. Sporadic trips over the next couple of years led to its identification as the U.S. destroyer *Murphy* (DD-603). The *Murphy* was cut in two by the tanker *Bulkoil* on October 20, 1943. The forward section of the *Murphy* sank with the loss of thirty-five officers and men. The after section was towed to port. A new forward section was constructed for the destroyer, and she was later returned to service.

Dan Bartone, skipper of the *Independence*, located the wreck in 2002 by using the same method that the *Seeker* had used: checking hang numbers. Dan Crowell, now owner of the *Seeker* (he bought the boat from Bill Nagle's widow, Ashley), repeatedly called the Naval Historical Center to complain that divers from the *Independence* were violating a gravesite by stripping the wreck of artifacts.

In 2003, Crowell complained so loud and so often that the Navy finally sent an investigator to Bartone's house. Bartone had not recovered any artifacts from the *Murphy*, and said as much to the investigator.

After Kohler returned from a *Murphy* trip aboard the *Independence*, Chatterton spotted a helm stand in the back of Kohler's truck. Chatterton turned informer on his fellow Shadow Diver by telling Crowell that the helm stand came from the *Murphy*. Crowell passed this information to his contacts in the Navy. The Navy sent an investigator to Kohler's house. Kohler denied that the helm stand came from the *Murphy*.

This ruckus eventuated in the passage of legislation that specifically prohibited the recovery of artifacts from all sunken Navy vessels anywhere in the world: a Congressional Act that I have christened *Murphy's* Law.

I wrote an article on the loss of the *Murphy* and the shenanigans that led to the passage of the law. The article was published in issue #3 of *Dive Chronicles* (Autumn 2005). Shortly thereafter, *Dive Chronicles* sponsored the Florida Dive Show, which took place Palm Beach on December 2-4, 2005.

At the show, Kohler thanked me for letting the story be known. He told me that it was important for people to be made aware of the truth, so that misconceptions did not take hold in the public consciousness. Taking him at his word, I asked some members of the Atlantic Wreck Divers to tell me about their experiences with Kohler.

Atlantic Wreck Divers

In order to obtain the history of the Atlantic Wreck Divers, I interviewed nine of the members: Steve Gatto, Pete Guglieri, Rick Jaszyn, Dennis Kessler, John Lachenmeyer, Tom Packer, Jeff Pagano, Pat Rooney, and Brad Sheard. All agreed that *Shadow Divers* grossly misrepresented the actions and attitudes of the group, and that the book portrayed Kohler's behavior in ways that conflicted with their memories of actual circumstances. Some of them shared with me their personal experiences with Kohler. Here are their stories.

On pages 133 through 137, *Shadow Divers* gave an account of the formation of the Atlantic Wreck Divers that was contested by the members of the group. The Atlantic Wreck Divers were never a "gang" that went by the name of "the Thugs," either formally or informally. "Thugs" was a criticism bestowed by *Shadow Divers.*

On page 136, it was written that the six founding members voted Kohler into the group by a show of upward pointing thumbs; while on page 340, it was written that he was one of the founding members. In addition to the lack of internal consistency, neither version was true.

While there was no official name or date when the Atlantic Wreck Divers began, the nucleus of the group began to form in 1982 when Tom Packer and Steve Gatto met Rick Jaszyn and Jeff Pagano while diving on the *White Star* out of Barnegat, New Jersey. The group quickly expanded to six by the spring of 1983, with the addition of Pagano's friend Jim Aitkenhead (known as Pinky or the Pinkster), and Bob Ehle. This tight knit group was considered the founding membership of what would become the Atlantic Wreck Divers.

Later that year, they met Dennis Kessler, Pete Guglieri, and Brad Sheard while diving out of Freeport, New York, and soon realized that they were kindred spirits. By 1984 they had become an integral part of the group, which was now nine members strong.

In 1985, Jaszyn began running charters on the *Sea Lion*, out of Brielle, New Jersey. Captain George Hoffman truly embraced the free spirit of the group, and was willing to take them to some of the deeper wrecks in the Mud Hole - wrecks that were seldom visited. They dived hard, and they played hard. The group thrived on friendship, camaraderie, and trust. If one person found a nest of artifacts, he would turn the rest of the group onto the location. According to Gatto, "A good day was when someone found an artifact; a great day was when everyone found an artifact." The group had no meetings, rules, or legal waivers. They simply dived.

Kohler heard about the diving they were doing and made his way onto the scene sometime during the 1985 season. Gatto's first impression was much like Pagano's: "I don't like this guy, he's bad news." But Kohler's heartfelt handshakes and eagerness to learn won out over their skepticism.

As their outlaw persona grew, Jaszyn decided that the group needed a name. He wanted a name that would separate the group from other groups. After several suggestions made by other members, Jaszyn decided to pay homage to Captain Hoffman for being one of the true deep diving pioneers in the region, by using the "Atlantic Wreck Diving" phrase on the back of T-shirts that Hoffman had made for his boat. Jaszyn modified the wording slightly, and the Atlantic Wreck Divers had a name.

Jaszyn knew that he wanted the biker style patches or 'colors' to reflect their outlaw image, and insisted that they be sewn onto denim jackets. Flipping through a brochure he came across the skull and crossbones, and adopted them as the official colors. And so, in the spring of 1986, the Atlantic Wreck Divers were officially born.

It was true that Kohler was known as Crackhead, but not for the reason that was given on page 139 of *Shadow Divers.*

Full Moon

On page 138, *Shadow Divers* claimed that the Atlantic Wreck Divers mooned charter boats that ran black-tie parties, threw beer cans at them, and broke into their trademark ditty. The members tossed beer cans overboard, but never threw them at other vessels (which a skipper would not allow). The ditty was not a trademark of the Atlantic Wreck Divers, but one that originated with the Dive Shop of New Jersey in 1980.

They mooned only one boat, they did it only one time, and they had a special reason for doing so. As they were returning from a dive trip, their boat passed the marina in which the *Sea Hunter* was docked. Lachenmeyer had sold his interest in the *Sea Hunter* to his partner, Sal Arena. According to Guglieri, Arena "screwed us out of a *Doria* trip and wouldn't pay us back the money, and then kicked us off his boat." *Shadow Divers* took this solitary incident and exaggerated it to standard practice.

Double Standard

With respect to the Atlantic Wreck Divers, on page 109 of *Shadow Divers* it was written that Chatterton "despised their overriding lust for tonnage, a collective instinct to take every last piece of crap from a wreck until their goody bags bloated with artifacts."

Perhaps "despised" should be replaced with "envied," for on the very next page, the pot called the kettle black by writing, "Chatterton and Nagle were planning to go back to the *Doria* early the next season, long before most boats would even consider tackling that wreck. Their mission: to haul every last artifact from the area and leave nothing."

On page 240 of *Shadow Divers*, Chatterton was quoted as criticizing the Atlantic Wreck Divers by saying, "What do they want, another plate from the *Oregon*? Another bowl like the one they got twelve bowls ago?" This sentiment did not prevent him from recovering duplicate items from the *Andrea Doria* and the *U-869*. His actions made it seem as if his philosophy of "one plate per wreck" applied to everyone but him.

It was also written on page 109, "None of them [the Atlantic Wreck Divers] seemed to Chatterton to love diving for knowledge or exploration." In fact, members conducted research on the shipwrecks that they had dived or planned to dive. Some members visited archives and libraries where they found articles, photographs, and deck plans that would not only enhance their appreciation of the wrecks, but would aid their exploration. They engaged in archival research long before Chatterton ever started wreck-diving.

The Atlantic Wreck Divers were innovative and open-minded. They were among the first wreck-divers to accept the concept of helium mixtures for deep exploration.

Diving Unction

On page 209 of *Shadow Divers*, it was alleged that one of Kohler's and Chatterton's guiding principles in recovering artifacts from the *U-869* was to not show disrespect for the dead by "rummaging through the pockets" of corpses. This lip-service sentiment contrasted sharply with actions that the book ascribed to them: on page 243 Chatterton recovered a boot; on page 249 he and Kohler recovered shoes. Bones were more likely to be found in boots and shoes than in pockets.

On page 248 of *Shadow Divers*, it was written that Kohler picked up a skull inside the *U-869*, and "placed it in such a way as to allow it to look out over the compartment and its mates." This passage was supposed to express his compassion.

Kohler's compassion for dead German sailors appeared to have been greater than his compassion for deceased wreck-divers. According to the account that was given on page 108, after Steve Feldman died, Kohler jumped at the opportunity to take his place: "He felt bad for the dead diver. But he had just one thought . . . 'You gotta get me on the next trip.' "

First Betrayal

On page 165 of *Shadow Divers*, it was written that Kohler ascribed to the fundamental values of the Atlantic Wreck Divers, "in which divers worked as a team for the good of the group." Actions speak louder than printed words. The Atlantic Wreck Divers are still rankled over Kohler's contraventions to their credo. One of the most glaring examples, which was left out of *Shadow Divers*, involved Pete Guglieri and Jeff Pagano.

Guglieri discovered a hot spot on the *Oregon*, a Cunard passenger liner that sank in 1886 off the south shore of Long Island. Near a pair of portholes he found a pristine china cup beneath a fallen hull plate. After the dive, he told Kohler and Pat Rooney what he had found. They each professed an interest in the portholes. Guglieri was more intrigued by the cup, because it was adorned with the name and crest of the shipping line.

Guglieri offered to take them to the spot so that they could recover the portholes, but he made them promise to leave cup alone. They both agreed. Under water, Guglieri pointed to the cup that he claimed as his own, then indicated the portholes. Kohler and Rooney recovered the portholes, but Guglieri was unable to extract the cup because it lay beyond his reach. Afterward, he told them that he hoped the recover the cup on the next trip to the wreck.

The following week, Kohler and Pagano obtained spots on another dive boat that was going to the *Oregon*. Kohler told Pagano that he had devised a scheme to reach Guglieri's cup. He wanted Pagano's help. Pagano expressed concern about Guglieri's prior claim. Kohler said that he had discussed the issue with Guglieri, and that it was okay with him if Kohler made a try for the cup. Pagano was so concerned that he asked Kohler again if he had permission from Guglieri to go for the cup. Kohler reassured him that Guglieri had sanctioned Kohler's plan.

In addition to the double tanks that they wore on their backs, they carried a single cylinder with them. With Pagano acting as his safety, Kohler doffed his doubles, donned the single, and managed to squeeze far enough under the hull plate to grab the cup.

Guglieri was furious when he heard about Kohler's deliberate breach of faith. Pagano was just as infuriated because Kohler had duped him into acting as an accomplice to his treachery.

On page 110, Kohler's ethic was stated as one in which "you don't jump another guy's claim."

Do Unto Others . . .

Another incident that still rankles the members involved some underwater sleight-of-hand that nearly got the group thrown off the *Sea Hawk*.

The Atlantic Wreck Divers chartered the *Sea Hawk*, Captain John Lachenmeyer, to take them to the Revenue Cutter *Mohawk*. When they arrived at the site, the *Eagle's Nest* was already tied in to the wreck. The skipper of the *Eagle's Nest* was Howard Klein. Lachenmeyer and Klein were friends as well as fellow members of the Eastern Dive Boat Association. Lachenmeyer dropped his grapnel well away from the *Eagle's Nest*.

Klein found a porthole. He did not have time to break it free on his first dive, so he marked it with his liftbag. After surfacing, he called Lachenmeyer and told him that he intended to recover the porthole on his second dive.

In the meantime, Kohler found Klein's porthole, removed the liftbag, attached the liftbag to an empty hole, knocked the porthole free, and sent the porthole to the surface on his own liftbag. He did not tell anyone that he had found Klein's porthole, the implication being that he had found a different porthole.

After Klein learned that his porthole was gone, he complained to Lachenmeyer. Lachenmeyer asked the Atlantic Wreck Divers to fess up. Tempers flared, but Kohler kept quiet. The situation was serious, for the accepted code among wreck-divers precluded one from taking an artifact when he knew that another diver was working on it.

In an attempt to rectify the situation, Guglieri kept asking Kohler if he was certain that he had not taken Klein's porthole. Kohler insisted that he had not. Finally, after giving Kohler plenty of time to come clean, Pat Rooney announced that he had seen Kohler remove

Klein's liftbag from the porthole.

In order to avoid potential repercussions, Kohler was told to give the porthole to Klein after the boats returned to port. Kohler would not do so. Lachenmeyer took it upon himself to go to the *Eagle's Nest's* dock and give the porthole to Klein.

Even though Klein was not a member of the Atlantic Wreck Divers, none of the other members would have considered taking an artifact on which he was working. The group's ethics applied to everyone, not just fellow members.

In relating this incident to me, Rooney commented dryly that Kohler "was our brain-dead child."

Double Dealing

In yet another act of betrayal involving the Atlantic Wreck Divers, Kohler turned against Tom Packer.

Packer wanted to recover one of the three auxiliary helms on the *Choapa*, a wreck that lay in the Mud Hole at an average depth of 200 feet, with washouts that went to 210. Visibility rarely exceeded eight feet. The *Choapa* was known among wreck-divers as one of the most challenging wrecks on the eastern seaboard.

Two of the helms were mounted on a steel shaft that measured one and three-quarters inches in diameter. To attune his muscles for the task, Packer practiced for two weeks prior to the dive by hacksawing through inch-thick reinforcing rods.

On the first dive of the trip - on September 14, 1991 - his planned bottom time expired when he was only a few strokes short of completing the cut through the shaft. Phred Cichowski, one of the *Sea Lion's* mates, completed the job after only a couple of minutes. The wheel turned, but he could not pull it through the A-frame bearing. After a short surface interval, Packer made a second dive of fourteen minutes duration. He turned and pulled the helm until it finally slid through the bearing. It made a distinct thud as it landed on the deck.

Packer secured a 250-pound liftbag to the helm.

Employing the standard safety procedure for the recovery of artifacts with a liftbag, he tied a sisal line to the helm, then unreeled the line as the liftbag rose. When the liftbag hit the surface and the line stopped unreeling, he cut the line and tied the bitter end to the starboard railing. This procedure served two purposes: it prevented the liftbag from drifting away in the current, and it acted as a guideline should the liftbag sink.

Kevin Brennan snorkeled to the helm and took photos. The liftbag must have had a leak, for it slowly started to submerge. Brennan tried to keep the bag afloat by blowing air into it. He got caught in the shrouds and was nearly pulled under the surface when the liftbag and the heavy wooden wheel sank to the bottom off the side of the wreck.

Packer was going up the sisal line as the helm was coming down. When he felt the line go limp in his hands, he knew immediately what was happening. He beat a frantic retreat back down to the wreck. He got wrapped in the line like a Christmas package and had to cut himself free. He landed on the mud where ambient light rarely reached. He fought to regain control of his senses, and located the wreck despite the utter blackness. He then ascended the anchor line in order to conduct his decompression.

Because he had cut the sisal line, there was no guideline to the helm. Packer made five more trips to the *Choapa* that year, but either poor visibility or the group's desire to dive on the midship bridge impeded him from swimming to the stern to conduct a search for the lost helm.

Brennan sent a photo of the helm to Packer. From the known depth of the wreck, and the angle of the sisal line in the picture, Packer extrapolated the farthest distance from the wreck that the helm could have reached.

After four more frustrating trips throughout the 1992 diving seasons, he and Steve Gatto were finally successful in relocating the helm on November 21. They returned to the railing to which the sisal line had been tied. They tied off a nylon line, dropped from the deck to the seabed, swam along the starboard side some fifty feet, and started a sweep along the muddy bottom. There was no ambient light, and visibility ranged between five and ten feet. Despite these ghastly conditions, they located the helm within five minutes. Packer put a 100-pound liftbag on the helm in order to lighten the load, and together they dragged it closer to the wreck.

Meanwhile, the weather kicked up. After they surfaced, Hoffman informed the group that they had to head for shore. Everyone felt exuberant nonetheless. Not only had Packer and Gatto found the proverbial needle in a haystack, but they had tied the nylon sweep line to the helm, thus establishing a permanent guideline between the helm and the wreck. Despite the sense of urgency, poor weather prevented any more trips that year.

The trip that was scheduled for Memorial Day in 1993 was blown out. The weather was better on June 5. Packer located the guideline, but instead of it leading him to the helm, it went straight down into the mud at an angle of 45°. He wrapped the line around his wrist and forearm, but was unable to pull the line out of the mud. Apparently, some part of the wreck had fallen onto the guideline during the winter. Because of conditions that were worse than normal, he could not determine if the line reappeared above the mud farther from the wreck. He was forced to leave in frustration.

After a dozen scheduled trips over the course of two years, he still had not come home with the helm.

At the time, Hoffman was the only skipper the Atlantic Wreck Divers trusted to take them to the *Choapa*. They chartered the *Sea Lion* several times again that year, whenever Hoffman had room in his schedule, but all except for one was blown out by high winds and heavy seas. Charters in the following years suffered a similar fate. Packer was either unable to charter the boat, was unable to fill it with divers who wanted to go to the *Choapa*, was unable to gain a favorable anchorage, or was stymied by inclement weather and poor visibility. He seemed destined never to recover the helm for which he had worked so hard.

Years passed. Hoffman passed away. The helm languished in the mud next to the wreck.

Kohler decided that he wanted the helm for himself. He secretly chartered another boat to take him to the wreck. He was unable to locate the helm. Packer heard about Kohler's duplicity, and called him to discuss the matter. Kohler maintained that Packer was not working hard enough on the project. Packer agreed that he could have been more diligent in recent years. Had anyone not a member of the Atlantic Wreck Divers found the helm, he would have been the first to congratulate him. But not Kohler. He was supposed to be a brother. Packer thought that Kohler should want to help him recover the helm in a spirit of fellowship, instead of working against him in order to recover it for himself. After all, it was Kohler who allegedly abided by the principle that "you don't jump another guy's claim." Apparently, there was a vast difference between his words and his actions.

The Atlantic Wreck Divers sided with Packer. They all felt that Kohler should not go after other people's artifacts, but should instead try to find his own.

In the meantime, Harold Moyers had a dive boat built. On August 13, 2005, he moved the *Big Mac* from Cape May to Brielle primarily to help Packer before Kohler spirited the helm away from him. Jon Hulburt, Greg Masi, and Bart Malone went along to lend assistance.

Packer and Moyers relocated the helm the following day. They established a new guideline between the railing and the relic. Even after fourteen years, Packer decided to wait one more day before making the actual recovery, so that he could photograph the helm on the bottom.

The *Big Mac* returned to the *Choapa* the next day. Diving alone, Packer took his pictures. Then Moyers took down a second anchor line and swam it out to the helm. Once the secondary line was secure, Moyers swam back to the wreck, severed the guideline, and ascended the anchor line.

After everyone was back on the boat, Moyers used the boat winch to haul the helm out of the mud and through the water column to the surface. The two old liftbags were still attached to the helm; they had been completely buried. Now they were filled to the brim with heavy mud. Packer cut the shrouds and let the liftbags drop to the bottom. The helm came aboard with ease. Patience and perseverance triumphed at last.

Retrospective

When Rick Jaszyn told me, "The worst decision I ever made was to let Richie Kohler dive with the club," he was reiterating sentiments that were shared by the other club members. Jaszyn said that Kohler "brown-nosed" the Atlantic Wreck Divers by carrying their tanks to the boat, and by helping them with their gear.

Despite his ingratiating behavior, most of the members were skeptical of him. Nonetheless, because Kohler bleated his eagerness to learn, they tried to instill in him the Atlantic Wreck Divers' code of ethics.

Today they feel regret. None of them now consider Kohler to be a member.

Packer told me that Kohler never seemed to understand what being an Atlantic Wreck Diver was all about. Becoming an Atlantic Wreck Diver was such an achievement for Kohler that it seemed to go straight to his head.

As Jaszyn lamented, "We created a monster."

Forever more, whenever Kohler looks at the colors of the Atlantic Wreck Divers, he will be reminded of how he betrayed his former friends.

As wreck-divers are wont to say, artifacts can be bought and sold but friendships must be earned.

EPILOGUE
The Emperor's New Clothes

"John Chatterton and Richie Kohler will stop at nothing to rewrite history."

- Dave Weich

Truth or Consequences?

I apologize to Dave Weich for taking his words out of context. The quote above was preceded by, "Braving pitch-black waters two hundred thirty feet below the ocean's surface to snake through the sub's tangled machinery in search of a clue, crossing the globe to pore through massive government archives and inter-view the world's foremost naval experts, . . . "

Weich's sentence was used to set the background for an interview with Robert Kurson for Powell's Books. I was struck by the essence and poignant criticism that the quote embodied.

The question that discriminating readers must now ask themselves is this: What exactly was *Shadow Divers*?

Was it a tall tale in the vein of Paul Bunyon or Baron Munchausen, containing Horatio Alger caricatures replete with Tom Swift dialogue spiced by Andrew Dice Clay expletives?

Was it an emaciated skeleton of facts surrounded by a fat body of fiction?

Was it a kernel of truth on a cob of lies?

Was it only a façade, like a movie set with store fronts but no buildings behind them?

Was it all smoke and mirrors?

Was it an insidious effort to hoodwink the public?

Was it a cunning attempt to rewrite history the way the book's contributors wished it could have been, or the way they wanted their personas to be perceived because their true inner selves lacked substance?

Was it a manipulative fabrication that was designed to present false images to a gullible and uninformed public, on the precept that perversions of the truth that were told often enough to a sufficient number of people could become accepted in the public eye as reality?

Was it a collage of imaginative vignettes that were assembled indiscriminately along the plot lines of a novel?

Was it a vapid sequel to Kurson's Three Stooges biography, with one knucklehead omitted?

Or was it nothing more than John and Richie's excellent adventure told with ludicrous hyperbole?

Shadow Divers contained at least three verifiable facts: the *U-869* was discovered, dived, and identified. My faithful readers must decide for themselves how much of the rest of the book was a product of imagination. My faithful readers must also decide how much of the dialogue was not simply reconstructed and synthesized, but was invented out of whole cloth for scenes that never occurred.

Shadow Divers concocted dialogue for people who were never interviewed, and in some cases for people who have long since been dead. The interjection of swearwords and gross vulgarities *can* be attributed to Chatterton and Kohler, for socially unacceptable language was an affectation of their speech pattern. But most other wreck-divers spoke without reliance on profane emphasis to make their points.

Shadow Divers treated the actions of other divers in cavalier fashion, in order to compare them unfavorably with the book's chosen heroes. This contrivance relied on making the media junkies look good by making other divers look bad.

One thing is certain: the two main characters that are portrayed in the book are artificial constructs - designer personalities, if you will. The way they were sanitized and glorified by Chatterton's hired writer, they bore little resemblance to the people I knew in real life, at least with respect to the actions and motives that were ascribed to them. *Shadow Divers* was *his* story, not history.

False Credits

Since Nagle's death, Chatterton has contrived to take sole credit for the discovery of the *U-869*. In my opinion, he has no more claim to such credit than the other twelve divers on the boat, and certainly not in place of Nagle, who obtained the wreck's location and who organized the discovery trip.

Shadow Divers gave credit to Chatterton for discovering the Ultra decrypts which identified the *U-869*, and which determined that it was proceeding to the precise location of its ultimate demise. Yet Mark McKellar actually unearthed this valuable information, and passed it along to Chatterton in a spirit of cooperation. In order to support its bogus contention, *Shadow Divers* did not even acknowledge McKellar's existence.

Shadow Divers credited Chatterton with spending numerous days in the archival facilities in Washington, DC, doing research that was in reality done by Barb Lander. In this context, her name was mentioned only in passing.

Robert Coppock suggested the circular run torpedo theory to account for what Chatterton and Kohler led him to believe was the only damage to the pressure hull. *Shadow Divers* downplayed Coppock's incredible research contributions, neglected to mention that he was the first to suggest the theory, and gave credit for the theory to Kohler and Chatterton (on pages 232 and 233). Ironically, they took credit for an untenable theory that has been indisputably disproven.

Shadow Divers made no mention of the attack that was prosecuted by the *Howard D. Crow* and the *Koiner*, and which resulted in the destruction of the *U-869*.

Shadow Divers gave credit to Chatterton for finding the body of Mark Ruggiero on the *Texas Tower*, when in fact Kevin England and John Moyer found the body.

Chatterton has contrived to take sole credit for conducting CPR on Chris Rouse, when in fact the part that he played was a minor role that was insubordinate to the roles of other divers on the boat that day, particularly Tom Packer, but also Steve Gatto and Steve McDougall - none of whom was so much as mentioned with respect to the tragic incident.

Shadow Divers credited Chatterton as the sole inspiration for opening the way to the Third Class Dining Room of the *Andrea Doria*, as the sole operator of the cutting torch, and as the sole installer of the gate that was intended to block access to divers on boats other than the *Seeker*. In reality, Nagle at the very least shared the inspiration, and may have been solely responsible for the inspiration. (The truth can never be known because he is deceased.) Nagle spent more time operating the torch than did Chatterton, and a host of other divers were required for assistance. The installation of the gate could not have been accomplished without a massive group effort.

In short, Nagle discovered the wreck, McKellar furnished the identity, Lander conducted the bulk of the research, Moyers ascertained how the U-boat was sunk - and Chatterton and Kohler took the credit, then made a career out of reputations that were based upon a foundation that was either faked, filched, or fictitious.

Newsmanship is the art of conveying a false impression without actually lying. *Shadow Divers* made no pretension to such a subterfuge.

Doublethink and the Ministry of Truth
The damage that was done by a book like *Shadow Divers* is difficult to assess and more difficult to undo. Unless its falsehoods are disputed, the inventions and inaccuracies could take permanent form. A prime example of this occurred when I interviewed Brad Sheard. He was on the boat when Gilligan and I recovered the "Closed for Inventory" sign. When I asked him about the incident, he stated at first that Guglieri and Kohler must have recovered the sign. After a little prompting, he realized with some astonishment that he

was wrong - that he was remembering the scene that he had recently read in the book, not the actual event as it occurred more than sixteen years earlier.

I told him, "Did it occur to you the other night how *Shadow Divers* has affected the public perception of the truth, when you remembered the version of the 'Closed for Inventory' sign the way it was written in the book, instead of the way the incident actually happened? Your more recent memory of reading that account in the book was pasted over your memory of the actual event."

Sheard knew the truth, yet even *he* was tricked into remembering the event differently. Imagine what must happen to uninformed readers whose *only* knowledge of events came from what was written in *Shadow Divers*. This is a powerful example of the irreparable harm that such a book can cause. It reminds me of the climactic scene in George Orwell's *1984*, in which Winston Smith finally conceded that two plus two equaled five. He was brainwashed to the point of concession in that what he was told was more valid than what he observed.

At what point does myth become historical tradition?

The Santa Claus Effect

All too often, once a person puts his faith in illusion, his beliefs cannot be changed no matter how compelling the later recognition of reality. People tend to believe what they hear first: the irrational condition of an unalterably closed mind that cannot accept - or that refuses to accept - the truth, because the process of change causes stressful mental effort, or because bitter reality is not as appealing as the fantasy world. Instead of accepting the unvarnished truth that is supported by evidence and testimony, these people prefer the comfort of their delusions.

Shadowy Divers

The easiest way to write historical fiction is to obtain the core of a story from actual history, alter and embellish it for the most dramatic presentation, then create courageous characters to suit the situations. I do this all the time in writing novels. In fiction, the goal is to achieve verisimilitude that suspends disbelief, rather than to adhere strictly to facts in true chronological sequence. Such latitude is not permissible in nonfiction.

Shadow Divers purported to be nonfiction. Nonfiction means fact. Fact means reality. Reality is an account of events as they actually happened in the order in which they occurred. Nonfiction means quoting eyewitnesses accurately, not ignoring their declarations in order to invent a more sensational story that hyped the featured characters.

Anything that does not conform to these rigid and uncompromising standards is not history, but fable or ideality: whether it be in the form of a book, a magazine article, a television show, a movie, or any other form of presentation. There is no room in nonfiction for invention, exaggeration, embellishment, hyperbole, or sensationalism. Those are the devices of fiction and falsehood.

It was written on page X in *Shadow Divers*, "This is their story. All of it is true and accurate. Nothing is imagined or interpreted, and no literary liberties have been taken." This reminds me of the conundrum in which one side of a playing card reads, "I never lie. The other side of this card is the truth," while the other side of the card reads, "I always lie. The other side of this card is the truth." My faithful readers must decide for themselves how much of *Shadow Divers* to believe.

It was also written on page X, "Everything was checked against multiple sources." If this statement were true, then the events that are described in the book would have included the names of participants who were hidden by anonymity, and those events would have been described the way in which the witnesses described them to me. Some of the people who disputed the published versions of their interviews were Steve Gatto, Pete Guglieri, Jon Hulburt, Howard Klein,

John Moyer, Pat Rooney, Norman Sakai, Brad Sheard, and John Yurga.

It was written on page 338, "Whenever possible, these stories were checked with the principals involved." Kurson did not interview me, or Gail Amarino, or Kevin England, or Rick Jaszyn, or Chris Jazmin, or Dennis Kessler, or John Lachenmeyer, or Steve McDougall, or Tom Packer, or Jeff Pagano, or any number of other divers who could have provided counterpoint to Chatterton's and Kohler's narcissistic version of events.

Kurson had ample opportunities to arrive at the truth of the circumstances, had he chosen to do so and had truth been his objective. He squandered those opportunities in order to improvise a seductive story that bore little if any resemblance to reality. The result was a book that lacked integrity, a book that perverted the truth, a book that perpetuated counterfeit dogma, a book that relied blatantly on juvenile machismo to achieve effect for audience appeal, a book in which history was adjusted in order to shift the limelight onto two imitation swashbucklers, a book which in the final analysis demonstrated complete absence of social conscience.

It was written on page 339, "Inconsistencies were slight, when they occurred. I used the consensus version of events to conclude, say, that a diver had been underwater for ten minutes rather than twelve." This statement implied that the greatest disparity of truth in the events that were described was a bottom time of two minutes. This implication may lull uninformed readers into believing that everything else that was written in *Shadow Divers* was gospel instead of gobbledygook, but I beg to differ.

"Ignorance is Strength" only in *1984*. In a court of law, once a witness commits perjury, all his testimony is automatically discredited. Which statements might be true and which are patently false cannot be determined without corroborating evidence. A witness who has been impeached loses his credibility for all time.

Shadow Divers Exposed is not a court of law. It is a forum in which a number of candid witnesses have given genuine accounts of events that were deformed and contorted in *Shadow Divers*. The primary purpose of the present volume is to leave a record of truth to contradict the fictions that made up its predecessor.

The present volume also pays tribute to the officers and men of the *Howard D. Crow* and *Koiner* for intentionally going in harm's way, and taking aggressive action that resulted in sinking one of the Fuhrer's U-boats.

The Moment of Truth

On page 208 of *Shadow Divers*, it was written about Chatterton and Kohler, "Their behavior would reflect on the sport for years." This was one of the few truisms that the book contained. Perhaps it was the only instance of understatement, for it may take decades to undo the damage that has been inflicted on the public by *Shadow Divers'* pompous disregard for the truth.

I often wonder if the author(s) seriously believed that their fabulous fairy tale would go unchallenged.

Interview Techniques

One quirk of memory is that people remember different things at different times. A person might remember one detail clearly at one time, then at another time remember something else clearly but be hazy about a detail that he remembered before. Recall depends upon how memory is triggered - a question that neurologists have been striving to answer for years.

An astute interviewer - and one who is sincerely seeking the truth - must be creative in order to elicit memories about incidents that occurred in the distant past. I have developed my own techniques for sparking memories. Some are specific while others are roundabout.

I start with a global question such as, "What do you remember about so-and-so?" I let the person ramble without interruption. Often, the story that develops is jumbled and undirected: it bounces back and forth through the timeframe of the incident. An interviewer must not alert the person of this seeming incoherence, or he may implant a mental block as the person tries to protect the integrity of his memory.

Coherence will come later, after the interviewer collates and assembles the seemingly discordant facts in their proper sequence. In free association, a person may remember details that he might not remember if the interviewer's questions are too specific.

When the person's spontaneous recollections begin to falter, I prompt him by asking pointed questions about things that he had already told me, in order to get him to elaborate and to flesh out the picture. Once his conscious memory is exhausted, I rely on three ways of pulling details from his subconscious.

One way to delve into latent memory is to get off the subject. Talking about unrelated issues or other events allows the hard memory to relax and clear the mind. I encourage conversation about topics that have nothing to do with the subject at hand. This is easy to do if I know the person. Slowly and subtly, I swing back to the subject of the interview. The person may now surprisingly remember details that had escaped him before. Once his recollection energy is regenerated, I may obtain additional pieces of the puzzle.

Another way to trigger repressed memories is to agree with the details of a certain incident, even if those details are contradicted by the facts or by the memories of other witnesses. For example, I might say, "I heard the same thing." This affirmation encourages the person to delve deeper into memory, and to evoke feelings that were associated with the event in question. It might make him doubt his previous recollection. I do *not* bring the person's attention to his change in viewpoint. Instead, I gently suggest disparities in the global picture.

The third way to spark memory is to refute certain details, even if I know from other sources that the accuracy of those details is not in question. This puts the person on the defensive. In order to defend his first recollection, he may be forced to delve deeper into memory in order to furnish additional details to bolster his claim.

All these methods enable me to reconstruct long-ago events to the best recollections of the people involved. But the process is not yet complete.

Transcription Errors

Next I transcribe my notes and recordings, and write a full account in a form that is both logical and chronological. Most important, I submit my written account to the person or persons who contributed recollections of the event, and ask for feedback. This measure achieves several goals.

First, it gives witnesses the opportunity to correct any errors that I may have made in transcribing their recollections. Second, when a witness reads a written transcript that summarizes his recollections and arranges them in order, he may see details that trigger more memories. Third, when one witness reads an account that is a compilation of recollections from a number of witnesses, the recollections of other witnesses might spark additional memories.

I encourage the person to make corrections and additions. After receiving feedback, I rewrite the account, submit the revised draft, and ask for feedback again. I continue this process until he (or they) is satisfied with the result. The process is long and laborious, and it creates a great deal of work for me because of the seemingly unending number of revisions that I have to make. But it results in an account in which everyone's input is consolidated, and which is as close to the truth as it can possibly be.

Consolidating the accounts of a single event from the perspective of multiple witnesses creates a problem of its own. When a witness reads the consolidated account, he might have difficulty in accepting the viewpoints or recollections of other witnesses, in which case he might object to the way the incident is presented.

Trying to get a witness to approve a consolidated account that differs from his personal recollections can lead to argument and debate, which sometimes end fruitlessly.

In a court of law, the jury decides which reconstruction of events to believe. A journalist must make that decision for himself to the best of his ability.

In cases in which a person's contribution is small, or in which brief contributions are scattered throughout different sections of the text, I read the various contributions with the contributor either in person or on the phone. This system provides the contributor with opportunity to refine his language for clarity.

Mistakes Still Happen

The result is not perfect. For example, when I wrote the history of wreck-diving in *The Lusitania Controversies*, I interviewed Pete Manchee about penetrations that he had made into the *Andrea Doria*. After going through the process that is described above, he approved my written account. Yet the final version contained a mistake that neither one of us caught until 2005.

In the published version, I wrote about one penetration that he made in 1988. In reality, he made a different penetration in 1988, and made that particular penetration in 1989. I wish I could state that the incorrect date was a typographical error, but it was not. I ascribed the years based upon the dates that were stamped on my slide mounts, some of which were partially illegible. Because he made deep penetrations in 1987, 1988, and 1989, he failed to notice the difference. As a result, the account was correct but the year was wrong.

I can understand how Manchee got confused about the dates. Having made more than fifty trips to the *Andrea Doria*, I have to admit that most of them run together in my mind. It is nearly impossible for me to remember who was on which trip when a certain incident happened, or in which year a certain event occurred. When I refer to my dive log and photographs, I am often surprised to find that my recollections were off by several years.

I doubt that perfection can ever be achieved. But a willing witness and an honest interviewer cannot be faulted for lapses in a person's memory. In any event, any errors that are incurred in this process are unintentional.

Inspiration

I would not have written this book without Harold Moyers' insistence. In the summer of 2004, he began to use me as a sounding board for his findings that surrounded the attacks of the *Howard D. Crow* and the *Koiner*. I reviewed his evidence and found it compelling. He had no difficulty in swaying me to accept his conclusion that the *U-869* was sunk by hedgehogs and depth charges, and not by a circular run torpedo.

As he continued to gather historical documentation to further support his conclusions, he suggested that the truth of the *U-869* must be made available to the public in written form. I did not think that the subject warranted the length of a book, and neither did he. I thought of writing an update for the subscribers of my website newsletter, which is read by thousands of Internet users, or perhaps a magazine article. I also intended to include the information in a book that I was writing: *The Fuhrer's U-boats in American Waters*.

Meanwhile, I kept hearing from an overwhelming number of dive buddies about the inaccuracies in *Shadow Divers*. I had not read the book, so I was blissfully unaware of its tendency toward urban legend. Moyers and many others in the wreck-diving community put the bug in my ear about the need to correct the legion of lies and deceptions that filled the pages of *Shadow Divers*. After reading it, I understood why so many of my friends were enraged by a book that purported to be a "true account," but which was far less than truthful.

For me, the ultimate stimulus to defend the cause

of righteous indignation was the Coast Guard boarding of Moyers' boat.

The genesis for a full-length book was not fully formulated until I hosted a gathering at my house after the boarding incident. In attendance were Steve Gatto, Jon Hulburt, John Moyer, and Harold Moyers. Gatto brought a copy of *Shadow Divers* that he had marked throughout with a highlighter: passages to which he took exception. We discussed at length the book's fabrications and falsifications. We all knew the truth of events because we had lived through them. After an hour of discussion, we had barely touched the surface of factual errors that were contained in the book.

This led Moyers to complain about his loss of faith, "I wonder about any book I read now." He also wondered how much actual truth was broadcast on television documentaries.

Gatto commented jokingly, "I wonder if World War Two even happened."

We all snickered. But behind our thin veil of laughter lurked some very real concern.

After airing the issues, it became obvious that Kurson had made a number of fatal errors in creating the spurious *Shadow Divers*: he declined to interview people whose testimony would have contradicted that of Chatterton and Kohler; people he interviewed did not have the opportunity to review the final product and make corrections; when a person's testimony contradicted a story as it was told in the book, that testimony was either ignored, or it was changed so that it no longer offered contradiction; words that were never spoken were put into the mouths of real individuals in order to add credibility to a nonfactual account.

Although the Coast Guard boarding incident provided the impetus for my zeal to redress factual distortions and unscrupulous behavior that I found unacceptable, Moyers still insisted that an article would suffice to correct the fallacies and sophisms of *Shadow Divers*. I now argued for a full-length book, because the inaccuracies were so many, so gross, and so enormous that no magazine would publish an article of the length that was needed to provide the counterpoint of truth.

The result was a volume that worked on a multitude of levels: it presented the real saga of the loss of the *U-869*; it put the discovery of the *U-869* into perspective with other U-boats that have been discovered in American waters; it provided an overview of the U-boat war through the stories of other U-boat losses; it bestowed homage to the officers and men of the *Howard D. Crow* and the *Koiner*, and it corrected some - but certainly not all - of the errors and distortions in *Shadow Divers*.

Thanks for the Memories

I could not have done justice to the present volume without the cooperation of a number of individuals who shared their recollections with me. I thank them all for telling me their version of events in which they participated. I wish I could have found more witnesses to corroborate the incidents that I covered, and to contradict a number of other incidents in *Shadow Divers* that I suspect are untrue but which I cannot adequately disprove without eyewitness testimony.

The diving community is somewhat fluid. Some divers enter the field as others leave it. Once a person drops out of the community to pursue other interests, the community frequently loses contact with him, and vice versa. Friendship is not broken; rather, communication is disrupted, in some cases forever. Divers within the community may not know the whereabouts of those who have left it. That explains why I was unable to trace some of the people I wished to interview.

Moyers found and interviewed surviving crewmembers of the destroyer escorts that sank the *U-869*. From the *Howard D. Crow* he interviewed Ken Denson, George King, Harold Muth, Robert Quigley, and Ted Siviec. From the *Koiner* he interviewed Charles Judson and Ralph Kern.

Jon Hulburt's contributions were many and varied. In addition to providing the background information on the *Andrea Doria* gate caper, he reviewed the manuscript with introspection that only he could provide. He has been in the forefront of wreck-diving since the early 1970's - not only as an explorer but also as an innovator. His historical perspective of the activity was as invaluable as his suggestions for changes that helped to improve the wording in the text.

Steve Gatto annotated *Shadow Divers* for inaccuracies. Both he and Tom Packer furnished true versions of events in which they participated. They provided a history of the Atlantic Wreck Divers, of which they were founding members.

Gatto, Packer, and John Moyer are icons in the wreck-diving community. Their contributions are too numerous to mention. They reviewed the manuscript in its entirety, and made many valuable suggestions that helped to improve the quality of the final draft.

Bonds of Friendship

It is quintessentially important that my non-diving readers understand the wonderful camaraderie that permeates the wreck-diving community. I have known some divers for decades, have become their friends, have shared their joys and sorrows, and have heard intimate details about their personal lives - yet I may never have been to their homes or met their families. This is the nature of the community. We meet largely on dive boats or at club meetings or at large-scale conferences, while engaging in the activities that we love. Then, after being apart for many years, we may meet again and act as if we never parted. We reminisce about old times as if the events of yesteryear occurred the day before.

While a few divers may have been driven through life and through their wreck-diving activities by their egos - stepping on the heads of others in order to attain what they perceived as personal success - most have been guided by an innate social tendency to belong to a brotherhood whose whole was greater than the sum of its parts, and within which a safe and successful dive was shared by all. For most of its members, the wreck-diving community was an extended family.

The wreck-diving community is largely a melting pot of people from all age groups, from numerous occupations, from many social ranks, from all income levels, from different cultural backgrounds, and from various religions. For the most part, they are devoted to diving on shipwrecks and to basic humanitarian principles. Equality is so much taken for granted that, on a dive boat, one might see a rich elderly professional socialite diving with a struggling young blue-collar worker - then sharing junk food and swapping stories after the dive.

The anger, hostility, bickering, and conflict that fulminated throughout the pages of *Shadow Divers* did not present a true perspective of the team spirit and fellowship that characterized the wreck-diving community. Such magnified contention was either a fabrication created by the author, or the thwarted perception of the author's partners and advisors. In reality, the byword of wreck-diving is camaraderie: a point that *Shadow Divers* missed entirely.

If I were granted three wishes, I would wish for peace, health, and prosperity for the world. If I were granted a fourth wish, I would wish for more friends. The greatest satisfaction that I have gained from wreck-diving has been the sheer number of friendships that I have forged throughout the years. I refuse to let a couple of rotten apples spoil the barrel.

APPENDIX ONE
U-boat Forensics

"I think you'd have a hard time disputing that it was a T-5 acoustic torpedo that sent it [the U-869] to the bottom."

- *John Chatterton*

Running in Circles

On page 66 of *Shadow Divers*, Chatterton was quoted as stating, "I know nothing about U-boats." Apparently, he knew nothing about torpedoes, either. Worse, he neglected to *learn* anything about them and how they functioned. On pages 232 and 233, Kohler and Chatterton explained how the *U-869* was sunk by its own torpedo. Throughout the years, they have persisted in propounding this circular run torpedo theory, despite the lack of any evidence to support it, and despite a wealth of evidence to contradict it.

The happenstance of self-destruction is not as far-fetched as it sounds. There are authenticated cases of submarines that suffered such a fate: American as well as German. A number of circumstances must conspire in order for a submarine to torpedo itself.

The submarine must have launched a torpedo (presumably at a target).

The torpedo's mechanical components must have malfunctioned in a very precise manner in order for it to circle back on the submarine that launched it.

The submarine must have been cruising on the surface or no deeper than periscope depth at the time that the torpedo commenced to circle.

Kohler and Chatterton claimed that *only* a direct hit by a torpedo could have caused the enormous hole in the pressure hull adjacent to the control room, that no other ordnance device could cause such "cataclysmic damage" (page 324), and that the German sailors were "blown apart and nearly vaporized by the explosion" (page 325).

The circular run torpedo theory may make sense to people who are unacquainted with the mechanisms involved, but the theory quickly falls apart in the water when the circumstances that are required for its effectuation are applied to the *U-869*. Nonetheless, once Kohler and Chatterton adopted the theory, they clung to it like strangling men on the gallows, clutching the tightened noose around their necks.

Let us examine their theoretical points one by one.

Depth Charge or Torpedo?

On page 151 of *Shadow Divers*, it was written, "the damage was likely caused by a force far greater than a depth charge."

Standard German torpedoes carried 617 pounds of high explosive (not 780 pounds as it was written on page 325 of *Shadow Divers*). The T-5 acoustic torpedo carried 604 pounds of high explosive, because the acoustical sensing device occupied some of the space that was allocated for the explosive charge in the standard torpedo.

The depth charges that were dropped on the *U-869* contained 600 pounds of high explosive. Although it was true that a T-5 acoustic torpedo carried a larger explosive charge than a depth charge, the difference was a matter of less than 1%.

One percent more explosive cannot be construed as "far" greater.

Unwarranted Assumptions

It is important for the reader to visualize the actual extent of the damage on the *U-869*. The wreck sits upright on a white sandy bottom. The pressure hull is pierced by two massive holes: the largest hole is located on the port side of the control room; the other hole is located on top of the after torpedo room. The blast that breached the control room detonated from the side. The blast that breached the torpedo room detonated from above.

In 2005, the control room hole measured thirty feet in length, encompassing the entire length of the control room plus about six feet of the officers quarters and six feet of the engine room. This hole stretched vertically from the seabed over the very top of the hull and beyond to the starboard side. The torpedo room hole measured ten feet across.

On February 4, 2006, Chatterton claimed on an Internet forum, "The wreck is virtually blown in two and has a 20 foot opening on the port side that demolished the pressure hull, the fuel bunker, and toppled the conning tower."

These naïve assumptions - that the wreck was virtually blown in two, and that the conning tower was toppled by the initial concussion - appear to be based upon the extent of the damage at the time of the wreck's discovery: as if the condition of the wreck in 1991 was exactly the same as it was in 1945. Because these assumptions are baseless, they cannot support a claim of a direct torpedo strike.

These assumptions fail to take into account some highly significant facts: that the hull alighted in an upright orientation, that the hull is contiguous, that the forward and after sections are in alignment, and that the wreck had deteriorated extensively in the forty-six years that passed between the sinking (in 1945) and Nagle's discovery (in 1991). They also fail to account for *perceptible* deterioration that occurred during the six years when Chatterton dived on the wreck. And they fail to account for additional deterioration that occurred during the nine years between Chatterton's last observation and the present time.

Orientation of the Wreck

A U-boat that was destroyed on the surface or in mid water generally settled to the bottom with a list. This was a function of progressive and unbalanced flooding as the U-boat sank out of control. Examples that are discussed elsewhere in the present volume are the *U-85*, the *U-352*, the *U-701*, and the *U-2513*. The *U-853* was scudding along the bottom at the time it was depth-charged. It settled upright, the same as the *U-869*.

If the pressure hull had been blown in two anywhere but right on the bottom, as Chatterton contended, then the hull would have folded or separated from structural failure either before it struck the seabed, or when either end struck the seabed before the other end. As noted above, the hull is contiguous with both bow and stern in alignment.

Damage to the Wreck

The *U-869* did not always appear to have been blown apart. Experienced wreck-divers know that shipwrecks exist in a constant state of flux. As I wrote in the *Primary Wreck-Diving Guide*, "A shipwreck is not a static singularity but a process at work . . . a dynamic system of degradation . . . Shipwrecks are not immortal; they are way stations to oblivion."

The two blast holes were not always as large as they are today. In 1991, the control room hole measured seventeen feet in length, and extended over the top of the compartment. By 1995, the hole measured twenty feet in length, and extended into the adjacent compartments. Chatterton failed to mention the progressive deterioration that occurred over a period of six years. As noted above, the hole has now stretched to thirty feet, and the starboard hull (opposite the blast hole) has a gap that measures two to three feet across and which extends from top to bottom.

The torpedo room hole measured nearly ten feet across in 1991. Although this hole has not grown appreciably, the torpedo loading hatch has gradually pivoted until it no longer points aft at a downward angle, but now stands almost vertical.

Chatterton's presumption - that the pressure hull was "virtually blown in two" - displayed a serious lack of understanding of the processes of collapse.

Submarine Comparison

Sixty-one years have passed since the *U-869* made its final plunge. The wreck does not appear today as it appeared in 1991. By extrapolation, it should not have appeared in 1991 the way it appeared in 1945.

At this point, it is worthwhile to educate uninformed readers on hull deterioration by exploring other sunken submarines. The *U-853* serves as a perfect case in point, because the *U-869* was a nearly perfect clone of the *U-853*. Both U-boats were Type IX-C-40's, and both were built at the Deschimag yard. The *U-853* was depth-charged to destruction on May 6, 1945. There were no survivors. (See Appendix Three for details.)

I first dived on the *U-853* in 1972. The hull was nearly intact except for a blast hole in the side of the after torpedo room. Tom Roach and I made a penetration into the *U-853* that was similar to the penetration that Chatterton made into the *U-869* twenty-five years later, but in the opposite direction. We had to remove our pony bottles in order to squeeze through restrictions. Whereas Chatterton entered a mammoth hole in the control room, then passed through the diesel engine room into the electric motor room, Roach and I entered the after torpedo room by squeezing through the small jagged blast hole, then proceeding forward into the electric motor room, thence through the diesel engine room to the control room.

Because the hull was essentially sealed, the mud that had accumulated on the bottom of the compartments was many feet thick, and undisturbed silt was piled to a height of several inches on every horizontal surface. My exhaust bubbles knocked scads of rust particles off the overhead; these particles then fell like flakes of black snow and obscured our exit route. I am forced to admit that the long penetration was a frightening experience.

In 2005, I made the same penetration alone and with ease. I did not even feel apprehensive. The blast hole in the after torpedo room was large enough to drive a truck through the opening. The pressure hull had so many rust holes, and so many cracked welds between the plates, that outside light peeked through in numerous places. When I reached the control room, I did not have to backtrack through the disturbed silt to the after torpedo room. Instead, I exited through a hole in the forward end of the control room. Much of the silt had been washed away by the water that flowed constantly through the wreck.

In 1972, the control room blast hole on the *U-853* was a slender crack about the size of a child's beach bucket whose plastic sides were pinched to the shape of a lozenge. By the 1980's, that hole was easily penetrable. Today you can fit a small car in it. The wreck that had once been a sealed tube now reminds me of a cylinder of rotten Swiss cheese.

The point that I am striving to make is this: if an inexperienced wreck-diver saw the *U-853* only as the wreck exists now, he might be misled into believing that the massive damage hole in front of the conning tower was always as large as it is today. I know that this was not the case - not only because I have seen the progression of deterioration of the pressure hull - but because I have seen the same process at work on hundreds of other wrecks.

A dive on a shipwreck is like a snapshot. One sees the wreck the way it appears at a precise moment in time. It may have looked different the year before, and it might look different a year hence. Change is ongoing: usually it is slow and subtle, but occasionally it is fast and dramatic (such as during a severe storm, or when supporting structures rust enough to collapse).

Today, merchant vessels that were sunk during World War One look as if an atomic bomb had detonated immediately above them. The present state of collapse or deterioration is not necessarily an indication of the appearance of a wreck shortly after its demise. Radical changes are generally observable only after many years have passed.

On the *U-869*, it is likely that the massive damage hole alongside to the control room was originally a

Appendix One

much small breach in the pressure hull, perhaps as small as that on the *U-853*. Those who study shipwrecks and the processes of collapse know that deterioration is accelerated at places where metal plates have been damaged. Wherever an explosion has distorted metal and stressed welds, rust spreads like gangrene in a flesh wound.

The Conning Tower Collapse

A prime example of conning tower collapse occurred on the U.S. submarine *Tarpon*. When Nagle and I made the discovery dive, in 1983, the wreck was almost completely intact. The bow was pointed and well defined, the forward gun mount stood proudly in place, and the conning tower - with its two lofty periscopes, radar mast, and antenna - reached skyward majestically.

I dived on the wreck annually for several years. In 1986, I saw that a tremendous change had taken place since the previous season. I found the conning tower lying on its side next to the port side of the wreck, with the periscopes partially buried in the seabed. One hundred feet off the wreck, I found the brass fairweather (the protective shield that surrounded the conning tower and external bridgeworks). The gun mount lay upside down in the sand to port, beneath the base to which it was once secured. A neophyte - seeing the wreck for the first time - may have jumped to the conclusion that the conning tower had been blown off its mounts by some tremendous explosion.

One can imagine a great winter storm reaching down through the water column to cause such wholesale destruction by means of underwater wave action. Deep ground swells punching the starboard side of the wreck could conceivably have knocked off the conning tower and gun mount. But how did the fairweather wind up a hundred feet away?

Far more inexplicable, the pointed bow was bent back to starboard so that it came to rest pointing aft at an angle of 110°. Strange gravity fluctuations could not account for such a change. The real culprit was less fanciful and actually quite common: a dragger or trawler.

It is impossible to determine how much damage has been done to shipwrecks by commercial fishing vessels whose down-gear snags in wreckage. I have seen many a dredge locked eternally in the side of a shipwreck. And I have often seen the damage that such fishing gear can do. The *Tarpon* was the most obvious and the worst case of damage that I ever encountered.

Imagine a clam dredge or fish trawl, which weighs many tons, dragged into the starboard side of the *Tarpon*. After the gear was caught, the vessel backed down on the trawl cable until it stood nearly over top of the down-gear. Lift hydraulics and engine thrust combined to haul the dredge upward and forward - in this case, over the hull of the submarine. The conning tower and gun mount must have snapped off at weld joints that were rusted and fatigued, then were dragged to the port side where they fell to the seabed. The fairweather must have clung to the dredge for another hundred feet before it broke free.

A different dredge must have accounted for the broken bow by snagging the tip and bending it back to its unnatural position.

It is likely that a similar event occurred on the *U-869*. This would account for the placement of the conning tower lying on its side next to the wreck. In support of this scenario, the snorkel tube - which rested in a recessed well on the *starboard* side of the U-boat, and which now lies on the seabed on the *port* side of the hull - could not have been blasted to its present location by a detonation against the port hull: it had to have been dragged there by a dredge that was hauled over the top of the hull from the starboard side. While the snorkel tube and head (or intake) lies in the debris field, the snorkel knuckle (or pivot) now lies at the bottom of the control room, where it must have fallen after the overhead (or ceiling) rusted away.

Indeed, all the debris and loose wreckage lies on the port side of the hull: exactly where it would have come to rest after a dredge had disassembled it.

In this scenario, a detonation occurred against the port side of the control room, breaching the pressure hull to a certain extent. The control room was the area with the most hull penetrations for pipes and valves, and therefore had the most welds. Welds corrode at a faster rate than the steel plates and pipes that they join. The metal was damaged initially by the explosion. The overstressed metal was prone to accelerated deterioration. The blast hole was enlarged by natural oxidation, expanding like the hole in the control room of the *U-853*. The weight of the conning tower pressed down against the pressure hull, causing the hull to sag on the side where the metal was weakened. A dredge completed the destruction.

This scenario also accounts for the absence of the guns.

Hang-ups

Before divers visited the *U-869* and learned that it was a U-boat, the wreck at that location was known as a "hang." A hang is a set of loran numbers or GPS coordinates that was found accidentally when a trawler or dragger snagged its net or dredge in an obstruction on the bottom.

Most hangs are rocks, reefs, ledges, or geological outcrops. About one in ten is a shipwreck. All too often, the net or dredge cannot be retrieved after it has been snagged or "hung." In order to avoid losing additional expensive gear, commercial fishing skippers maintain records of these nasty places to shun. They often share their book of "numbers" with fellow anglers so that, when they are dragging their gear over the vast ocean bottom - which they do like gardeners who are mowing the lawn - they can avoid these dangerous but unidentified obstructions.

The elder Bogan of the family probably obtained the numbers of the *U-869* from a friend in the business. Head boat skippers almost *never* share their numbers, because each hang represents a valuable resource:

guaranteed fish for his customers. A head boat skipper who can "produce" will attract more customers than one who cannot. He does not want his competitors to horn in on his secret fishing spots.

Two scallop dredges are jammed in the wreckage of the control room; one of them rests on top of the snorkel. These tangible hangs not only serve as evidence of the origination of the numbers, but they support the scenario in which a dredge or some other part of fishing gear could have dragged the conning tower off its rusting perch.

Neither Chatterton, Kohler, nor *Shadow Divers* made any mention of the presence of dredges or the absence of guns. They simply ignored what they were unable to explain.

Striking Evidence to the Contrary

As noted above, Chatterton envisioned that the *U-869* was "virtually blown in two" by its own torpedo. In *Shadow Divers*, it was written that the men inside were "vaporized." On pages 325 and 326, it was written that "rippling sheets of air pressure" were responsible for "sling-shotting some crewmen off ceilings and walls and one another;" that "bodies would have been rag-dolled off machinery and other structures;" that "men in adjoining rooms likely also died immediately from the concussion or from being hurricaned into machinery;" and that "corpses - many of them likely missing heads or limbs - would have begun a crooked float to the surface."

On page 325, it was written, "Steel doors were blown open. So strong was the blast that it bowed the steel hatch leading into the diesel motor room." (What *Shadow Divers* called a steel hatch is actually known as a watertight door.)

Such extravagant exaggeration displays uncommon ignorance, and does not paint a true picture of events that would have occurred. U-boat protocol and survivors' accounts of the aftermath of a powerful detonation against the pressure hull are readily available in submarine literature. (Note the high survival rate of men aboard the *U-701*, in Appendix Two.)

The watertight doors that separated compartments were not closed, neither in routine service nor while undergoing attack. The doors were left open in order to enable the men to communicate, and to permit free movement of the crew. When a U-boat crash-dived, crewmembers often assisted the downward angle of the bow by running through the boat into the forward torpedo room, where their human weight was used as additional ballast.

After the HMS *Trenchant* torpedoed and sank the *U-859*, the British submarine rescued seventeen survivors who had opened the hatches and swum for the surface.

The *U-305* - a strong suspect for a circular run torpedo - had time to transmit a radio message after being struck by a torpedo that was allegedly its own.

The USS *Tang* fired a conventional gyro-stabilized torpedo whose rudder jammed, causing the torpedo to circle back on the surfaced submarine and detonate against the hull near the stern, forward of the after torpedo room - only six seconds after it was launched. Ten men escaped from the conning tower. Forty-five men reached the forward torpedo room before the submarine struck the bottom. The Japanese depth-charged the submarine on the seabed. Trapped survivors attempted to escape. No one knows how many men reached the surface alive, but the Japanese picked up five of them (or nine - sources vary).

In these and other known incidents, no one was vaporized, sling-shotted, rag-dolled, or hurricaned. No heads or limbs were torn off by rippling sheets of air pressure. The submarines flooded and sank. Most of the men survived. No twenty-foot hole resulted. For additional information concerning real-life U-boat survival stories, the interested reader is directed to the accounts of the *U-701* in Appendix Two, the *U-352* in Appendix Three, and the *U-550* in Appendix Four.

The facts demolish the argument for a direct torpedo strike that blew the wreck in two and caused human disintegration and bodily separation.

The Smokeless Gun

Chatterton and Kohler have contended - and continue to contend - that they possessed the smoking gun that proved conclusively the validity of their circular run torpedo theory. They point digits at a brass detonator head that was found on top of the wreck near the forward torpedo loading hatch. A photograph of this detonator head was published in *The Last Dive*, along with the caption, "The head of the torpedo that sank the U-Who."

On page 325 of *Shadow Divers*, it was written that the men in the control room must have been "blown apart and nearly vaporized by the explosion." Yet, if Kohler and Chatterton are to be believed, the detonator head survived this titanic explosion in nearly perfect condition, complete with its arming device and detonating whiskers. Their scenario stretched the bounds of credulity far beyond the breaking point.

The only thing that is circular about this so-called proof of the circular run torpedo theory is the tautological argument that surrounds its assumption.

Was Anyone Listening?

On October 11, 1992, John Yurga recovered the detonator head that is referred to in the section above. (A detonator head is also known as a pistol, or exploder.) He knew that the detonator head had nothing to do with sinking the *U-869*, because he personally removed the primer before placing the brass cone in his mesh bag. If the primer was intact, then the torpedo to which it was attached could not have been detonated.

The arming device consisted of a two-bladed propeller. The propeller had to turn a specified number of revolutions in order to arm the torpedo. The arming range was set at 400 meters (about one quarter of a mile). When Yurga recovered the torpedo head, a small

wire was threaded through the nose projection to prevent the propeller from spinning and from accidentally
arming itself prematurely.

All four detonating whiskers were intact when he
first picked up the warhead. Two of the whiskers broke
off in his bag. The purpose of the angled whiskers was
to trigger the detonator in the event that the torpedo
struck the target at an angle that was greater than 20°,
in which case the central firing pin might not close the
firing circuit.

Yurga was still wearing his drysuit when he
removed the detonator head from his mesh bag,
showed it to Chatterton, and announced, "I removed
the primer on the bottom." His pronouncement is clearly audible on Steve McDougall's videotape. Chatterton
was standing right in front of Yurga at the time, asking
him questions. Was he not listening to Yurga? Did he
ignore Yurga's verbal disclosure?

Yurga *never* contended that he recovered the detonator of the torpedo that sank the *U-869*. Chatterton
and Kohler made that contention through wishful
thinking. They accounted for the existence of the
undamaged detonator head by adopting a "glancing
blow" theory. According to this theory, the circular run
torpedo struck the hull of the U-boat with a glancing
blow that snapped off the detonator head, notwithstanding which the torpedo *detonated anyway* without
damaging the detonator head and leaving the primer,
the detonating whiskers, and the still-wired arming
propeller intact.

German torpedo explosive consisted of a mixture of
trinitrotoluene (TNT), hexanitrophenylamine, and aluminum. The propagation rate of this explosive exceeds
22,000 feet per second (about four miles per second).
The glancing blow theory would have the uninformed
public believe that the explosion vaporized the pressure
hull instantaneously without catching up to the detonator head.

Torpedo detonators were stowed in boxes in the torpedo room. The head was not placed on a torpedo until

the torpedo was about to be loaded in a tube. Yurga's torpedo head was designated for a torpedo that had not yet been loaded. It is more likely that the box that held the torpedo head floated or was forced out of the hatch by rushing water. He found the detonator within inches of the torpedo loading hatch.

Finally, the type of detonator head that Yurga recovered was a combination impact and magnetic influence detonator (it could be set for either one). This type of detonator was not used on the T-5 acoustic torpedo. T-5 detonators were recessed into the side of the warhead; the forward end of the torpedo was reserved for the listening microphones.

Can You Hear Me Now?

Robert Coppock initially thought that a circling torpedo would have homed in on the U-boat's propeller noise, and therefore should have struck the hull farther aft than the control room. In order to account for the location of the damage, he proposed a scenario in which the sound operator heard the torpedo's approach on his hydrophone, and alerted the skipper of imminent danger. Neuerberg then ordered an immediate avoidance maneuver. In water that was too shallow for a U-boat to dive, it would have turned either toward or away from the direction of approach.

McKellar informed Coppock that, according to divers' reports, the rudder was in the amidship position. The rudder position implied that the U-boat was not trying to outmaneuver its own torpedo at the time of its destruction.

Proponents of the circular run torpedo theory then suggested that the torpedo must have homed in on mechanical components in the hydraulic systems in the control room. One of my correspondents who disagrees with this interpretation is Robert Marble, a Senior Chief Torpedoman who was qualified in submarines. He wrote, "Below ten knots the target's noise (in this case, the *U-869*), would not be sufficient to activate the homing system. The Type IX-40 could not make 10 knots submerged. The T-5 was a passive-acoustic torpedo and depended on propeller cavitation noises at a frequency of 24.5 khz [kilohertz]."

He added that the homing device was inoperative for the first 400 meters, which allowed the U-boat to keep clear. After the acoustical device was activated, it locked onto the loudest noise. The torpedo would then home in on the propeller cavitation of the target, and not the cavitation that was generated by the slow revolutions of the U-boat's propeller.

Marble's arguments are persuasive.

Furthermore, because the Germans were well aware of deficiencies in the gyroscopic mechanism that guided the torpedo, U-boat skippers were warned to submerge to a depth of 200 feet immediately after launching an acoustic torpedo. The running depth of a torpedo was preset in the tube so that it would not pass beneath the hull of its target without detonating. By submerging deep, a circling torpedo would pass harmlessly over the top of the U-boat that launched it.

The absence of a torpedo from one of the tubes might provide circumstantial evidence. At the present state of deterioration, the torpedo tube doors have not fallen off their hydraulic hinges. In fact, videotape footage of the exterior shutter doors shows that all of them are closed. That none is open and ready for action implies that the *U-869* was not in the process of launching a torpedo at the time of its loss, or that it had not launched a torpedo in the seconds prior to its loss.

Kohler and Chatterton would be well advised to account for this fact in order to obtain evidence to bolster - or torpedo - their theory.

A Hole in the Theory

Another hole in the circular run torpedo theory is the one that pierces the top of the after torpedo room. This hole is separated from the hole in the control room by a distance of seventy-five feet. A torpedo striking the control room cannot account for the hole in the after torpedo room.

Shadow Divers gave this hole short shrift. It was mentioned only in passing. On page 163: "The damaged area had been blasted open by some external force." On page 209 it was described as "the blown-out deck section that led to the aft torpedo room."

The book offered no explanation for the hole's existence. The hole was not even mentioned in the imaginary sinking scenario that appeared on pages 324 to 326. Ironically, the hole was shown in the artist's conception that was used as the frontispiece.

Ignoring the cause of the hole cannot make it go away.

After Moyers announced his finding of the incident report of the *Howard D. Crow* and the *Koiner*, Kohler and Chatterton defended their circular run torpedo theory by claiming that the destroyer escort attacks must have occurred *after* the U-boat sank itself, and that the blast hole in the after torpedo room - which they had not even considered before, and which could be attributed to a hedgehog - must be the result of this later attack, or perhaps the result of some other attack that went unrecorded.

The plausibility of such an occurrence was well documented in the war diary of the Eastern Sea Frontier, in convoy reports and in antisubmarine warfare reports. It was standard practice for escort vessels to launch hedgehogs or drop depth charges on any suspicious sonar contact, in the off chance that it might be a U-boat lurking on the bottom. As a result of this Navy protocol, many shipwrecks were damaged by wartime exuberance. However, contact reports were *always* recorded, whether it was just a sonar contact or an actual attack. Within the parameters of positional accuracy, some of these attacks were made on targets that are now known to be shipwrecks.

After grudgingly admitting the reality of Moyers' findings, Chatterton wrote on an Internet forum, "It makes sense to me that the *Crow* and *Koiner* depth charged the already sunken *U869*. This accounts for the damage to the stern, that appears to have no link to the actual sinking itself."

At the cost of being repetitious, on page 185 of *Shadow Divers*, Chatterton was quoted as saying, "Not a single thing happened anywhere near our wreck site during the entire war. Nothing." He seems to want it both ways: on one hand nothing happened, while on the other hand a later attack accounted for the hole.

Furthermore, Chatterton's presumption implied that the *U-869* had to have torpedoed itself before February 11. The *U-869* must have made an exceptionally fast transatlantic crossing in order to reach the wreck site in time to fire a torpedo at a target that Chatterton could not find.

Distant Target

Initially, Kohler and Chatterton relied on the *Harper's Ferry* incident to create a target for the *U-869's* errant torpedo. The *Harper's Ferry* was a T-2 tanker that was traveling independently from the Ulithi Islands in Micronesia to New York City. At 9 o'clock on the night of February 16, 1945 - one day prior to her arrival in port - a patrol plane passed the tanker's port side and dropped a flare off her stern. Visibility in the darkness was about half a mile.

The *Harper's Ferry* was zigzagging in accordance with Navy instructions. She immediately put her stern to the flare and increased engine revolutions to flank speed. The flare burned with intense brilliance. The plane dropped a second flare near the first. According to the armed guard engagement report, "Master and Gunnery Officer saw unidentified object in area of illumination on port quarter. Opened fire with stern gun, 5"/38. Range set at 3200 yards. Spotted first shot as short about 200 to 300 yds. Second shot could not be observed as flare had settled in the sea. Two (2) rounds expended. No further firing. Ten minutes later two (2) more flares were dropped but were too far astern and nearly out of visibility by the bridge on the ship."

Kohler and Chatterton wondered if the *U-869* launched a torpedo at the *Harper's Ferry* - one that was unseen by those on board the tanker, and whose detonation was unheard.

From the incident report: "Position approximately 38° 58' N. and 72° 25' W."

This attack location measures 51 nautical miles (or 58 statute miles) from the site of the *U-869*. This enormous distance from the wreck makes the *Harper's Ferry* an unlikely target of opportunity. It presupposes that the *U-869* - with its conning tower blown off and its men vaporized - traveled more than 50 miles before sinking with all hands. Such a scenario is untenable, as Kohler and Chatterton were forced to admit in the final report that they compiled and issued on March 1, 1998.

Shadow Divers ignored the target vessel issue entirely, and neglected to mention the report that is noted above. To make matters worse, it was written on page 187 of *Shadow Divers*, "Not a single event or observation had been recorded within sixty miles of the wreck site." This statement contradicted not only the existence of the *Harper's Ferry* incident with respect to distance, but a couple of dozen other incidents that are recounted in Chapter Three of the present volume.

Shadow Divers emphasized its own idiocy by stating on page 181, "During the war, not a single incident - not a piece of flotsam, a washed-up life jacket, the body of a sailor, an oil slick, even a puff of smoke - had occurred anywhere near the wreck site."

My faithful readers must decide for themselves whether these quotations reflect sloppy research, Three Stooges hyperbole, or a combination of both.

The question that all these quotations beg is: At what vessel did the *U-869* launch a T-5 acoustic torpedo? *Shadow Divers* did not even address the issue, much less explain it. Nor did *Shadow Divers* deign to mention that both the *U-869's* snorkel and attack periscope are in their retracted positions.

In any case, T-5 acoustic torpedoes were used against armed escorts, not against merchant vessels. See below for additional explanation.

Destruction In Motion

The circular run torpedo theory - the way Kohler and Chatterton explained it - missed the target for another reason. The U-boat could not have been proceeding on the surface, at periscope depth, or anywhere in mid-water when the hull was virtually blown in two and the conning tower was toppled. If it had, it would have planed away from the conning tower as the wreckage fell straight to the seabed.

The only way to explain the blown-off conning tower coming to rest next to the control room is to surmise that the U-boat was on or slightly above the bottom at the moment of destruction. But U-boats did not launch torpedoes from two hundred feet. They launched torpedoes from the surface or from periscope depth.

The hedgehog and depth-charge scenario can explain the wreck perfectly. A hedgehog detonated against the deck above the after torpedo room. Water rushing through the breach in the hull dragged the U-boat to the bottom. The follow-up depth-charge attack breached the hull next to the control room.

Before a depth charge was dropped, a selector switch on the detonator head was set so that the charge would detonate at a predetermined depth. The settings were calibrated in 50-foot increments. The diameter of the hull of a Type IX-C-40 was twenty-two feet. If the *U-869* were sitting on the bottom, or proceeding slowly just above the bottom, a depth charge that was set to detonate at 200 feet would have exploded at the depth of the hull.

Torpedo Mechanics

The standard German torpedo measured 23 feet in length and 21 inches in diameter. There were several different types of torpedo. Each type was designated by the means of propulsion and by the model evolution. As design improvements were made during the war, the number of designations proliferated.

There were two means of propulsion. The G7a was driven by burning alcohol. After ignition, combustion was supported by compressed air from a tank. The resulting gas and steam powered a turbine which spun the propeller. The G7e was driven by an electric motor that was powered by batteries.

In this shorthand method, the "G" was an arbitrary designation equivalent to "Mark" or "Mk" in the U.S. Navy. The "7" designated the length in meters. The "a" stood for air; the "e" stood for electric. Only G7 torpedoes were used on submarines; other sizes were used on different types of warships.

Alcohol and compressed-air torpedoes left a stream of bubbles on the surface. Torpedoes that were driven by an electric motor left no telltale exhaust.

The first model was T-1. By the end of the war, the models most commonly in use were the T-3 and the T-5. (These model designations may also be written as T3 and T5, and with Roman numerals as T III and T V.) Thus a full descriptive designation might be T-3 (G7e), or conversely, G7e T-3.

Several types of detonators were used. The contact exploder detonated on impact against the side of the hull below the waterline. The magnetic influence pistol was triggered by the magnetic field of the hull as the torpedo passed beneath the target. This proximity feature was more effective in sinking ships because the upward force of an explosion was more destructive than a sideways force.

Most torpedoes were equipped with a combination detonator so that either function could be selected prior to launching. Both functions could be selected at the same time.

The guidance system was an important component of a torpedo. Early torpedoes ran in a straight line out of the launching tube. Later systems could be programmed to turn the torpedo once after leaving the tube, after which it traveled in a straight line. The FaT and LuT torpedoes could be programmed to run straight for a given distance, then zigzag. The FaT and LuT torpedoes were effective against convoys. The course was directed by a gyroscopic steering device.

Home, Home on the Range

The acoustic homing torpedo was designed for protection against warships that were in pursuit. A hydrostatic mechanism controlled the depth by manipulating a horizontal fin. The depth could not change because the hydrostatic pressure was preset. The depth control mechanism was basically the same for all torpedoes of all nations in both wars.

The detonator head was fitted with microphones on either side, each of which was flush mounted in indents. Because the rudder had only three positions - full left, center, and full right - the swing from left to right could be pronounced. Essentially, the torpedo turned in one direction until the signal faded from one microphone and was detected by the other, at which point the torpedo swung in the opposite direction: much like snake slithering through the grass. If it were visible, the track to the target would look like a horizontal sine wave. The side-to-side motion was gradually reduced as the torpedo approached the target, where rudder adjustments became more responsive.

An electric torpedo could travel at 30 knots in a straight line. The snakelike track of an acoustic torpedo reduced the effective closing speed to as little as 16 knots. This slow approach speed made the acoustic torpedo a poor choice for sinking merchant vessels. It was used primarily against attacking warships, in which case the torpedo and the target were on approaching courses. The torpedo could then turn into the loud cavitation noise that was generated by the propellers as the warship passed nearby.

Escorts learned to defeat acoustic torpedoes by towing noisemakers (called "foxers"), or by varying propeller revolutions. As Marble noted above, the sensors of the acoustic torpedo were designed to detect propeller revolutions at a frequency of 24.5 kilohertz. This was the frequency that was generated by propellers that drove a vessel at approximately fifteen knots. The microphone could not detect an escort vessel that proceeded considerably faster or slower than fifteen knots.

Crash Dive

There were problems with the steering mechanism of the T-5 acoustic torpedo. Sometimes the rudder jammed, causing the torpedo to turn in one direction and not turn back. When this occurred, the torpedo turned in circles until it ran out of fuel. U-boat Control issued appropriate warnings, and recommended that U-boats dive to 200 feet after firing an acoustic torpedo. A circular runner would then pass harmlessly overhead.

The guidance system and the depth-setting device were separate mechanisms. In order for the *U-869* to be struck by its own torpedo as the U-boat sat on or slightly above the bottom, not only would the torpedo have had to circle back on the U-boat, but it would have had to chase the target down to 200 feet: something that the hydrostatic pressure device was not designed to do. The hydrostatic pressure plate responded only to changes in water pressure, not to sound.

Two simultaneous malfunctions, one of which was not possible, were required to account for the *U-869* torpedoing itself according to the Chatterton-Kohler theory.

Chatterton and Kohler postulated an impossible scenario without making any attempt to explain the mechanism by which it could have worked. Apparently, uninformed readers were expected to accept their scenario on faith, without questioning the validity of the theory.

Curse on Evidence

Steve Gatto spent the better part of half an hour explaining to Kurson why no one but Chatterton and Kohler believed in the circular run torpedo theory. Kurson seemed to be astonished at Gatto's revelations. Chatterton and Kohler had never even suggested to him that the *U-869* could have been sunk by any mechanism other than a circling torpedo.

Kurson kept asking questions, and Gatto kept providing answers. In the process, Gatto provided much of the information and many of the logical deductions that are included in this Appendix.

Yet Kurson chose to ignore the opposing viewpoint that was held by numerous wreck-divers, in order to promote a theory that no one advanced but Chatterton and Kohler. Kurson's refusal to so much as mention the existence of an alternative hypothesis speaks of worse than poor journalism; it speaks of intentional desecration of available facts.

APPENDIX TWO
Contemporaneous
U-boat Discoveries

"To strive, to seek, to find, and not to yield."
- Alfred Tennyson

Misconception

Shadow Divers was written in such a way as to lead its uninformed readers to believe that the discovery of a U-boat was an unprecedented and inimitable event. Nothing could be farther from the truth. Between June 1985 and June 1993, no fewer than seven U-boats were discovered in American waters. Another was discovered in 2001 (for details, see *U-166* in Appendix Four).

Nor are U-boats rare: three others (*U-85*, *U-352*, and *U-853*) have been visited by recreational divers since the 1970's, and are among the most often dived shipwrecks on the eastern seaboard.

The *U-85* is a Type VII-B. The *U-352* is a Type VII-C. The *U-853* is a Type IX-C-40; not only is it identical to the *U-869*, but it was built at the same shipyard (Deschimag).

Of the seven discoveries, Don DeMaria discovered one (*U-2513*); Bill Nagle discovered one (*U-869*); Uwe Lovas discovered two (*U-701* and *U-1105*); Ken Clayton and this author discovered three (*U-117*, *U-140*, and *UB-148*).

With respect to the discovery date of the *U-869*, the *U-1105* was discovered six years before; both the *U-701* and the *U-2513* were discovered two years before; the *U-117* and the *U-140* were discovered one year after; and the *UB-148* was discovered two years after. Thus the discovery of the *U-869* was sandwiched between six other discoveries: three before and three after.

Nagle's discovery was accidental. The discoveries of the other six U-boats were the result of years of dedicated search efforts. This rash of U-boat discoveries commenced in 1985. They helped to highlight the rich history of German U-boat warfare in American waters.

As noted in Chapter One and Appendix Four, the *U-166* was located in 1986 but was not properly identified until 2001.

U-1105: the Infamous Black Panther

Germany has consistently led the world in the design of military submarines, from the very onset before the Great War until the end of World War Two. Germany has built more U-boats than all the other countries in the world combined. Rare they are not.

The *U-1105* represented only one of many technological advances that German engineers developed during World War Two. Its hull was the standard Type VII-C design. Construction was completed in 1944 at the shipyard of Nordsee-Werke in Emden, Germany.

The outer steel plates were covered with a synthetic rubber skin whose purpose was to make the U-boat invisible to Allied sonar. Normally, a sound wave (or ping) reflected off a U-boat's steel hull, and was returned to the source of transmission: much like system of echolocation that bats utilize when they fly in the dark, and when they snatch insects out of the air. The rubber coating absorbed sound waves, making the U-boat difficult if not impossible to detect. Furthermore, the rubber blocks, or tiles, streamlined the hull by rounding the sharp metal angles of any protuberances. This smoothing effect not only deflected sound waves away from the source of transmission, but, because it reduced dynamic drag, it enabled the U-boat to cleave faster through the water.

The attribute that made it possible for the *U-1105* to slink through the water undetected earned it the sobriquet of Black Panther.

From Defeat to Test Vessel

Because it was constructed so late in the war, the *U-1105* made only one war patrol before Germany's unconditional surrender. During that patrol it sank the HMS *Redmill*, with the loss of thirty-two British lives. After Germany's capitulation, the *U-1105* surrendered to Allied forces, and was escorted to Ireland for internment. The U.S. then took possession of the U-boat. It was taken to Portsmouth, New Hampshire, where American engineers conducted studies of the experimental rubber skin.

Throughout most of 1948 and 1949, the Black Panther was moored off Piney Point, where the Potomac River flows into the Chesapeake Bay. Most of the time she was moored underwater at a depth of 30 feet, while underwater testing proceeded. The U-boat was raised at the end of August 1949. It was towed to a place nearby, where the depth of water was 90 feet. Here the Black Panther was used for its final test: it was scuttled by means of a depth charge. The Navy conducted diving operations on the hull until the end of October.

The location of the site was duly noted. Then, as the Navy had learned as much as it was possible to learn about the anti-detection coating, the Black Panther was dismissed from its collective mind.

Moment of Insight

The deck log of the *Windlass* noted the location as 38° 8' 10" north latitude, and 76° 33' 10" west longitude. It also provided a compass bearing of 273.5° true, 200 yards from Piney Point Light. The Navy circulated a report that provided only the latitude and longitude. Due to a typographical error, the two numbers in the longitude were transposed: "76" became "67." This placed the wreck more than 500 miles eastward of its true location: some 400 miles off the coast of Maryland, where the water was thousands of feet deep.

Uwe Lovas loved U-boats. He loved to dive on U-boats, he loved to read about U-boats, and he loved to research U-boats. His researches led him to Naval Historical Center in Washington, DC, where he studied the reports on lost and scuttled U-boats that might conceivably lie in diveable depths. When he read about the

Black Panther, he wondered why the Navy would go to the trouble of towing the U-boat so far out to sea before scuttling it. Then he saw a photograph of the depth charge as it detonated beneath its hull. The shore was visible in the background!

Lovas was perplexed. He wondered about the possibility of a discrepancy in the coordinates that were given for the location of the test. He quickly formulated the theory that the longitude numbers must have been transposed. When he switched the numbers, he found a wreck symbol on the nautical chart of the Chesapeake Bay.

Using his own boat, he had no difficulty in confirming his hypothesis. There was a wreck exactly where the symbol showed one on the chart. On June 29, 1985, he and his friend Alan Russell became the first people in thirty-six years to see the Black Panther's sleek ebony hull.

U-701 on Patrol

Lovas did not stop with the discovery of the *U-1105.* He put the discovery behind him, then set out to discover another long-lost U-boat: a Type VII-C whose construction was completed in 1941 at the shipyard of Stulcken Sohn, in Hamburg, Germany.

The *U-701* arrived in American waters in June 1942. Its purpose was twofold: to sow mines at the approaches to the Chesapeake Bay, and to torpedo Allied merchant vessels. Kapitanleutnant Horst Degen pursued both goals assiduously. Unfortunately for his crew, Degen was more arrogant than he was observant: twice he was caught napping on the surface.

The first time was June 12. A patrol plane zoomed down from the clouds with the wind screaming past its wings. Degen crash-dived, but the U-boat reached a depth of only 40 feet when five depth charges straddled the barely submerged hull. "Lights failed and instrument glasses were smashed in the control room, but the damage was slight and quickly repaired."

Degen laid his mines, then slunk into deeper water.

The infernal devices waited in silence to do their dirty work for the Fatherland. The mammoth tankers *Robert C. Tuttle* and *Esso Augusta* detonated two of the mines.

My father was a gunnery sergeant in the Army. At that time, Domenic was on duty at one of Virginia's coastal bunkers. He witnessed the explosions, and remembered that day vividly for the rest of his life.

Both tankers were damaged but were not sunk. They were repaired and returned to service.

The *Kingston Ceylonite* was not so fortunate. She was a 160-foot-long trawler that had been converted to an armed escort by replacing her trawl gear with depth-charge racks, by the addition of a 4-inch gun on her bow, and by the addition of machine guns that were mounted amidships in armored tubs.

"The trawler suddenly went up in two terrific explosions which blew her to bits. The first apparently was a mine, the second the ship's magazine." The *Kingston Ceylonite* sank in two minutes. Seventeen British sailors were sent undeservedly to an early grave.

The last ship to be sunk by Degen's mines was the *Santore.* The freighter sank in three minutes, with the loss of three lives.

On the night of June 19-20, Degen chanced upon the guardship *YP-389* off the Diamond Shoals. She was another converted fishing trawler that was pressed into service by the U.S. Navy for coastal defense. In a bloody, one-sided battle, Degen blasted her unarmored hull with a combination of shrapnel shot, high explosives, and incendiary shells, which Degen described as "a wasteful and untidy piece of work." The *YP-389* was riddled with holes and set afire. Five men died. The rest jumped overboard. They bobbed in the gentle ocean swells until the following morning. By that time, another man had died from his injuries. Thirteen survivors suffered from burns and shrapnel wounds, six of them seriously.

Degen torpedoed the *British Freedom* on June 27. The tanker refused to sink, despite a hole that measured fifteen feet in length along her starboard side. She managed to reach Norfolk under her own steam.

In retaliation, the convoy escort *St. Augustine* detected the U-boat on her sound gear, and drove in with a well-executed depth-charge attack. She dropped five cans so close to the descending U-boat that the "electric motors were put out of commission temporarily and the glass of gauges in the conning tower was broken." Another attack knocked out the U-boat's air-circulators. Degen got away after a harrowing series of follow-up attacks.

On June 28, Degen torpedoed and sank the *William Rockefeller*. The tanker sank without loss of life. Degen took another pummeling from Coast Guard cutters and aircraft.

Out of Circulation

The U-boat's air-circulators could not be repaired at sea. Degen was forced to surface periodically in order to ventilate the boat. The stench was bad in itself, but the oxygen-depleted air was unhealthy for the men, and the build-up of carbon dioxide made them drowsy and listless.

No ships were sighted for a week and a half. The crew suffered from the doldrums of inactivity. Despite the damage to his boat, Degen refused to terminate the mission early.

July 7 found the U-boat cruising on the surface in broad daylight. The sky was clear and the sea was smooth. Four lookouts clustered in the conning tower, each scanning a ninety degree quadrant through binoculars that were glued to their eyes. In addition to Degen were Oberleutnant zur See Junker, Leutnant zur See Bazies, and Obersteuermann Kunert.

Suddenly Junker shouted, "Airplane, there!"

Without a word, Bazies and Kunert dived down the hatch.

Degen said, "You saw it too late."

"Yes," Junker replied.

The awful whine of screaming airplane engines

chased them down the hatch. The ballast tanks were flooded and all the vents were closed. The *U-701* went into a crash dive. All too soon came the terrible explosions of two aerial depth charges.

It Came from Shangri-La

The plane was an Army A-29 bomber with the impersonal designation *#9-92-392*. It was attached to the 396th Bombardment Squadron. When it left Cherry Point Field, North Carolina for a routine anti-submarine patrol off Cape Hatteras, it carried a crew of five: Second Lieutenant Harry Kane (pilot), Second Lieutenant Murray (Navigator), Corporal C.E. Bellamy (bombardier), Corporal L.P. Flowers (radio operator), and Corporal P.L. Broussard (engineer). The plane was armed with one 50-caliber and five 30-caliber machine guns, and held three 325-pound depth charges in its bomb carriage.

For four hours the plane's engines droned noisily some fifteen hundred feet above a placid sea. Murray dead-reckoned their course as he spotted landmarks. A lively chatter kept the crew alert to their task. It was like every other patrol they had flown.

Kane: "I was flying in lower broken clouds with visibility about ten miles when off to my left at a distance of about seven miles, I first sighted this boat through an opening in the clouds. Its heading was between 300 and 330 degrees. I immediately made a sharp turn to the left in order to get a closer look and investigate."

It took only moments to realize that the vessel was a U-boat that was proceeding with its decks awash. Instantly the men prepared for action. Kane began his descent for a bombing run.

"At a distance of approximately two miles, the submarine commenced to dive, taking about fifteen seconds to get under the water. When we got over it, we were at an altitude of 50 feet and our speed was about 220 mph. The submarine was then about 10 to 15 feet under water and his swirl from diving was quite pronounced. The navigator and bombardier could easily discern all its outlines and superstructure. We dropped three depth charges, in train; the first fell 25 feet short, the second 100 feet further on, and the third 50 feet beyond the second. Both second and the third depth charges either fell on the submarine or slid off the left side. The second was aft of the conning tower and the third between the bow and the conning tower."

Crash Dive to the Bottom!

The effect on the U-boat was devastating. A summary of Degen's interrogation stated, "The submarine was approximately five meters under surface when the first bomb made a direct hit on the topside of the stern of the submarine, tearing a large hole which put out of commission the first engine and caused water to rush in. The second bomb made a direct hit on the topside just aft of the conning tower which tore a large hole and put out of commission all of the engines and mechanisms."

Other detail comes from the Translation of Statement Prepared by Kapitanleutnant Horst Degen While Held as Prisoner of War at Camp Devens, Mass. "2 bull's eyes—air bombs. All instruments out of order. Tanks blown. Within 1 to 2 minutes control room and conning tower filled with water. Ship had list to starboard of approximately 20 degrees. C/T [conning tower] hatch opened easily. Ship is at a depth of about 15–20 meters and no longer able to surface. Depth of water about 80–100 meters."

Elsewhere, Degen noted that the *U-701* settled on an even keel listing to starboard at 30 degrees, and that the depth was 60 meters.

Accounts of escape from the sinking U-boat were incoherent and contradictory, in one sense understandable considering the circumstances of stress, in another purposely obfuscatory. As water cascaded into the compartments through breaches in the pressure hull, and spurted out of disjointed seats and sprung valves, the *U-701* headed down on its last dive. So fast did it plummet, and so intent on escape were the survivors, that there was no time to pull the lever that released the rubber life raft. They were literally burped out of the conning tower hatch in the last remaining bubble of air, most without life preservers or escape lungs.

Aerial Jubilation

Kane: "About fifteen seconds after the depth charges were released, a light blue substance appeared about 25 feet to the left of the slick caused by the third depth charge. This started a slight bubbling on the surface. As it increased in intensity, a man popped up in the middle of it."

The bomber crew was ecstatic. They shouted and cheered madly at what was absolute proof that they had sunk their sub. One man after another popped up through the glistening air bubble, until eighteen of them floated together on the blue Atlantic swells.

An ONI (Office of Naval Intelligence) summary of interrogations stated, "one torpedo man stated he was asleep in the bow compartment at the time of the attack. He said the main lighting failed, but the emergency lights were still on. He made his way to the control room to ask whether they were to abandon ship. He then struggled back to the bow compartment - perhaps to get lifesaving apparatus or some treasured personal possession - and when he again reached the control room water was waist deep."

Kane: "As we continued to circle, at an altitude of about 300 feet, we noticed another group of men about 100 yards from the first group. There were also about fifteen men in this group. Quite a few of the men were wearing what appeared to be black swimming trunks. I would venture to say that they were Germans. Their complexion was rather light and one of them was exceedingly bald. While circling around the survivors, we dropped four life vests. All this time, Corporal Flowers, the radio operator, was transmitting in detail just what had happened."

The passage of time between the appearance of the

first group of men and that of the second is unclear, but it may have been as long as thirty minutes - implying that the U-boat lay unmoving on the bottom.

Struggle with Survival

Because a sea was kicking up, the two groups were prevented from seeing one other; each assumed that they were the only survivors. The group that escaped through the conning tower hatch consisted of eighteen men; the group that escaped from the bow numbered approximately fifteen. The remainder of the complement of forty-three men must have drowned inside the boat.

The men were ill-prepared for survival at sea. Most wore only trunks because of the U-boat's oppressive heat. Degen: "We had three escape lungs and one life preserver, and in addition two small life preservers which had been thrown to us by the airplane (landplane). Force of sea, 4. The plane circled about several times, threw smoke floats into the sea and then departed." Ironically, Degen recognized the plane as the same type that had attacked the *U-701* when it first entered the Eastern Sea Frontier.

According to one official document, Kane, "upon sighting a Panamanian freighter left scene of attack and signaled the freighter to follow and pick up the survivors of the destroyed submarine. The freighter acknowledged receipt of the message but failed to comply with instructions." Was this a deliberate act of disobedience? The merchant marine surely had no love for the curs who sank their ships and left their crews to die. "The plane then returned to the attack area but was unable to locate survivors. Large quantities of oil, however, were visible for four or five miles."

Another official document stated that Kane spotted a Coast Guard vessel five miles away. After dropping the smoke bomb, he "proceeded to the vicinity of this craft. He quickly informed the Coast Guard by Aldis lamp and radio, of the sinking of the submarine and the plight of the survivors and then returned as nearly as possible to the site of the sinking and the survivors. The crew of the bomber did not see the men again but they circled the area until the Coast Guard patrol vessel was right below, that is, in the area of the sinking. Kane then informed the vessel that he would have to leave the area because of shortage of fuel, which he reluctantly did at 1630, two and one half hours after the attack."

Degen; "We sighted the plane again, apparently in search of us, but it was unable to find us again because of the rough sea, even though we had remained close together."

A cruel combination of circumstances left the German sailors stranded in the broad reaches of the sea. The Gulf Stream current propelled them northward at nearly two knots. The slight chop made the low-lying heads indiscernible from whitecaps. Either Murray's navigation was off, or he did not take the drift into account.

The *CGC-472* searched diligently without success. The *PC-480*, which was escorting a convoy twenty-five miles away, was called off duty to help locate the U-boat's survivors.

As evening settled in, Boatswain's Mate Hansel and Midshipman Lange decided to swim to shore. Neither Hansel nor Lange were ever seen again. Then came darkness and uncertainty. With as many as five men clinging to one life preserver, their physical resources were severely strained. Around nine o'clock, Coxswain Etzweiler was unable to support himself any longer, and drowned. In group one, eighteen was whittled down to fifteen.

Night - and Day

The long, dark night dragged on. The men kicked, coughed, gagged, and fought to keep their heads out of the water. The loneliness was interminable.

Degen: "We consoled ourselves with hope in the morrow. A few of us were ready to give up, but these we cheered up, so that we were all still together when it became light again."

But with light came heat. The men were smeared with oil: an irritant that got into their eyes and the pores of their skin, but which mitigated the effects of sunburn. They had no food and, worse, no drinking water. Salt stung their lips, and sickening seawater found their tongues and throats. Their suffering was terrible.

Degen: "Around 1200 a Coast Guard ship passed within 2,000 meters of us at slow speed. Despite our cries and waving we remained unnoticed. The ship passed out of sight. Although we all hoped that it would return, some of the men now gave up. Damrow and Schmidtmeyer were delirious as though in fever. Around 1400 the following drowned, one after another: Damrow, Schmidtmeyer, Grundler, Bahr, Weiland, Schuller." Half the group was dead. "We saw many airplanes - apparently we were still being sought."

A massive air-sea search and rescue operation was taking place. Army, Navy, and Coast Guard planes were alerted of the situation. They flew in a steady treadmill past the reported sinking position, which was already in doubt. Both the *CGC 472* and the *PC-480* were combing the ocean off the Diamond Shoals, or following an oil slick that measured some fifteen miles in length.

For the beleaguered German sailors, the entire day passed without relief of their fears, their waning strength, their growling stomachs, their parched throats. They lay on their backs, clinging to the few bits of jetsam that they possessed, and clenched shut their eyes against the hot, blinding sun. Time and again, waves washed over faces that were now burnt raw. Seawater splashed into their eyes, nose, and mouth: a constant anguish. Two firemen died: Bosse and Fischer. And then there were seven.

Sometime late in the day the men from group one received a revelation when a man from group two appeared in their midst. Degen: "We came across apprentice seaman Laskowski, who wore two escape lungs and who was still very fresh. He reported that several more of the crew had escaped, among others the first and second watch officers."

Another Night - Another Day

Despair set in. "With the oncoming darkness we huddled close together in order to survive in this way also the second night. Fortunately the sea subsided. We found a lemon and a coconut. Each man received a swallow of cocoanut milk, a piece of the meat and everyone had the opportunity to suck the lemon. A tremendous refreshment! Our thirst was awful, and the large quantities of salt water burned mouth, nose, and stomach. (The cocoanut was opened by Vaupel after the greatest exertion with the help of the oxygen flask from the escape lung.)"

A believer would claim divine intervention, but the food was more likely flotsam from a torpedoed merchant vessel and was therefore the offering of innocent men who were killed for the sake of Germany's territorial expansion. Besides, the meager repast was not the savior of all the enemy aggressors. Despite Laskowski's freshness and double buoyancy, he died, as did Leu and Michalek. "All three were delirious and yelled terribly." They were down to five.

Degen: "At dawn my strength began to leave me too. I seem to recollect that I talked nonsense and that Kunert kept on quieting me. As the sea was still like a pond, I kept up the practice of discarding my life preserver, saying that I would swim to shore. I assumed that with a few strokes I would feel bottom under my feet and would be able to stand up, but every time I tried this I went under. That would bring me up again and I would swim back to my life preserver. This occurrence must have happened many times. Then I lost consciousness."

About the time that Degen passed out, another patrol left the Naval Air Station at Elizabeth City, North Carolina to look for the men. Belonging to Squadron ZP-14, the *K-8* was a lighter-than-air craft better known as a blimp. It's pilot was Ensign G.S. Middleton. The *K-*

8 proceeded southeast to the Wimble Shoals Light
Buoy, then picked up an oil slick which it followed
northward.

Found at Last

At 11:55 a.m., the *K-8* became the Germans' salva-
tion when it "located the first survivor, who appeared to
be strong and uninjured. The search was continued in
the same area. Two more survivors were located within
a short time. A status report - giving their position and
the state of the survivors - was sent to the Coast Guard
Station at Elizabeth City. The report included the fact
that weather conditions were such that a Coast Guard
plane could land at sea."

The search continued, and survivor number four
was located approximately one-quarter of a mile from
the group of three. A life raft was then lowered to the
strongest survivor, in the hope that he would be able to
help other survivors. Shortly thereafter, food, blankets,
a first aid kit, a knife, and drinking water were lowered
to the survivors in the raft. The first survivor to board
the raft was directed to the other survivors; one by one
he took them on board.

The blimp then continued the search to the east. It
followed the slick and debris to its source, some fifteen
miles away.

"Along this route, three dead men in life jackets
were found. They were being attended by several
sharks. There were many life jackets noted to be floating among the seaweed, slick, and debris. While returning to the life raft, three other survivors were located by
the *K-8* approximately five miles from the raft, also separated by one-quarter to one-half miles."

The survivors were found ninety miles from where
the *U-701* went down.

Rescue

Degen: "I awakened as though I had been asleep
when I suddenly heard myself called. About 30 meters
away sat Kunert, Vaupel and Grootheer making for me

in a white rubber boat. I was taken into the boat as Kunert was about to open a can of pineapple with a knife. Out of a can already opened Grootheer gave me tomatoes to eat, and all the while a Zeppelin airship circled about us."

Meanwhile, Elizabeth City was a beehive of activity as word circulated about the German survivors. Plane No. 167 prepared for take-off. The pilot of the J2-F5 was Lieutenant Commander Richard Burke.

"He located the *K-8* at 1423 and after scouting the vicinity for a few minutes, he also saw the seven survivors scattered over an area of eight miles. Landing on the water where the *K-8* had dropped flares to indicate wind direction and to spot the first survivors, he first proceeded to pick up the three individual scattered survivors and then taxied about five miles west to the life raft and took on board the remaining survivors. Rescue operations were completed at 1535, and during the actual operation, another Coast Guard plane, Type J-4F, Flying Fortress, circled the area taking pictures."

Degen was completely naked, and so far gone that his memory of the rescue was faulty. "As the coastal waters are thoroughly oily, we were completely covered with a thick black layer of oil. Now, while in the boat, the sun shone down upon us, and this resulted in a terrible sunburn. . . . A large flying boat arrived and took us on board. We were given water and hot coffee. All four of us were completely finished. . . . We were delivered to the Navy Hospital at Norfolk where we were treated with the greatest care and attention and made into human beings once more. There we found three other survivors: Seaman Seldte, Apprentice Seaman Faust, Seaman Schwendel." All three were from group two.

While Degen was in delirium, Kundt passed away.

After surviving the forty-nine-hour ordeal afloat, at the end of which he slipped into and out of consciousness, it is understandable that he never noticed the other three men who were already on the plane, or that he believed that he had not gotten sunburned until the final hour, or that he did not realize that he was covered with oil from his own U-boat, and that the major oil spills came from the tanker that he had sunk and from other ships that had been torpedoed by his fellow pack wolves.

In rationalistic terms, the real tragedy of the *U-701* was not the death and suffering of its crewmembers, but the fatalities and injuries that the U-boat inflicted upon innocent people who did not wish to be enslaved by a cruel and inhuman government. Perhaps upon reflection, even Degen came to accept the deaths of his shipmates as just retribution for the suffering that they and their kind had inflicted upon so many innocent men, women, and children, whose greatest crime in life was the occupation of land which Germany was brutally attempting to possess.

Interrogation

Degen's memory also failed to record the medical attention that was offered by the Coast Guard Pharmacist's Mate aboard the plane. "All were given mild stimulants, water, coffee, whiskey, and sandwiches. A hypodermic was administered to Captain Degen. . . . One of them badly weakened and exhausted stated 'you come joost in time, odderwise, I die.' All except the Captain asked for cigarettes."

Other than their skins, the German sailors saved surprisingly little. The records are unclear. "Four of the survivors were naked and three had no bathing trunks." Elsewhere, "Four pairs of swimming trunks and two escape lungs and one rubber life jacket constituted the sole effects."

Within three hours of rescue, the U-boat crew underwent interrogation at the Norfolk Navy Yard. ONI reported that the men "with one exception, were fairly security-minded, but not to the degree generally encountered. Degen had probably admonished his crew not to divulge matters of military importance, but a number of factors - his own garrulousness, his independent interpretation of security, the swiftness of the sinking, and the prompt preliminary interrogation - contributed to weaken the resistance of the survivors to incisive questioning."

From the U-boat crew, ONI learned the entire history of the *U-701's* construction, trials, and first two missions - although selectively left out was the loss of an officer who was washed overboard in the North Sea. Degen related the highpoints of his background in the German navy, including names, dates, and places of negligible intelligence value. Degen was proud to be Erich Topp's protege: he "taught me all I know."

ONI noted, "the condition of the survivors unquestionably weakened their resistance to questioning. As the prisoners recovered, their defenses against interrogation stiffened."

Little did ONI know how devious was Degen's apparent candor. He readily admitted to attacking ships on dates that coincided with the attacks against the *YP-389*, *British Freedom*, and *William Rockefeller*, but left out all mention of his mine-laying operations in the Chesapeake Bay approaches. He did not brag about the four ships that ran afoul of his "infernal devices," even though a radio transmission from headquarters praised him for the success of that phase of his mission.

On the contrary, "Degen held the opinion that shallow waters presented opportunities to mine-laying U-boats, both in the paths of convoys and at harbor entrances. He admitted the possibility of large U-boats carrying mines, but said such matters are held secret."

By such deceptive sincerity did Degen keep the biggest secret of all. Not until after the war did he receive credit for his "kills" off Virginia Beach, and for the unholy ruckus that was caused by enemy incursion into a supposedly protected area. In that he was a true patriot to his country.

Interned

On July 11, after two days in the hospital, Degen received an unexpected honor. Kane and the entire crew of the bomber that sank his boat visited him at his bedside, "and inquired after our well being." Little was recorded of this historic event that was unique in the annals of war.

The next day, the crew of the *U-701* boarded a train bound for Fort Devens, Massachusetts, "where we shall now pass the days of our detention as prisoners of war. We are being correctly handled and receive good treatment. There is plenty of good food to eat."

Certainly, German prisoners received better treatment than American POW's received at the hand of the Nazis.

Although the *U-701* did not reach its first birthday (July 16), its crew celebrated four birthdays in American POW camps. During that time, Degen wrote to Admiral Karl Doenitz requesting decorations for the surviving crew members. (The Red Cross reported the men's names through Axis contacts.) For Gunter Kunert, who held Degen's head out of the water for so many hours and saved his captain from drowning, he requested the Iron Cross, First Class. For the others he requested the Iron Cross, Second Class. His gratitude and love for his men were unfailing.

In June 1946, all seven survivors were repatriated in good health.

Location, Location, Location

With one U-boat discovery to his credit, Uwe Lovas dedicated himself to discovering another. First he had to ascertain the most likely area in which to commence his search. He quickly discounted Degen's observations of depth. Instead, he worked on the presumption that Degen intentionally lied in order to prevent ONI from learning that the U-boat lay in shallow water. Degen did not want Navy divers to recover his precious Enigma machine and code books.

If the *U-701* sank at a depth of 200 feet, as Degen claimed (or 250 to 300 feet, as he also claimed), so many men could not have made it to the surface unaided by either flotation or breathing apparatus: a practical impossibility from the depth ascribed by Degen. One man might make it, possibly two or more, but not thirty-three out of forty-three men. The high rate of successful escape implied shallow depth. Ergo, the U-boat lay in shallow water, and Degen tried to hide the fact.

Degen claimed to have seen the funnel and masts of a sunken ship toward shore. A review of the ESF records revealed that of the four wrecks that were still exposed at that time on the Diamond Shoals, only the *Empire Thrush* showed its funnel and both masts. Crucial to finding the *U-701* was locating the *Empire Thrush*. Lovas figured that if he could find the British freighter, he could then concentrate his search efforts eastward of the wreck, gradually working out to deeper depths.

Search Preliminaries

Uwe Lovas, his brother Ron, and Alan Russell spent three years in the quest to find the resting place of the *U-701*.

The Diamond Shoals is a dynamic area where the Labrador current from the north collides with the Gulf Stream from the south. As the two currents buck each other - either head on or with glancing blows - the seabed is churned like snow in a winter storm, forming drifts that were large enough to swallow a shipwreck. A depth recorder showed a bottom with dunes like undulating sine waves. A side-scan sonar was equally as useless.

Lovas decided that their needs would be better served by a magnetometer: a device that detected anomalies in the Earth's magnetic field, such as those that are produced by large concentrations of iron or steel of which a ship's hull is constructed. Lovas not only built his own magnetometer, he wrote the software program to drive it!

This was no easy task: it took forty versions of the software before he developed a program without bugs. By interfacing the magnetometer's computer program with the boat's loran unit, he could recreate his daily plot at home, see exactly what ground was covered, review the "hits" that signified anomalies, and return to each "hit" with precision and reliability. Instead of hauling nets and "hanging" on a wreck, he dragged an electronic web whose return signal pinpointed magnetic masses. The strength of the anomaly determined the size of the target. What's more, a magnetometer could detect anomalies that were buried in the sand and, therefore, hidden from the beams of scanners and depth recorders.

The Search - and Success

First the trio "magged" the seabed where the official records placed the *Empire Thrush*. They found the site, but the wreck was covered by so much sand that almost none of it was exposed. Using that as a starting point, they then worked their way offshore in a cone-shaped pattern. The "magging" continued for days, for week, for years.

The end of a search that rivaled in enterprise the quest of the golden fleece, came on June 25, 1989. Unfortunately, neither Lovas nor his companions realized at the time that they had driven over the *U-701*. It was only one of several targets that they had "magged" that day, and not the highest on their list of priorities for checking. It was at the extreme edge of the grid square that was drawn around the U-boat's most likely position.

It was not until weeks later, while reviewing the data in his computer files, that Lovas decided that the "hit" that was recorded that day should be investigated further. In wreck-diving protocol, a wreck is not officially discovered until it is dived. Bad weather and other distractions, not the least of which was Alan Russell leaving the country because of his job, prevented the Lovas brothers from diving on the site until August 27.

As Uwe had suspected, the wreck was the *U-701*. The reason it presented such a small target was that the hull was almost totally buried. Only the conning tower and deck gun protruded above the ever-shifting sand.

U-2513

In March of 1981, I made the first of many treks to Key West, Florida. Jon Hulburt and Bill Nagle accompanied me. The three of us made the 1,300 trip in Nagle's diesel pickup truck.

Billy Deans had just started running trips to the *Wilkes-Barre*, a U.S. cruiser that the Navy had scuttled in an underwater explosives test. The wreck lay in 250 feet of clear blue water. Bristling with guns that protruded from turrets, it was the most picturesque shipwreck I had ever seen. I returned annually for the rest of the decade, making countless dives to the wreck and to the seabed around it. Once I swam through a washout under the keel, where I recorded a maximum depth of 260 feet. A dive on the *Wilkes-Barre* was a tremendous experience.

In the mid-1980's, I gave Deans a packet of information about an prototype U-boat known as Type XXI. Construction of the *U-2513* was completed in 1945 at the Blohm & Voss shipyard in Hamburg, but Germany surrendered before sea trials were performed. The U-boat never saw action. The Allies took possession of Germany's U-boats. Ownership of the *U-2513* was transferred to the U.S. Navy. A Navy crew took the U-boat to the United States, where naval engineers scrutinized its ultramodern features. The Type XXI was radically different from any submarine that had ever been designed - or even contemplated.

The *U-2513* was the most important U-boat in the world. This experimental U-boat presented a distinctive hull form that was designed to move underwater at more than twice the speed of conventional U-boats. It also incorporated a host of other technological innovations. It has often been said that if the Type XXI had reached full-scale production a year before the end of the war, it would have posed a serious threat to Allied supremacy of the seas.

The Type XXI became the model for the modern submarine fleet. Its hull configuration was used as a template for American nuclear subs.

After the Navy completed its studies, the U-boat was towed to a position that lay west of the Dry Tortugas. The Navy then utilized the submarine for one final test: a rocket attack. The attack was eminently successful.

I accumulated documentation that included the latitude and longitude. The *U-2513* lay at a depth of 210 feet.

I convinced Deans to poll his boating acquaintances about hang numbers in the area. At first he put the U-boat on the back burner. I kept sending him reminders, but he was so busy developing his dive shop and charter business that he had little time for a project that was more important to me than it was to him. My persistence paid off in 1989.

The *Misteriosa*

Deans found someone who thought he knew the location of the wreck. His name was Don DeMaria. I made a special junket to Key West to determine if he was right.

DeMaria was a fisherman of a different sort: he did not catch fish with hooks or trawls, but with plastic bottles and a butterfly net. He collected live tropicals for sale to aquariums and pet stores. Sometimes he had to dive deep for rarer species. He got to know Deans because Key West was such a small community, and not many divers needed double-tank fills. DeMaria had friends among the commercial draggers; it was from them that he obtained three sets of hang numbers that purported to be shipwrecks. He even confirmed that one of them had the appearance of a submarine on a depth recorder.

The wrecks lay twenty to thirty miles west of the Dry Tortugas, a remote island group that was located sixty to seventy miles west of Key West. DeMaria worked from his own boat, the *Misteriosa*, and although he had never run charters, he was willing to give it a try. Also participating in the trip were three fellow U-boat enthusiasts: Hank Keatts, a college professor who taught marine sciences; Brian Skerry, a salesperson for a cardboard box company, but who had a degree in film production and who was working his way into underwater photography; and Frank Benoit, a mechanic.

The boat ride from Key West to the Dry Tortugas took all day. We anchored in the protected harbor in the shadow of Fort Jefferson, then left from there at dawn. DeMaria had no trouble in locating the wreck. It was the *U-2513*, just as he had predicted. The date was September 12, 1989.

Circuit of the Wreck

The first day I went on a tour with Brian Skerry. We circumnavigated the listing hull, examined the sleek conning tower, and petted a turtle on the seabed. In visibility that extended more than forty feet laterally, we saw rockets littering the sand like confetti on a parade ground. These rockets were duds that failed to detonate on impact, perhaps because they missed the target, or perhaps because they struck at an angle so oblique that the firing pin in the nose failed to engage. In either case, the lethal warheads were very much alive. Each missile measured some four feet in length. A metal shroud encircled the four stabilizing vanes on the tail.

We returned to the protection of the Dry Tortugas that night, then went back to the wreck in the morning. I went into the water alone this time, and had one of the scariest moments of my life (exclusive of combat). The seas were a bit bouncy - just enough to make the boat ride up and down the waves, possibly enough to jerk the grapnel out of the wreck. I checked the grapnel when I reached the bottom. It appeared secure.

One might suppose that squeezing through a jagged damage hole, and penetrating solo for more than fifty feet, past hanging cables and debris to the forward torpedo room, would be the feat that caused my fright - but one would be wrong.

A Ride on the Wild Side

At the end of my dive I noticed that the grapnel had slipped from its original emplacement and was dragging along the port side of the hull. No one else noticed because they completed their dive on the starboard side and converged with the anchor line above the wreck. With a long decompression to face, I thought I'd better rehook the grapnel so the boat would not go adrift and wallow sideways in the troughs. Imagine my horror when I beheld the true state of affairs: the trailing grapnel had snatched a rocket by the tail, and two of the tines were hooked firmly in the shroud.

Worse yet, the rise and fall of growing seas yanked the anchor line up and down. When the boat rode up on top of a crest, the rocket was lifted clear off the bottom. When the boat fell into the following trough, the nose cone slammed down hard against the sand. The action was that of a pile driver with three feet of ram travel.

I was stricken with fear. If the warhead exploded, the concussion would kill everyone in the water, including those who were decompressing a couple hundred feet up the line. They would never know what hit them. Neither would I, for that matter, although I might see the flash a millisecond before I felt the concussion. Death would be instantaneous.

I knelt on the sand next to the wreck in a posture that was strangely reminiscent of prayer. On the rocket's next downward plunge, I gripped the cylindrical body with the idea of twisting it out of the grapnel's clutches. So powerful was the upward thrust of the anchor line that the rocket was yanked right out of my hands. When the nose cone plunked into the sand again I made another grab, better prepared for the violent boost, and held on fast. This time I was lifted bodily with the rocket some three feet off the bottom. My wetsuit-clad body was then scraped up and down the barnacle-encrusted hull as if I were a speck of hardened grease clinging to the bristles of a bottlebrush. I held on for several swipes before I was ripped off, battered and bruised by the jerking rocket, and flung aside, thoroughly thrashed.

Without hesitation, I leaped back into the fracas. I wrapped the fingers of my left hand around the sharpened metal edge of the shroud. With my other hand I seized the shank of the grapnel. For an instant I tried to pull the rocket and grapnel together, in order to separate the tines from the shroud as one might free a fishhook from a snag. But the tines were not simply curled under the shroud; they were wedged between the vanes. I might as well have tried to bend an iron bar with my hands at either end. Then the instant passed and the rocket plunged to earth, crashed, was yanked up, attained burnout altitude, and began the cycle over again.

I held on fiercely. Each periodic burst of speed was attended by a spell of slack. During these transient moments, I fought to maintain my grip and jiggle the rocket off its overhead launching pad. Between times, I was wrenched vertically to and fro like a piston rod on the camshaft of a high speed engine. My arms were being jerked out of their sockets.

All this while, the anchor line was sliding sideways along the hull, adding another vector of abrasion. To gain a stable position with respect to the rocket and the grapnel, I bent at the waist and brought my knees forward, then quickly wrapped my legs around the lurching metal cylinder. I rode the rocket like a rodeo cowboy on a maddened bucking bronco, or perhaps like some maniacal child on a pogo stick in a storm.

I hoped that straddling the rocket would enable me to apply sufficient leverage to pry the grapnel out of the shroud. No way. My wetsuit was grated like Parmesan cheese, and I was thwacked on the head by the anchor chain. Despite the terror of the moment, I was surmounted by my sardonic sense of humor: I could not help but think of the scene in *Dr. Strangelove* in which Slim Pickens rode bareback on an atomic bomb as it dropped from the bay of a jet.

I pulled and shook the shank to no avail. The tines

might just as well have been welded to the vanes. Despite my best efforts, I could not free the grapnel from the shroud. I was running out of air. I had to leave. Dizzily, I pushed away from the rocket, watched helplessly as the nose cone continued to wallop the sand, then caught my breath as I made my slow ascent.

For the next hour and a half, I agonized over that unguided missile that wâs impacting itself on the bottom. My decompressing buddies were blissfully ignorant. On the boat, I warned DeMaria to be careful in pulling up the grapnel. He tugged the anchor line a couple of times, then the rope parted. We lost both the grapnel and the rocket. I was relieved.

Diving Beyond the Limit

In 1989, Ken Clayton and I joined forces to locate a number of ultra deep wrecks off the coast of Virginia. Our first target was the U.S. battleship *Washington.* We located the wreck in August (one month prior to my dive on the *U-2513*). Steve Gatto, Tom Packer, Jon Hulburt, and Greg Masi shared the discovery dive with us.

This dive caused us to re-evaluate our deepwater regimen. We breathed air down to a depth of 290 feet. I was blitzed. And the other wrecks that we wanted to find were supposed to be deeper! Nitrogen narcosis was not our only problem. At that depth, we had to be concerned about oxygen toxicity. The element that sustained life on the surface was deadly poisonous under such extraordinary pressures.

The extreme dives that we planned for 1990 required different breathing media: exotic mixes of helium blended with oxygen. Helium was an inert gas that was neither toxic nor narcotic. Breathing such a mixture was the only way that we could expect to survive the dives on the sunken German fleet.

General Billy Mitchell: Aviation Advocate

Flash back to 1921. Billy Mitchell was as controversial general as the U.S. Army ever produced. He saw only reason, and was forced during his entire career to combat unthinking conventions. Then, as today, there was plenty of irrationality to fight. Mitchell's big bone of contention was the impotence of naval power in light of a technological innovation that was advanced considerably by the Great War: the airplane.

Mitchell knew before anyone else that his high-speed gnats in the sky could wreak havoc on ponderous, slow-moving warships as they plied the coastal waters. Although the war had produced a recognizable body of evidence to support his views, the Navy and its career officers - who were steeped in age-old traditions of naval might - did not want to accept it. Mitchell set out to prove it to them.

The way he chose to do this was by demonstration. The ships that he wanted to sink by aerial bombardment were eleven German warships that had been taken from Germany by the U.S. government as war reparations. These warships were:

> *Ostfriesland* (battleship)
> *Frankfurt* (cruiser)
> *G-102* (destroyer)
> *S-132* (destroyer)
> *V-43* (destroyer)
> *U-111* (submarine)
> *U-117* (submarine)
> *U-140* (submarine)
> *UB-88* (submarine)
> *UB-148* (submarine)
> *UC-97* (submarine)

U.S. Navy personnel were placed in command of the fleet. The six U-boats reached the United States in the spring of 1919. The five surface vessels arrived the following year. Of the surface vessels, only the *Ostfriesland* crossed the Atlantic under its own steam; the others were towed.

U-boats on Parade

The U-boats led a wide and varied career, galloping

along the coast and stopping in port cities where they were exhibited to the public as part of the Victory Bond Drive. With the U.S. treasury in great debt, the U-boats became advertisements that encouraged people to buy bonds for the much-needed Liberty Loan. By the end of the summer, the U-boats were withdrawn from public viewing. They were consigned to Naval engineers, who disemboweled them like beached whales in order to study their design and mechanical systems.

Just as the *U-2513* served one generation and one war later, these six U-boats served to inform naval engineers how superior Germany technology was compared to U.S. submarine construction. The Navy's initial findings indicated:

"(a) The Diesel engines of these submarines are superior to any other Diesel engines in any other submarines in commission in the world.
"(b) The periscopes are equal, if not superior, to any other periscope.
"(c) The radius of action of these boats, type for type, is greater than that obtained by other nations.
"(d) Their double hull method of construction is probably superior to other types of construction, so far as protection against depth bombs is concerned."

Lieutenant Commander Holbrook Gibson, Commander of Submarine Repair Division, did not want to make a report because of the adverse effect that this knowledge might have within the Navy bureau. Although information released to the news media stated otherwise, due to the studies on U-boat diesel engines, the engines of the U.S. Submarines *S-10*, *S-11*, *S-12*, and *S-13*, were redesigned, using U-boat engines as models.

Preliminary Bombing Tests

Mitchell fought long and hard to convince his superior officers to afford him the opportunity to demonstrate the bomber's might. Eventually, against its will, the Navy was forced to accede to Mitchell's demands because of political persuasion. During June and July of 1921, most of the ex-German warships were towed to the Southern Drill Grounds for a two-part exercise: some to be bombed by Mitchell's airplanes, others to be shelled by Navy warships.

More important politically than the means of destruction was the actuality itself: according to the terms of the Armistice, all German naval vessels were to be either scrapped or scuttled irretrievably by August 9, 1921. They could not be saved as relics.

Mitchell overcame quite a few problems in conducting his aerial display, least of which was the availability of ships to sink. The First Provisional Air Brigade needed planes, practice, and bombs. Mitchell mustered every biplane that the Army possessed. He personally led flights of bombers over the target ship *San Marcos* (ex-*Texas*, a U.S. battleship). The *San Marcos* lay off Tangier Island in the Chesapeake Bay. Mitchell's airmen made run after run, until they reached a score of 94% hits.

Mitchell Prepares for Real

The biggest aerial bomb that was then in existence was a 1,000-pounder: suitable against a submarine, but not large enough to sink a battleship. Mitchell ordered specially made bombs for the real test against the German big ships: one-hundred-fifty 2,000-pounders, and seventy-five 4,000-pounders.

The Navy did everything it could to stymie Mitchell's plans: it appealed directly to Washington, claiming that the general was a madman, that the country needed a stronger Navy and had no allocations for an air force, and that planes could have no effect against thickly armored warships. When the Navy lost the battle to prevent Mitchell from gaining support for his bombing experiments, it tried to have the target ships placed so far offshore that the airplanes would be forced to operate at the extreme limit of their range: the fuel capacity of early biplanes was not great. When Mitchell got wind of this final subversion, he put pressure in the proper places and got the ships moved closer to shore. The orders that were finally issued called for all ships to be scuttled "beyond the fifty fathom curve."

(A fathom is not a linear measure, but a measurement of depth. One fathom equals 6 feet of depth. Fifty fathoms equals 300 feet.)

The *UB-88* was shelled by the *Wickes* off San Pedro, California; it sank in 300 feet of water. The *UC-97* was shelled and sunk by the gunboat *Wilmette* in Lake Michigan, where the depth exceeded 200 feet. (Strictly speaking, this depth did not meet the depth requirement that the Navy established. However, the terms of the Armistice required only that the German warships be scuttled in depths from they could not be recovered. In 1921, 200 feet exceeded salvage capability.) The *U-111* sank far off the Virginia coast, at a depth of 266 fathoms, after the *Falcon* detonated scuttling charges inside the pressure hull.

Of the three U-boats that were to be scuttled off the Virginia Capes, Mitchell's planes were allowed to bomb only one: the *U-117*. The *U-140* and the *UB-148* were sunk by gunfire from Navy warships.

Bombed to Perdition

The aerial bombardment of the *U-117* was a glowing success. Mitchell deployed six flights of planes to make bombing runs. The three planes in the first flight straddled the anchored U-boat, and a direct hit from a plane in the second flight sent her to the bottom. The Navy made excuses: the *U-117* was a small unarmored submarine. The effect on a large capital ship would not be so dramatic.

Meanwhile, destroyers shelled the remaining two U-boats with far less proficiency. The *Dickerson* fired thirty-nine shots at the *U-140*, of which nineteen scored hits. It took an hour and twenty-four minutes for the U-boat to sink. The *Sicard* scored twenty hits out of forty shots fired at the *UB-148*. It took eleven minutes to register the first hit, and another twenty-nine minutes for the U-boat to sink.

A self-serving Navy memorandum stated succinctly, "Valuable data secured from destruction." Had
Naval officers been open-minded, they would have realized that the most valuable datum was that aerial bombardment was more effective than shelling.

By July 13, Mitchell was ready to attack the *G-102*
with eighteen SE-5 pursuit planes that were armed
with machine guns and light bombs, De Havillands that
were armed with 100-pound bombs, and Martin
bombers that were armed with 600-pounders. The SE-
5's raked the decks with pinpoint precision, and riddled
the hull from bow to stern. Mitchell waved off the De
Havillands and brought in the heavy bombers straight-
away. Twenty minutes later, the *G-102* lay at the bottom of the sea. The Navy was still unimpressed, making excuses for the destroyer's quick demise.

Two days later, rather than to let Mitchell repeat his
performance, Navy ships sank the other two German
destroyers by gunfire: the *S-132* by the *Delaware* and
the *Herbert*, the *V-43* by the *Florida*.

Bigger Ship, More Bombs

Next on Mitchell's agenda was the *Frankfurt*. The
Navy insisted, with good reason for a change, that he
pummel the cruiser with small bombs first, then work
his way up to the larger ones. Flight after flight of
planes dropped 100-pounders all morning, with long
intervals between attacks during which observers from
the *Shawmut* boarded the derelict and inspected the
damage. In this instance, the Navy was methodical in
studying the results, finding that even 250- and 300-
pound bombs were unable to penetrate the upper
decks. Goats and other animals, which were stationed
topside to simulate human crews, were found dead and
macerated, but the ship itself was intact.

Navy inspectors, smugly deciding that aerial bombs
alone could never sink the cruiser, ordered the *North
Dakota* to prepare a time bomb. Then came Mitchell's
Armageddon with the 600-pounders that were dropped

by Martin bombers. They rained down so fast and furiously that the *Frankfurt* was immediately shrouded in spray. Tons of seawater fell upon the decks. Crews on board the observation vessels ran for cover, as steel fragments ripped across the water for more than a mile. Before the attack could be called off, so that observers could board and make damage assessments, the *Frankfurt* slipped beneath the waves. Photographic planes recorded with a vengeance the dramatic events of July 18.

The Ultimate Test

The ultimate test was yet to come. The *Ostfriesland* was protected by twelve inches of armor plate; she had four skins for protection against mines and torpedoes; she had so many watertight compartments that it was thought impossible to sink her. At the Battle of Jutland, she survived a mine explosion and eighteen hits from large shells. She was a floating fortress of arms and armament.

On July 20, the *Henderson* was packed to the gunwales with over three hundred distinguished guests; in addition to some fifty reporters there were eight Senators, twelve Congressmen, three Cabinet members (the Secretaries of War, Navy, and Agriculture), and foreign observers from England, France, Spain, Portugal, Brazil, and Japan. The *Pennsylvania* was packed with admirals, generals, and other high ranking military officers.

The day dawned miserably, with thirty-knot winds whipping the sea to a froth. Mitchell and his flyboys sat idly at Langley Field, awaiting the call to strike. When nothing was heard by 1300, Mitchell jumped in his Osprey and flew out to sea. The Navy wanted to call off the attack because of weather. Mitchell insisted that the bombing raid be carried out as planned, stating that his planes could fly under the conditions then prevailing, if Navy men could observe under them. He went so far as to order his planes into the air without Naval approval.

The Navy was struck by his impudence, but permitted the attack to proceed. Unfortunately, the 250-pound bombs did little damage to the *Ostfriesland's* steel hide. Mitchell's planes landed in a blinding rainstorm as reporters were racing for shore aboard the *Leary* to report that the battleship was "absolutely intact and undamaged." Many seasick VIP's also returned to shore, convinced that the planes had lost the day.

Mitchell was not to be dissuaded from his convictions. The next morning found him arming his planes with blockbuster 2,000-pound bombs. At first he was allowed to drop only the 1,000-pounders. Two scored direct hits, and the Navy called off the rest of the attack so they could send observers aboard. They found the *Ostfriesland* so badly torn up that they were unable to go below the third deck. They peered through gaping bomb holes at the water seeping in below.

Then came the big bombs. One by one, seven Martin and Handley Page bombers made their drops, aiming for near misses so that the underwater detonations created shock waves that pummeled the hull, and spreading their attacks so that each tremendous waterspout had time to settle before the next plane came in for its bombing run. The concussion of exploding bombs was so severe that observation vessels shook and trembled when the shock wave reached them. Planes at an altitude of 3,000 feet rocked violently. Thousands of tons of water descended upon the *Ostfriesland's* decks.

The third bomb scored a direct hit on the forecastle. It tore a frightful hole in the hull and started a raging fire. Another near miss lifted the battleship visibly out of the water. Bomb number five fell near the stern. The *Ostfriesland* commenced to settle aft. By the time the sixth bomb landed, the after two turrets were underwater. The battleship's bow nosed upward, the ship rolled onto its port side, and it disappeared from view. A Handley Page delivered the final stroke by dropping the last bomb on the huge vortex of escaping air.

Day of Infamy

Although Mitchell was ecstatic, the Navy refused to accept the implications of his success. It continued to denigrate the general's allegations that a strong and separate air force would change the tide of future warfare. Mitchell refused to back down from his position. Soon, he was railroaded out of the country on foreign assignments that were intended to lose him in red tape and obscurity. Eventually, as he maintained his verbal attack against Naval ignorance, using the press as his sounding board, he was brought up on charges of subversion, and court-martialed.

Mitchell was in nationwide headlines for months. His trial was the news of the decade. In a kangaroo military court, the general was eventually "suspended from rank, command and duty with the forfeiture of all pay and allowances for five years."

This censure did not prevent Mitchell's predictions from coming true. As early as 1923, he forecast the buildup of Japanese air power, and outlined in detail how they would attack Pearl Harbor and Clark Field. It happened exactly as stated in his report - a report that was pigeonholed by military minds that were not prepared to face American vulnerability.

Obviously, the Honorable G. Katsuda, member of the House of Peers of Tokyo, was more impressed by the aerial display of might than his American counterparts. He was on board the *Shawmut* as an observer when the *Ostfriesland* was successfully bombed and sunk. Ironically, when the Japanese bombed Hawaii's battleship row two decades later, the *Shawmut* (renamed *Oglala*) was sunk at her berth during the attack.

Perhaps July 21, 1921 was the real day of infamy.

The Billy Mitchell Wrecks

Such was the rich and forgotten history of what I named the Billy Mitchell wrecks. In order to locate them, I accessed the deck logs of a number of the warships that were anchored in the vicinity during the bombing tests. From those logs I obtained the names of other vessels that were part of the observation fleet. Clayton took my list of additional vessels, and accessed *their* logs.

Each log recorded the vessel's position at anchor, as well as the bearings of and approximate distances to the other vessels in sight, including the German warships. I obtained a hydrographic chart that showed three prominent wreck symbols. Clayton plotted the vessel positions on the chart, and extended the bearings from each one to the approximated distances of the German vessels. This spider web of extrapolated lines converged on the target anchorage sites.

Both Clayton and I curried the favor of skippers who shared their "hang" logs with us. The southernmost wreck symbol coincided with the loran coordinates of an unknown trawler hang that I obtained from Trueman Seamans. Clayton obtained additional hang numbers from commercial fishermen Robert Hollowell and Lenwood Marten, who confirmed that the numbers that we already possessed were accurate, and who provided additional numbers in the vicinity.

Diving to Extremes

Researching and locating the wrecks was only part of the job. Now we had to dive on them. Because northeast wreck-divers had never dived on wrecks that lay so deep, we had to learn a great deal about helium mixtures, gas management, consumption rates, equivalent narcotic depths, decompression theory, oxygen tolerances, central nervous system toxicity, oxygen analysis, accelerated decompression rates, drysuit inflation gases, partial pressure blending, and even such esoteric subjects as isobaric counterdiffusion with respect to gas absorption and elimination. We also had to relearn how to wear diapers on dives that exceeded two and a half hours in length.

Bill Hamilton, the first decompression software guru, suggested the proper heliox mixture to breathe for the depth that we anticipated reaching, and generated the decompression schedule that we were to follow during our ascent. It would not be fair to call the gas mix and ascent schedule "guesswork." But the algorithm that he had developed was purely theoretical: an extrapolation that was based upon currently accepted medical hypotheses that existed in controversial flux. Hamilton's software application was accepted as safe and practical, but it was not proven by in-water experimentation. We were the guinea pigs who volunteered to establish the program's validity.

I organized an expedition to the Civil War ironclad *Monitor* for the first two weeks in July 1990. The *Monitor* lay at a depth of 230 feet off the Diamond Shoals of North Carolina. This gave me the opportunity to experiment with helium blends for bottom gas, and with nitrox blends for accelerated decompression. (See *Ironclad Legacy* for full details.)

A month later, Pete Manchee joined Clayton and me for the discovery dive on the *Ostfriesland*, which lay at a depth of 380 feet. The historic date was August 10, 1990. I was apprehensive, but Clayton said that he was going to make this dive or die in the attempt. I hoped that his sentiment reflected enthusiasm and hype rather than hope.

I carried five tanks on the dive: one was a 40-cubic-foot pony bottle that was filled with argon for drysuit inflation; of the other four, each held 120 cubic feet of gas. I wore double tanks on my back, and I carried a single tank slung on either side of me. One single tank carried a travel mix of heliox that consisted of 16% oxygen and 84% helium, which I breathed down to the high side of the wreck, at a depth of 320 feet. Then I switched to my doubles, which contained the bottom mix that consisted of 12% oxygen and 88% helium. I breathed this gas for the bottom portion of the dive and during the deep part of the ascent to 320 feet, at which point I switched back to my travel mix. I also carried a video camera.

This was extreme diving to the nth degree.

Support divers placed tanks on the anchor line at

predetermined depths. These tanks contained nitrox blends that we intended to breathe in order to accelerate decompression.

A full description of our successful dive on the *Ostfriesland* is beyond the scope of the present volume. Suffice it to say that it took us six minutes to reach the wreck, after which we spent ten minutes in exploration, followed by two hours and twenty minutes of decompression. Our first decompression stop was at 180 feet: deeper than most recreational divers have ever gone.

None of us had set out to prove anything, either to ourselves or to the world. We simply wanted to dive on a wreck on which no one had ever dived before. In the process of pursuing a personal goal, we demonstrated incidentally that the commonly accepted depth barrier was an imaginary construct: a limitation of human perception.

For deep wreck-divers, that barrier was forever broken.

Interested readers are referred to *The Lusitania Controversies*, which contains the history of wreck-diving, the evolution of technical diving, full details of the *Ostfriesland* dive, and the culminating expedition to the *Lusitania*.

Onward and Downward

The deepwater discoveries that Clayton and I initiated did not end with the *Ostfriesland*. We returned several times to the German battleship, but at the same time we proceeded with our long-range plan to dive on the other scuttled warships. Two of the destroyers have eluded our efforts - and so far, no one has picked up the thread to search for them - but we found the other five wrecks.

Clayton and I dived on the destroyer *G-102*, which we found at a depth of 350 feet. The deepest one was the cruiser *Frankfurt*, which lay at a depth of 420 feet. My buddies on that dive were Steve Gatto, Tom Packer, and Jon Hulburt. In the course of our comprehensive discovery endeavors, we found all three U-boats that were scuttled in the 1921 tests.

The discovery of the U-boats was secondary to our prime purpose, and, in retrospect, somewhat anticlimactic: they were the shallowest of the sunken German warships. They were not, however, without historic import.

U-140

At a depth of 200 feet, the cerulean blue water below me showed no sign of ending. I raised my eyebrows at Ken Clayton. He shrugged. The current was strong and my arms were feeling the strain of the pull down the anchor line. We paused for a moment to rest. It was not good to get out of breath at depth, so we paced ourselves accordingly. We did not know how deep we had to go to touch the wreck that we hoped lay silently on the bottom.

At 210 feet, the water continued greenish blue and featureless. At 220 it was the same. At 230 I began to see a dim ghostly outline. At 240 the shadowy shape took on definite form. It was the hull of a sunken ship.

Ambient light visibility extended nearly 50 feet: the result of Gulf Stream intrusion which sometimes brushed the offshore waters of Virginia. At 250 feet I could see the hull distinctly. The side that faced us rose vertically to an upper edge that curved back to form the deck; the plating was remarkably well preserved. The thinly encrusted metal cast little reflected light, and the overall dull gray was mottled with splotches of lighter shades in a nearly monochromatic design.

What I could see of the hull so far looked very much like that of a submarine.

My exhilaration turned to anxiety when I saw that the grapnel had not hooked the hull, but the sand!

The grapnel had dragged over the top of the wreck, fallen to the white sandy bottom on the down-current side, and snagged with a single tine on something that was entirely buried. With a vicelike grip on the anchor line, in case the grapnel suddenly pulled free, I dropped to the sand to examine the stability of the hook.

Although only one tine had caught, it was gripped firmly on the edge of a thick steel plate only a foot from where the hull met the sand. No matter how hard I twisted and yanked, I could not move the grapnel against the force of the current. I raised my eyebrows at Clayton, who hovered above me and oversaw my actions. He nodded.

I let got of the line. Instinctively I felt behind my tanks for my decompression reel, just in case of an emergency. My depth gauge registered 266 feet. We kicked upward and alighted upon the deck about fifteen feet above the bottom. What looked like the end extended to our left, so we went right.

In just a minute or two we reached an upthrust structure that was distinctly discernible as a conning tower. And not the conning tower of an American sub, but of a German U-boat. And not just any U-boat, but a World War *One* U-boat.

Germany launched a deadly U-boat offensive against the American East Coast in 1918. During a six-month spree, half a dozen U-boats spread death and destruction among neutral and Allied merchant shipping, sail and steam, resulting in the loss of more than one hundred vessels, including the U.S. armored cruiser *San Diego*. These U-boats laid mines along shipping lanes and in harbor approaches, shelled unarmed merchantmen, placed bombs in the holds of vessels and set their crews adrift, and torpedoed ships without warning - all as part of the Kaiser's bid to dominate the world.

The *U-140* accounted for seven of these shipping losses, totaling 30,594 tons. Now the Hun lay in an unmarked grave in the same ocean where its victims lay equally unmarked.

We were the first to touch one of the Kaiser's U-boats that was sunk in American waters. The date was June 6, 1992. The divers who followed us down to the wreck were Ric Culliton, Peter Feuerle, Alexander Hamilton, Jon Hulburt, Barb Lander, Bart Malone, John Moyer, Gene Peterson, Brad Sheard, Brian Skerry, and Harvey Storck.

UB-148

The next U-boat on our discovery agenda was the *UB-148*. According to our historical documentation, the wreck lay close to the *U-140* in about the same depth. We had promising numbers. We anchored into the *U-140* for the benefit of those who had not dived it before. The rest of us saved our surface interval and waited to dive on the "new" U-boat - hoping, of course, that we could find it.

Chris Stone went down alone. When he returned, Mike Hillier, captain of the *Miss Lindsey*, could not get the grapnel out. Stone bounced down and cut the tines free from the net in which they were caught. Afterward, listening to Stone describe the wreck, Clayton and I had a creepy feeling that either he had been narked the whole time despite breathing mixed gas, or . . .

Hillier had gotten the numbers mixed up and took us to the wrong coordinates. Thus Chris Stone made not only the first dive on the *UB-148*, but the first *two* dives! The date was August 23, 1992.

With the wreck rehooked, Clayton and I dived separately and alone, although our paths crossed several times on the bottom and on the anchor line: characteristic wreck diving buddy technique. Thirty feet of ambient light graced the bottom, but I cringed when I saw how tenuous the grapnel was set: it had caught in a twisted knot of netting that was stretched taught to a point some fifteen feet off a break in the hull. The strain of the boat prevented me from budging the grapnel to reset it in metal. When I examined the net closely, I saw with relief that within the mass of rope and twine a thick steel cable lay embedded. I went exploring.

About twenty feet of the bow had been blown off, exposing two long bronze torpedo tubes, one of which lay almost completely free and appeared to be easily recoverable. The ten-foot gap between the forward compartment and the pressure hull was knitted together by the net in which the grapnel was hooked. The wreck sat upright, and the shell of the conning tower rose about eight above the rusting deck. Twenty feet off the port side of the conning tower, a string of buoys floated a net off the bottom like a thick lace curtain that was suspended from rods. Abaft the conning tower, on top of the hull, gaped a hole the size of a double door. I should have been able to peer into the engine room, but the interior was filled with sand and silt to within three feet of the rim.

The depth to the bottom was 275 feet. Peter Hess and Barb Lander shared the discovery dive.

U-117

The reason we looked for the *U-117* last, despite its importance in our overall quest to dive those particular vessels that were sunk by Mitchell's bombers, was a function of progressive depth exploration. Naval records indicated that the *U-117* went down where the water was 300 feet deep. We were working our way down, so to speak.

From historical accounts, we chose the most probable location and correlated it with the hang numbers that we had in the area. After hours of searching with no result, we resignedly moved off site to check out another set of numbers nearby, but only 230 feet deep. Any unexplored wreck could be interesting.

This time we got lucky and found the numbers right on target. Clayton and Peter Hess went down first. Just as they began their ascent, the grapnel pulled out and the boat went adrift, so the rest of us had to wait out their decompression before entertaining the possibility of a dive. When they finally emerged from the water, we were as astonished as they to learn that the wreck was that of a submarine! The date was June 5, 1993.

I knew of three U.S. submarines that had been scuttled off the Virginia coast, and concluded that we must have stumbled onto one of them. When we rehooked, the anchor chain fell across the edge of the conning tower, which I studied in detail without observing anything that provided clues to the sub's identity. Dark, dismal conditions prevailed on the bottom, almost like a night dive. I did not stray far. Dive buddy

Barb Lander stayed within touching distance the entire time, as much for my comfort as for hers. Don Koontz also dived on the wreck on that discovery day.

For two years we agonized over which sub it could be. Then we returned on a day when visibility exceeded fifty feet ambient. I took a grand tour from end to end. It was immediately obvious how the wreck's location became known: the towing yokes of two trawler rigs, expensive shipwreck locator devices, were firmly implanted in the starboard hull.

Not until I examined the stern carefully, and compared my drawing with historical photos, did I recognize the distinctive slope as the after deck above the minelaying tubes. It was the *U-117* all along, misplaced by both leagues and fathoms.

Through those tubes once slid the mines that sank the *Chaparra* and the *San Saba* off the New Jersey coast, the *Saetia* off of Maryland, and the *Mirlo* off of North Carolina. Through one of the tubes in the bow had sped the torpedo that sank the *Sommerstad* off Long Island's southern shore, in that long ago August when war raged over the world.

There is more to behold and explore on these wrecks than I have seen for myself or described. They are three of a kind, if you will, together comprising a rare insight into Germany's first undersea and most effective killing machine, and the precursor of deadly events to come a generation later.

To dive on the Kaiser's U-boats is to touch the heart of history.

APPENDIX THREE
Shallow-Water U-boats

"The only thing that ever really frightened me during the war was the U-boat peril."
- Winston Churchill

U-85 (Type VII-B)

Until April 1942, the East Coast U-boat war was both a howling success (viewed through German eyes) and a horrifying disaster (to the men of the merchant marine and the U.S. Navy.) With near impunity, torpedoes ripped through the coastal fleet with devastating effect. Ships were being sunk on an almost daily basis, while the brave sailors who manned them suffered horribly and died anonymously. Those who lived through the deadly ordeals returned to the sea with the courage of their kind.

Besides engaging the enemy on two fronts (the Germans in Europe, the Japanese in the Pacific), the Navy had to fight a defensive war at home. Its resources were severely strained. Men, machines, and materiel needed to protect coastal shipping were in short supply. But as the war entered its fifth month, the fortification of the eastern seaboard eased into high gear. Blimps, airplanes, and a mosquito fleet of small boats aided warships in pursuit of the underwater enemy. Training and tactical exercises sharpened skills that had been learned vicariously. Aggression became the watchword.

Meanwhile, the underwater snipers shot and submerged, torpedoed and ran, skulked by night and cowered by day.

Into this beehive of activity charged the *U-85*. Oberleutnant zur See Eberhard Greger was the U-boat's first and only captain. Greger and the *U-85* made three war patrols in the North Atlantic with very little success. On September 9, 1941 he fired a spread of torpedoes into Convoy SC-42 but made no hits. Still dogging the convoy, the following day "the *U-85* made two attacks. In the first one hit was observed, and one detonation heard beyond. In the second attack two detonations were heard, but these must have been depth charges dropped by HMCS *Skeena*." Greger reported three ships sunk and one probably damaged, but only the 4,748-ton *Thistleglen* went to the bottom.

After another attack, on January 21, 1942, "the *U-85* heard two detonations and after 10 minutes observed the damaged ship in sinking condition with a heavy list." Greger tried to take credit for sinking a 9,000-ton vessel, but no Allied ships were reported lost. On February 9, Greger made his second confirmed kill: the 5,408-ton *Empire Fuselier*.

March 21, 1942 found the *U-85* on its way to the American shooting gallery. The crossing took barely three weeks. Then the U-boat cruised offshore between New York and North Carolina, reaching as far south as Wimble Shoals. During this time it was credited with sinking the 4,904-ton *Chr. Knudsen*, which left New York on April 8, bound for Capetown, South Africa, and which disappeared without a trace. Then came the night of April 13-14, the *U-85's* time of reckoning.

USS *Roper*

Patrolling the arena was the U.S. destroyer *Roper*. The *Roper* was a flush-deck, four-stack destroyer that was built a generation earlier, in 1919. She was a sister ship of the *Jacob Jones*, the destroyer that had been torpedoed and sunk off the coast of Delaware by the *U-578*, six weeks earlier. Only eleven men survived out of a crew of one hundred forty-five.

The *Roper* was no stranger to war. On April 1, she came upon the survivors of the passenger-freighter *City of New York*. The people had been adrift in rafts and lifeboats for three days. One woman gave birth in a lifeboat, and after their rescue she named her son Jesse Roper in honor of the ship that saved their lives.

The night of April 13 was exceptionally clear: the stars shone bright on a placid sea. The destroyer's twin propellers churned surface plankton to a bioluminescent wake. The light on Bodie Island, North Carolina, offered a bearing point for the *Roper's* navigator. In addition to her normal complement, the *Roper* had on board the Commander of Destroyer Division Fifty-four, Commander Stanley Cook Norton. The evident U-boat activity that was concentrated off the Diamond Shoals kept the lookouts alert and the crew and on their toes. Understandably, Lieutenant Commander Hamilton Wilcox Howe conned his ship with extreme caution.

The *Roper* plowed the sea at a steady eighteen knots, on a heading of 162°. At six minutes past midnight she made a radar contact bearing 190° at a range of 2,700 yards. "Immediately afterwards the sound man, echo ranging from bow to bow, heard rapidly turning propellers at a range and bearing that coincided with those obtained by the Radar operator. Then, almost dead ahead, the lookout picked up what appeared to be the wake of a small vessel running away at high speed. Range decreased very slowly, so the *Roper* raised her speed to twenty knots."

His suspicions aroused, Lieutenant Commander Howe rang general quarters. All duty personnel raced to their combat stations. "Orders were given to prepare the machine guns, the three inch battery, the torpedoes and the depth charges for action. As the chase began the Executive Officer went to the flying bridge to keep the Conning Officer informed of the movements of the leading ship."

The unknown vessel sent no recognition signals. Instead, it began a series of course changes that were obviously evasive. Although no one aboard the *Roper* knew it yet, they had a U-boat on the run. It was trapped on the surface in shallow water where it could not escape by submerging. The U-boat turned to port in increments, testing the *Roper* to determine if it had been spotted. The distance between them closed.

First Blood

The *Roper* was not fooled, nor was Lieutenant Commander Howe taking chances. With the fate of the *Jacob Jones* so vividly on his mind, he kept his ship slightly off the fleeing U-boat's starboard quarter. The *Roper* gradually overtook the U-boat. As the range was decreased to 700 yards and contact was imminent, Greger reacted predictably, like a cornered rabbit. He fired a torpedo from his stern tube and tried to hit the destroyer "down the throat." Howe's prescience saved his ship. Sailors held their breaths as they watched the deadly fish slide close past the port side and across the *Roper's* wake.

The U-boat made a radical turn to starboard. Its turning radius was tighter than the destroyer's, permitting it to turn inside the other's circle. Ensign Kenneth MacLean Tebo held a steady helm throughout the battle, keeping a sharp eye on the dark ghostly image.

Lieutenant William Winfield Vanous, Executive Officer, directed the training of the 24-inch searchlight and brightly illuminated the enemy's conning tower; already, German sailors were pouring out of the hatch and preparing the deck gun for action.

Chief Boatswain's Mate Jack Edwin Wright spotted his target, pulled the trigger of his 50-caliber machine gun, and with deadly accuracy poured a steady stream of tracers into the men on the deck of the U-boat. Several German gunners were picked up physically by the force of the bullets and hurled into the water. As more men scrambled to take their place, they were scythed down like stalks of wheat. The conning tower became a charnel house of the dead and dying. Moreover, at such close range, the projectiles penetrated the ballast tanks; the U-boat's outer skin was soon riddled with holes.

While the Germans were kept from loading and firing their deck gun, the *Roper's* 3-inch gun came on line. Coxswain Harry Heyman, "a gun captain who had never before been in charge of a gun during firing," spotted his shots with such precision that he soon landed an explosive shell at the waterline below the conning tower, breaching the hull and making it impossible for the U-boat to dive.

Like rats deserting a sinking ship, German sailors poured out of the conning tower hatch and cowered behind the shearwater. The U-boat began to lose headway. The *Roper* turned at her maximum rate and prepared to fire a torpedo. Singly and in small groups the Germans jumped from the U-boat's bulbous tank on the side away from the incoming shells. The U-boat slowly came to a stop and settled by the stern, as if scuttling ports had been opened aft. By the time the *Roper's* turn brought her behind the U-boat, it had slipped beneath the sea.

Definite Destruction

Not sure whether this was a trick maneuver, the *Roper* drove in on the spot where the U-boat had disappeared. The screams of thirty-five to forty German sailors were clearly audible to the men aboard the *Roper* as the destroyer passed through the area where they had abandoned ship, "but the *Roper* was more immediately concerned with the certain destruction of the enemy than with the rescue of the personnel." The torpedo was secured, and a barrage of eleven depth charges was laid down "at a position determined upon by an eye estimate and an excellent sound contact." Each depth charge weighed three hundred pounds, and was set to go off at fifty feet below the surface. Racks, Y-guns, and K-guns delivered the attack.

The *Roper* held a straight and steady course away from the position of the submerged or sunken U-boat. Because U-boats were known to work in consort, there was the ever-present possibility that another pack wolf might be lurking nearby. This "made the conduct of any rescue work before daylight far too dangerous to risk." With her antenna sweeping and sound gear pinging continuously, the *Roper* searched throughout the night for other signs of the enemy. No one got any sleep.

At dawn, a Navy PBY plane flown by Lieutenant C.V. Horrigan swooped over the area to conduct a visual search. In the light of day, oil slicks and a large field of debris could be seen. Horrigan dropped a depth charge on a particularly suspicious area. Two more planes appeared on the scene; they dropped smoke floats to draw attention to bodies on the surface. The *Roper* drove into the area just after 7 a.m., launched two lifeboats, "and commenced recovering bodies and floating articles." At all times at least one plane circled the destroyer for protection against other U-boats. At one time as many as seven planes of various types flew cover for recovery operations. An observation blimp arrived at 7:30. The potential situation was too serious to leave anything to fate.

Dead and Buried

"At 0750 the first boat returned with five bodies, and at 0834 hoisting of fifteen more bodies by means of a small davit was commenced. At 0850 the sound operator detected a sharp echo at a range of 2700 yards."

Was this another U-boat? Leaving the two lifeboats to continue their grisly task, the *Roper* proceeded at high speed toward the target. Seven minutes later she dropped four depth-charges in a straight line at seven second intervals, producing "one very large air bubble and one smaller one . . . together with fresh oil. The airship and one plane dropped flares on the spot, and the airship reported the continuation of the air bubbles." The anti-submarine action report stated, "This is believed to be same submarine depth-charged after 0006 contact."

Altogether, "twenty-nine bodies were recovered. Among other things six escape lungs were found. Two bodies had mouth-piece tubing in their mouths, indicating escape after the submarine sank. While picking up the bodies, a number of empty life jackets were noted. Two additional bodies were permitted to sink after their clothing was searched by an officer in the boat." No explanation was given for why these bodies were let go; it is likely that they were so damaged by explosives that they were falling apart or that very little flesh remained to hold them together.

At ten o'clock two more depth charges were dropped "to further blast submarine depth-charged on previous attacks. Charges were let go over largest air bubble." The U-boat did not move, and air bubbles persisted. The *Roper* placed an orange colored buoy some two hundred fifty yards away from the largest air bubble.

That afternoon the *Roper* docked at Lynnhaven Roads, Virginia. The German bodies were transferred to the Naval tug *Sciota*, which later delivered them to the Naval Operating Base at Norfolk, Virginia. There they were photographed, examined, and placed in shrouds. All clothing and personal effects were saved. The next afternoon the bodies, each in a plain pine box, were trucked under escort to nearby Hampton National Cemetery. Prisoners from Fort Monroe dug twenty-nine graves.

As dusk approached, a select group of military personnel gathered at the grave site. Not until after dark, and in relative secrecy, were services commenced. The coffins were lowered into the ground. Two Navy chaplains officiated: Lieutenant Wilbur Wheeler read Catholic services, Lieutenant (j.g.) Rainus Lundquist read the Protestant version. In strict military fashion, the vanquished enemy was saluted by three volleys while a bugler sounded taps.

The German sailors received a finer peace than they had offered to their victims.

Under Wraps

Oddly, no mention of this decisive victory was released to the press until three weeks after the event. Even then the published account was meager and garbled, not by newspaper reporters but in the original Navy communiqué. By that time, so many false claims had been issued for the morale of the public that the authentic account paled by comparison. The story was spiced by the following falsity, "With the action over as suddenly as it had begun, the destroyer circled around and the crew, who minutes before had been manning the guns, went to the rails to help lift the surviving members of the submarine crew out of the water."

By coincidence, two days later part of a U-boat crew was captured off the North Carolina coast. (See *U-352*, below.) No mention of that incident was ever released to the public because German spies had access to American newspapers.

Not until July 23, 1942, after the U-boats had been firmly trounced and forcibly beaten out of the Eastern Sea Frontier, did the Navy announce the truth of the secret burial. Still, no mention was made of the U-boat's number; no names of deceased were made known. Outside the highest Naval circles the fate of the *U-85* was couched in anonymity.

Meritorious Service

Citations were in the offing for the alert and aggressive crew of the *Roper*. Admiral A.S. Carpender, Commander Destroyers, U.S. Atlantic Fleet, wrote, "The attack on an enemy submarine by the USS *Roper* was conducted with courage, skill, intelligence and determination, in the best traditions of the Naval Service. Its successful prosecution, which resulted in the destruction of the submarine, reflects great credit on the commanding officer, officers, and men of the *Roper*, and on the commander of Destroyer Division 54, who by his advice and guidance assisted in the conduct of the engagement."

In addition to the key figures already named, six members of the gun crew received commendations; gun captain Harry Heyman was recommended for the Navy Cross. The *Roper*'s forward stack was emblazoned with a large star on both port and starboard sides, to "indicate the first attack made by the vessel which resulted in positive evidence of destruction of an enemy submarine." Furthermore, every crewman was authorized to wear a distinctive sleeve device in the form of a silver star.

Navy Divers on the *U-85*

Diving operations on the *U-85* commenced almost

immediately. The U.S. Navy's Experimental Diving Unit was brought in to conduct a survey and learn what it could about German submarines. Several days were spent dragging for and grappling the sunken U-boat, and establishing mooring buoys. A diver actually alighted upon the wooden deck on April 26. He reported that the "submarine appeared to be lying on its starboard side. Inspected submarine forward to bow and returned to the descending line. No apparent damage except to clearing lines noted."

The next day, the *Kewaydin* fouled the marker buoys and descending line during increasing winds and seas. The buoy was replaced by the end of the day, but the seas were too rough to continue operations.

April 28 dawned with bettering conditions. The USCGC *Cuyahoga* relieved the British armed trawler as guardship while the *Kewaydin* repeated the laborious task of dragging, grappling, and setting mooring lines. This time the first diver who was put down "made descending line fast to cleat on port side of submarine just forward of gun."

Six dives were made throughout the day, with the following conditions noted: "(a) Submarine listed to starboard practically on its side - angle of deck with bottom about 80°. (b) Forward on port side several stanchions torn away. Hull appeared intact. (c) No other damage noted except clearing lines torn loose. (d) Forward gun swung forward and to port slightly elevated with tompion in place. (e) 20 mm. AA gun aft of conning tower in place, lines and wires fouled with it. (f) Conning tower apparently undamaged. (g) Upper conning tower hatch open with lubricating oil coming up through hatch below." The *Roper's* shell damage could not be seen because the U-boat lay on the ruptured ballast tank.

Furthermore, the wood deck was intact, the conning tower showed no signs of damage by shell fire, vents to all tanks were open, salvage air lines were collapsed ("probably due to the effects of depth charges"), numerous openings in the hull were open or partially open, the lower conning tower hatch was closed but not dogged, and all compartments were flooded. The bow and stern planes and propellers were undamaged.

On April 29, the Navy salvage tug *Falcon* arrived and took over diving operations. The *Cuyahoga* remained as guardship and quarters for observers. After the *Roper* fought so assiduously to send the *U-85* to the bottom, divers spent the next week trying to bring it back up to the surface. They closed the conning tower hatch, traced salvage air lines, manufactured fittings, then connected surface-supplied hoses and pumped air into the hull. Most of the external piping was collapsed; air that did pass spurted out of the compartments "like sprinkling system."

The 20-mm anti-aircraft gun was removed and recovered for study. Also brought up were the gun sights for the 88-mm deck gun, and instruments from the bridge: the night firing device, the gyro pelorus repeater, and the gyro steering repeater. One diver noted that the forward torpedo tube doors were open and ready for action. On the other hand, the ready ammunition stowage locker near the deck gun was found empty. Disassembly of the deck gun was begun but not completed.

Of historic interest was a picture that was painted on the forward high part of the conning tower, depicting a "wild boar with rose in mouth."

Diving was secured on May 4 with the following recommendation: "Combining the information contained in the USS *Roper* report of action with that gained by divers, it is my opinion that this vessel was thoroughly and efficiently scuttled by her crew, and that successful salvage can be accomplished only by extensive pontooning operations."

The Navy had better things to do. The machine of destruction was abandoned to the greatest of all destructive forces: the elements of nature.

Condition of the Wreck
Although there were no other reports about activity

on the sunken U-boat, the wreck as it exists today seems to have undergone further damage than that observed by Navy divers in 1942. The bow truncates sharply at the end of the pressure hull; the forward portion of the outer hull, or skin, is missing. The torpedo tubes protrude from the end and are separated so that the parts with the outer doors and massive hinges lie loose in the sand, partially or completely buried. A field of debris lies in front of the main wreckage and is scattered back along the starboard side. Rumor has it that the bow was blown off by private salvors.

Oddly, the angle of tilt is no more than 45°. Sand has built up high on the port side of the wreck, while the starboard side is exposed to a much deeper depth. Ocean currents scour the stern somewhat, but most of the time the propellers are covered with sand. However, this condition can change from year to year, and the amount of exposure can vary considerably. Due to the prevailing current, sand has piled against the port side of the hull nearly level with the tilted deck, while the starboard side drops down a good ten feet, to 90 feet.

Most of the thin, outer skin has rusted through to reveal the pressure hull underneath. When I first dived on the wreck in the 1970's, a spare torpedo was exposed forward of the conning tower; it was stored outside the pressure hull but inside the outer skin. This torpedo disappeared sometime in the 1990's. Since a torpedo weighs around 3,500 pounds, this was no simple salvage task. Yet no one has come forward to take credit for the job. Rumor has it that Navy divers recovered the torpedo as a training exercise.

The forward torpedo room is accessible through the torpedo loading hatch, but after penetrating six or eight feet forward, the room is filled with sand to within a foot of the overhead.

The control room can be accessed through the large damaged area below the starboard side of the conning tower. The interior at this point is a complicated maze of pipes and beams strung together with a cat's cradle of electrical wires. The conning tower hatch is open, but very small; because the lower hatch is also open it is possible to crawl through the conning tower and into the control room. The conning tower is in the process of separating from the hull; already it is possible to get an arm into the gap.

From inside the control room one can proceed aft around the periscope housing and go through the after control room doorway all the way to the galley hatch. However, it is a bit of a squeeze due to interior dunes. Complete silt-out must be expected behind a diver crawling through such close confines.

One can either exit through the galley hatch, or duck under it and go farther aft - at least until one is pressed against the overhead by sand that seems to build up higher with each passing year. The silt inside is thick.

The after torpedo loading hatch is open, but an iron bar bolted across it from the inside prevents a diver wearing tanks from entering. Only by removing all paraphernalia and using a long breathing hose can one squeeze past the barrier.

U-352 (Type VII-C)

Compared to all the U-boats that Germany sent to war, the life span of the *U-352* was probably about average. More than eighty percent of operational U-boats (most of them constructed after the onset of hostilities) did not live long enough to enjoy peace; likewise for the crews. The very underwater machines of destruction that wrought such havoc and caused the deaths and suffering of so many innocent people became iron coffins for many of those who operated them.

Typical of the breed was the *U-352*. It was commissioned in October 1941 by the U-boat Acceptance Commission, in Kiel, Germany. After a five-week shakedown cruise in the Baltic Sea, and a short sortie for tactical exercises, the end of November found it docked in Flensburg for "minor repairs and adjustment." It remained there throughout December, thus permitting the crew frequent leaves at home before their first war patrol. In mid-January, the *U-352* returned to Kiel to take on torpedoes and provisions. It departed soon afterward for its operational area off Iceland.

According to official Navy documents, "The complement of the *U-352* consisted of 3 officers, 1 midshipman, 18 petty officers, and 24 men." Kapitanleutnant Hellmut Rathke was thirty-two years old, but thirteen of the forty-six men were under twenty-one years of age.

Rathke scored no successes during five weeks at sea. He once spotted a merchant ship and prepared to attack, but was stymied by British corvettes. They harried him with depth charges that exploded uncomfortably close. At other times, land-based aircraft attacked with such vehemence that he was forced to submerge. On one occasion he fired a spread of four torpedoes at a destroyer, but they all missed their mark. The true value of the Iron Cross - supposedly bestowed for excellence in the line of battle - can be measured by the fact that three of them were awarded to crewmembers after a cruise that was an utter failure; it may have been a morale booster, but it certainly did not reflect skill or achievement.

March found the *U-352* in St. Nazaire, the U-boat base on the French coast. For several weeks the boat underwent repairs and reprovisioning. It departed in the first week in April for the three-week Atlantic crossing to the U.S. eastern seaboard. At that time U-boat depredations were at their highest. Any U-boat commander worth his salt could not fail to achieve success in the "great American turkey shoot." Tankers and freighters were being sunk with such regularity that the ocean bottom was almost literally paved with steel.

America Bound

Rathke was ordered to patrol the area off the Diamond Shoals of North Carolina, dubbed "torpedo alley" by U.S. Navy pundits to describe the great number of ships that were lost there due to enemy action. However, by the time the *U-352* reached the American eastern seaboard in May, U-boat activity was on the wane. The *U-85* had been sunk two weeks earlier. The coast was patrolled by ever-growing numbers of military craft: Coast Guard cutters, Navy gunboats, converted yachts, bombers, and blimps. What the Germans called the "second happy time" was nearing its end.

Instead of watching for isolated merchant vessels that were plying the shipping lanes, and picking them off with "eels," the *U-352* spent most of its time crash-diving to avoid aerial detection, or running submerged so as not to be spotted by patrol boats and planes. It was the life of a gopher. On those occasions when Rathke was able to prosecute attacks against unsuspecting merchant ships, the results he achieved were negative. He was a man thirsting for water in a house full of spigots. Perhaps that was what led him to make an insane daylight attack against the fully armed U.S. Coast Guard cutter *Icarus*. A vessel only 165 feet long must have seemed easy pickings.

Lieutenant (jg) E.D. Howard was at the conn of the *Icarus* on the afternoon of May 9, 1942. The Coast Guard cutter was en route from New York to Key West, traveling independently at fourteen knots. The sea was smooth. Visibility was about nine miles with a slight haze. At 4:25 p.m., there was still three hours of sunlight remaining in the day. As the Executive Officer, Lieutenant Howard paid particular attention to making certain that the helmsman followed the prescribed zigzag pattern.

Icarus Attacks

The sound equipment suddenly indicated an underwater contact described as "rather mushy." It was a mere one hundred yards away, "a wee bit off port bow." The XO immediately rang General Quarters and called the ship's captain to the bridge. Lieutenant Maurice Jester took charge of the *Icarus*. Four minutes after the initial contact, a torpedo detonated some two hundred yards off the port quarter.

Rathke, already lacking in skill, had run out of luck

as well. The torpedo he fired at the *Icarus* had detonated prematurely, not only allowing the cutter to escape but divulging the U-boat's location.

Lieutenant Jester: "Contact drew to port quarter. The submarine attempted to hide in our previous wake. We heard the propeller noises of the submarine." He ordered the course of the *Icarus* reversed. The cutter bore down on the clearly discernible swirl of bubbles that was caused by the torpedo's explosion. In an official interview, Lieutenant Jester described events with military precision and succinctness.

"At this time, we dropped five depth charges, in a diamond pattern. It was later learned that this attack destroyed the submarine's periscope, and killed the Conning Officer. We then reversed course. At 1645 EWT, we dropped three depth charges, in a "V" pattern. At this point, we observed large air bubbles on the surface. The submarine then attempted to surface, as the machinery had been disabled. We reversed course again, and dropped one depth charge, at 1708 EWT. At 1709 EWT, the submarine surfaced down by stern. We then opened fire with our 3" gun, and scored seven hits, on the hull and conning tower of the submarine. At 1711 EWT, the crew of the submarine was seen to be abandoning ship. At 1714 EWT, the submarine sank, and we then ceased fire."

During the forty-five-minute engagement, Rathke did all he could to slink away. The U-boat twisted and turned like a worm on a hot tarred road. As depth charges landed with unerring precision, "gauges and glasses were smashed in the control room. The deck was littered with broken gear. Lockers burst open. Crockery and other loose objects were flung about the boat. The crew was shaken up. All lights except the emergency system failed." The engines also halted momentarily.

With one man already dead and the rest sure to follow, Rathke had no choice but to surrender. The men donned Draeger lungs and lifejackets as Rathke ordered the ballast tanks blown. As soon as the U-boat reached the surface he gave the order to abandon ship. Thirty-three men burst from the hatch under a hail of shells from the smoking guns of the *Icarus*. The Germans had no opportunity to return fire: it was all they could do to jump into the water and hide behind the U-boat's perforated hull. Thirteen men did not make it out of the U-boat.

The *U-352* went down for the last time. On the surface, German sailors floated on the sea like flotsam, and supplicated for rescue.

Survivors Afloat

On each of her sweeps the *Icarus* had gone as far as a thousand yards before turning in for another attack. Now, as she returned to where the *U-352* had come to rest, she saw the group of men drifting away in the current. On the ocean there are no sign posts, so each time the cutter drove in to attack, there was no way to ascertain if the sonar target she was approaching was the same one that she had just passed over, or if it was another, altogether different target. Plotting a course by dead reckoning did not yield the pinpoint accuracy of modern GPS. Since merchant marine survivors often attested to U-boats working in consort, the Navy mind was set on the possibility that another U-boat might be lurking in the vicinity. To stop and pick up survivors meant to expose the *Icarus* to potential counter attack. Lieutenant Jester could not make such a decision on his own; it had to come from fleet command.

Communications Officer Ensign C.C. Poole sent a plain language message on the Navy frequency at 2716 kilocycles: "Have sunk submarine. 30 to 40 men in water. Shall *Icarus* pick up any of the men." When no answer was received from either Norfolk or Princess Anne, the same message was transmitted to Charleston, on 355 kilocycles. The message was received and receipted, but no message was forthcoming. Seventeen minutes later Ensign Poole asked, "Have you any message for us?" The answer was "No."

By this time the *Icarus* had completed another figure-eight loop. Again the sound gear made contact with a target. Was it the U-boat that was already sunk, or a brother wolf? Lieutenant Jester drove over an area of erupting bubbles and dropped a single depth charge. By this time the survivors of the *U-352* had drifted far enough away to escape injury from concussion. Rathke made the best of his time in the water by shouting "warnings to his men not to give any information to their rescuers." He also applied a tourniquet to the stump of Machinist's Mate Gerd Reussel's severed leg.

Nine minutes after his last message, Ensign Poole transmitted another. "Shall *Icarus* pick up any survivors?" Seven minutes after that: "32 German submarine men in water. Shall we pick them up?" The poor German sailors were as likely to drown in red tape as in the Atlantic swells. At last, the Commandant of the Sixth Naval District favored the *Icarus* with a reply: "Pick up survivors. Bring to Charleston."

Now if Lieutenant Jester lost his ship to further German aggression, he was at least acting under direct orders that would save his career in the event of a court-martial. "At 1750 EWT, we stopped and picked up 33 survivors, including 4 wounded. One of the wounded, who had lost a leg, died at 2215. One member of the crew lost an arm, and one had a fractured wrist, with possibly a bullet inside. One member had a slight wound on his hand. Each member of the submarine crew was searched as he came aboard the *Icarus*. All were equipped with life jackets and lungs, of the most excellent quality. Thirty members of the crew were placed under guard. Two members were placed in sick bay."

Ensign Poole's next message was triumphant: "Contacted submarine, destroyed same. Lat 32-12-1/2, long 73-75. Have 33 of her crew members on board. Proceeding Charleston with survivors."

Prisoners of War

Rathke had finally done something noteworthy: he became the first German submariner to be captured off the American coast.

The Sixth Naval District appeared to be unable to keep up with events. An hour and a half after the *Icarus* departed from the site of the engagement, she received a message from the Commandant: "Buoy spot with secure anchor. Recover sample oil and surface and all floating debris." Then: "Request that all information concerning *Icarus* incident be treated strictly confidential."

Rathke, for one, intended to fulfill this final request. Because Ensign Jester did not separate the German officers from their men, during the trip to Charleston there was ample opportunity for Rathke to get "the prisoners together to give them instructions about the story they would tell. He told them not to mingle with German girls, if they should be placed where they would have occasion for such association. He told them not to forget their comrades who had died, and also not to forget anything he had told them the preceding night."

The *Icarus* tied up at the wharf in Charleston, South Carolina, at 11:30 the following morning. The German prisoners were marched off her deck with the same precision with which they had abandoned their sinking U-boat. They ignored the military fanfare and, despite the gravity of their plight, exhibited high morale. They received better treatment at the hands of the enemy than they had been led to expect after listening to years of German propaganda. (While in the water, the man who had lost his arm waved his stump and begged not to be machine-gunned.) Gerd Reussel was "buried with full military honors in Post Section, grave No. 18, National Cemetery, Beaufort, S.C."

Intelligence Report

According to the Office of Naval Intelligence, "A brief preliminary interrogation was made shortly after the men were landed in the United States. Thereafter they were taken to a place of temporary internment where Rathke was permitted to maintain direct control over his men. A stern disciplinarian, Rathke kept a strict

surveillance over his men during this temporary internment. Ample evidence of this can be found in the list of
punishments meted out to his men for various delin-
quencies."

After more thorough interrogation, ONI found that,
"though courteous to a fault and cultivated, Rathke has
been conspicuously arrogant in complaining of his
treatment as a prisoner and in assuming unwarranted
control of his men following their internment. He pro-
fesses unqualified admiration for Hitler and National
Socialism." And, "Rathke spoke of Hitler as a 'genius'
who has unified all the German peoples of Europe. . . .
Rathke said Hitler was not only a military genius but 'a
genius in everything'."

The character references made by Naval interroga-
tors pertained only to Rathke, and not to his men. So
disliked was Rathke by his crew that after repatriation
he was banned from the annual survivor's reunions.

Salvage Attempt

The intelligence gained from Rathke and his crew
left much to be desired. Hoping that it might learn more
from steel than from flesh, the Navy decided to salvage
the *U-352*: if not the entire hull then at least its log and
code books and cipher machine. The Navy tug *Umpqua*
departed Charleston on May 19, but "it was not until
May 23 that the submarine was located. Using a buoy
anchor chain as a descending line, a dive was made by
C.E. Meyer, TM2c, USN, who reported after coming to
the surface that he had examined the bow of the submarine which had a deep gash in it. The submarine laid
on its starboard side at the angle of about 60° but in as
much as the diver had only enough line to give him a
20-foot radius of activity, a more thorough examination
of the entire ship could not be made at that time.

"The following day diving operations were continued
when it was hoped to enter the conning tower; however, it was impossible for the *Umpqua* to remain in one
position and after many unsuccessful attempts to relocate the submarine, operations on this day were dis-

continued.

"There were no escort vessels available on May 25th to afford the *Umpqua* protection, but on May 26th and for the three following days further efforts to locate the wreck were not successful."

If the Navy seems to have given up too easily, it must be remembered that there was a war going on, and the services of tugs and escorts were sorely needed elsewhere. Besides, those in positions of higher authority were privy to the knowledge that German cipher machines had long been in Allied hands, and that German naval codes had long since been broken.

Subsequent Attack

Nearly three months after the sinking of the *U-352*, on August 7, the British armed trawler HMS *Stella Polaris* "established a sharp metallic contact that was a submarine beyond doubt and with the excellent policy of 'shooting first - questions later,' she went in to attack. This was in the vicinity of the *U-352*. She dropped three patterns of depth charges which brought large air bubbles and additional oil to the surface. Then 5 minutes later a raft appeared. Excitement ran high when it was believed that another enemy submarine had been destroyed." The raft was covered with German writing, and contained "a red distress flag mounted on a 5-foot staff which could be broken in three joints.

"The *Stella Polaris* then dropped a pattern of 12 depth charges which brought more oil to the surface and then, developing a leak, stood by until 2030 when, after buoying the position, she departed for Morehead City. The following day the Coast Guard cutters *474* and *480* located the buoy and both dropped depth charges that failed to bring up wreckage or bodies, although oil came to the surface after each attack. It was at this time believed that a definite 'kill' had been made and the decision to conduct diving operations and search for the sunken submarine was reached."

The tug *P.F. Martin* was called in and a diver was put down. He found "hard smooth sand with pock marks in the ocean bottom, and also depth charge arbors and a quantity of dead fish, but no submarine. The area was dragged with a grapnel and two hours later a solid object was hooked and buoyed; the following day a diver, using the buoy anchor line as a guide, located the submarine."

On the third dive "a piece of wreckage was brought to the surface. The wreckage consisted of a twenty foot section of upper deck grating, presumably the hatch over the upper deck torpedo storage containers." Diving operations were secured because of a two and a half knot current, and because of the discovery of five unexploded depth charges that lay scattered around the wreck.

Unfortunately for the war record of the *Stella Polaris*, the divers also found entangled in the hull a three-inch wire hawser and a two-and-a-half-inch manila line, both of which had been lost in May during salvage operations on the *U-352*. The *Stella Polaris* had rediscovered the wreck and had added to its destruction.

Search and Discovery

Thereafter the *U-352* remained dormant until it was located once again in 1975, this time by wreck divers who were bound and determined to find it. It was not an easy task. George Purifoy told the story to me. Among others, Claude Hall had already spent considerable energy in the search when he passed the torch to Purifoy and his friends Rod Gross and Dale McCullough. The trio chartered local fishing boats to take them to the coordinates that had been recorded by the Navy. The position was given in latitude and longitude, and had to be converted to loran-A, the chain in use at the time and one known for lack of reliability. It sometimes took three to four hours to find a *known* wreck site.

Week after week throughout the summer, they ran grids with a Fathometer. Eighty percent of the time they did not even get wet. Sometimes they quit early enough to permit them to make a dive on the way home. The search was costly, time consuming, and frustrating in the extreme.

With a depth recorder for determining bottom contours, it was necessary to drive exactly over top of a wreck before it showed up as a spike on the graph. Still the weeks went by, and still they had nothing to show for their efforts. The monitor showed no trace of any wreckage whatsoever: the oscilloscope was flatlined like an EEG on a dead person.

Finally, Purifoy bought his own boat and rented a loran-C unit. Loran-C had just come out on the market. Armed with this equipment, he and his companions began running grid patterns in the suspected area. On the very first pass they ran over a target that showed promise. Because of the smooth hull, they had trouble grappling the wreck. When Purifoy went down the anchor line he knew that their quest was over. The grapnel's tines had caught in the conning tower. With two-hundred-foot visibility, he could see both ends of the wreck, and knew for certain that it was a U-boat.

The *U-352* lay a mile and a quarter from the coordinates that had been established by the Navy after diving on the site. This was a prime example of how far off a sextant sighting could be on a known location.

Bureaucratic Intervention

Although the wreck had been worked over hard by successive depth charge attacks, the pressure hull remained unruptured. The outer skin was gone, either blasted or rusted away, as was the conning tower: the U-boat appeared like a stripped down model with the pumps and valves, which were normally hidden under deck plates, now exposed to the sea. The deck gun and periscopes were the most prominent features. White, hard sand provided a sturdy platform that not only kept the hull from settling into the seabed, but along with warm Gulf Stream currents, helped to maintain visibility in ranges that generally exceed one hundred feet.

Although the *U-352's* hull had so far survived numerous depth charge attacks as well as the natural ravages of the sea, it was in imminent peril of annihilation from a much more insidious force: bureaucracy. In 1978, Senator Lowell Weicker, a Republican from Connecticut, strayed into an area where he was definitely out of his state. Hearing that the sunken U-boat contained unexploded ordnance, and that recreational divers visited the site regularly, he decided that the wreck should be placed off-limits. He called the *U-352* a "time bomb" waiting to explode. Exerting his senatorial influence, he eventually dropped a bomb where none had been before.

Under his direction, the U.S. Navy was ordered to survey the wreck in order to assess its potential danger to recreational divers. While national defense was more in the realm of the Navy's tactical area of responsibility, it was forced to condescend to political pressures and to conduct an investigation of the U-boat's live ordnance. What they found came as no surprise to local divers: exposed torpedoes and scattered 88-mm projectiles. Nor was this a situation with which the Navy had not dealt before.

Every once in a while, a dragger hauled in its net and found a lost mine or expended torpedo that was leftover from World War Two. At least one such incident led to disaster. On July 23, 1965, the fishing trawler *Snoopy* raised its net to dump its load of fish in the hold when, to the horror of the crew, a live torpedo slammed against the hull. The detonation killed eight men and sank the trawler with a "big bang followed by smoke."

Sometimes, children who were playing in the sand near old gun emplacements dug up live warheads. Concerned parents turned them over to local police, who then called the Explosive Ordnance Division to take charge of the warhead. The EOD handled these cases by delicately transporting all live (or suspected live) ordnance to a disposal range, where it was covered with dynamite which was then detonated, thus destroying the old and supposedly unstable explosives. Never was anything disarmed. Reporters of these events described the resultant blasts without bothering to mention that the large explosions were not caused by the old ordnance, but by the dynamite that was used to destroy it. This has led people (and Senators) to believe that all antique ordnance can explode spontaneously, like some Jack-in-the-box waiting for someone to flip its lid.

Now there came the hue and cry that the EOD might blow up the *U-352* as a way of discarding the ordnance it carried. The repercussions from Weicker's naïveté were pronounced: local businesses and charter operators claimed that "this option may adversely impact the area's recreational assets." The National Environmental Policy Act demanded an environmental impact statement because of the wreck's function as an artificial reef. German nationals claimed that the U-boat was a war memorial that still entombed some of the U-boat's crew.

Sanctimony

The loudest voice of protest was the latter, in the spokesperson of Captain Dieter Ehrhardt, the naval liaison for the German Embassy in Washington. "My government prefers to leave wreckage from World War II at the bottom of the sea, to give the dead sailors rest." He was further outraged over rumors that divers were removing from the *U-352* the bones of those dead sailors, and exhibiting them as curiosities. "Generally speaking, the boat is a cemetery, and nobody wants to disturb a cemetery. It is not good, if you are in a cemetery, to pull dead bodies out of the earth." That depends.

Land based cemeteries are often reclaimed for more useful purposes: housing, highways, and shopping malls. It is a common practice to disinter bodies and relocate them to newly established, out-of-the-way lots. Many warships have been demolished because they presented a hazard to navigation, and a way had to be cleared for safe shipping. In the case of the *U-853* (see below), bones were recovered and returned to the

Fatherland in piety toward the deceased.

There is no overriding rule of human nature, cultural ethics, or political prerogative that governs the disposal of human remains. Bodies can be buried, burned, or donated to science. Nor do people's beliefs concerning physical remains conform to any system of reason: whereas some individuals hold the corpse to be a sacrosanct receptacle with deep religious overtones, others regard it as nothing more than an inanimate object that was merely the carrier for the soul, persona, or consciousness.

Philosophical considerations aside, which German government had a proper claim on war graves: East Germany, West Germany, or the Third Reich to which the men and machines belonged but which no longer existed? Perhaps the only majority consent that can be counted upon was that skulls and skeletal remains should not be displayed as trophies. Yet, I have been to many museums that showcased skeletons in glass enclosures. In one Canadian maritime museum, I saw the skull of a passenger of the *Empress of Ireland* proudly exhibited in a lighted cabinet that was surrounded by other artifacts that had been recovered from the wreck.

Although clearly out of his depth, Weicker gained a great deal of publicity for his cause (and for his image) by diving on the wreck himself. Media attention focused on Weicker and his belief by claiming that the Navy was "worried" over the sunken U-boat. Such newspaper hype could not be farther from the truth. In actuality, the Navy had no concerns whatsoever concerning the *U-352*. It would rather have forgotten Weicker and his self-aggrandizing promotional stance, especially when he accused the Navy of foot-dragging when, after a year and a half, it had done nothing pursuant to his demands.

Ordnance Disposal Operation

Finally, in the summer of 1980, senatorial will presided, and the Navy mounted an expedition to the wreck that was costly to the taxpayer, bothersome to the marine life, face-saving to German nationals, senseless to sport divers, and only partially gratifying to Weicker. Perhaps the only good that came of it was an exercise for Navy divers in which they could hone their skills.

After exhaustive administrative preparations that included the accumulation of equipment and the assignment of personnel, the Navy salvage vessel *Hoist* got underway on May 27, 1980 for an operation that lasted six full weeks. For two days and nights, working around the clock, the *Hoist* towed a side-scan sonar fish over four different positions found among Navy records. "However, no probable contacts were made." It was not until May 29 that the "decision was made to ask the Squadron to make arrangements for commercial assistance from Morehead City in locating the submarine."

Voila! What insight. "Using loran charlie navigation, *Atlantis II* located and buoyed off *U-352* within 20 minutes." (I wonder how much money was spent on fuel and wages before someone thought of the obvious?)

Initial diving operations (on scuba) consisted of tying a series of radar buoys to the bow, conning tower, and stern of the wreck in order to determine its heading, which was northeast, so that a six-point moor could be established. This took two days. On May 31 the first survey was conducted. Using the MK 12 Surface Supplied Diving System with three hundred feet of hose, and taking pictures with a UDATS camera, they found that "the submarine is at rest on a sandy bottom, with a 65–75 degree starboard list. Divers reported soundings of 110 feet at the stern and amidship, and 116 feet at the bow. A variety of sea life linger in the vicinity of the submarine, including a school of barracuda. The forward 30 feet of the bow hull section is broken and down at an angle of 30 degrees. The entire submarine is heavily encrusted in barnacles, 75 percent of the decking is missing and only structural framing remains attached to the pressure hull. Approximately 20 per cent of the starboard hull is submerged in the sandy bottom, and an air lift or falcon nozzle could be used to remove this sand to gain access for a complete hull inspection. As previously mentioned, the submarine's outer shell is badly deteriorated and all that remains is the structural framing attached to the very accessible pressure hull which is in good shape. Because of the 65–75 degree starboard list, divers were unable to determine whether or not the two starboard forward torpedo tube outer doors are opened. Number two torpedo tube (upper port tube) is broken in half and number four tube (lower port tube) is intact but divers were unable to confirm the presence of any torpedoes. Although the external survey revealed that no torpedoes are stowed topside on the maindeck, a torpedo warhead was discovered wedged in the deck framing approximately 30 feet forward of the conning tower, above the forward torpedo room. The warhead is intact with exploder removed. The forward torpedo loading hatch is open and the hatch cover is missing. Divers passed survey of conning tower to continue looking aft. The messdecks hatch and after torpedo loading hatch are both open and both hatch covers are missing. Divers reported that after torpedo loading hatch is blocked by two six inch diameter pipes, possibly vents. Divers moved further aft and determined stern torpedo outer door is opened and approximately 2.5 feet of a torpedo extends out the stern tube."

They also found a single 88-mm shell in the sand, twenty-five feet off the starboard side.

The next day, divers found that "the upper conning tower hatch is open and is lying in the bottom of the conning tower. The lower conning tower hatch, which allows access into the control room, is partially open. Divers reported that the ready service aft of the 88mm gun mount is completely deteriorated. Only the gun mount base remains intact . . . divers entered the forward torpedo room through the forward torpedo loading hatch and began the internal search. Divers reported ed the forward torpedo room contains a considerable amount of mud, sand and silt. The presence of unexploded ordnance could not be determined at this time. However, two horizontal HP air flasks were identified extending between frames 26 and 37 on the port side, partially covered by mud and sand. A violet colored Petroleum Oil Lubricant (POL) product is present in the overhead with a depth of approximately 8 inches. A square water tight door (door missing) provides access between the petty officer's compartment and the forward torpedo room. At about frame 45 within the petty officer's compartment, an approximate rectangular shaped 18 inch by 24 inch hole passes through the pressure hull in the overhead and into the sea. Upon completion of the brief internal survey of the forward torpedo room and the petty officer's compartment, divers prepared for the X-ray of the stern torpedo. The radiation exposure device is heavy and required two divers to horse it around into position. ... An exposure was taken and the preliminary picture indicated the torpedo is unarmed."

On June 2, divers commenced the removal of mud and sand from the forward torpedo room (in order to "make the final determination as to the presence of unexploded ordnance") by implanting a jet. Bad weather, strong currents, and hard-packed mud conspired to make this a difficult and time consuming job. Not until June 11 were they able to excavate down as far as the deck plates. Still, more torpedoes might be stowed below the deck plates. "Several divers attempted to release the inner torpedo tube locking device using a 36 inch aluminum pipe wrench, but were unsuccessful.

Then came a couple days of bad weather, one day of good, a couple more days of bad. "Probing by hand in the bilges revealed no evidence of any torpedoes/unexploded ordnance in the excavation. Four air flasks, extended between frames 25 to 36, were positively identified within the forward torpedo room. Two lie end to end along the port side bulkhead and two lie end to end along the starboard side bulkhead."

June 17: "The lower port torpedo tube was found to

be cracked and the battery section of a torpedo was visible. The lower port torpedo tube is cracked approximately 3 to 4 feet outside of the pressure hull which would indicate the torpedo inside is broken in the center section." Also, "Alongside the starboard quarter, approximately 10 feet from the submarines side, divers located the end of a torpedo center section... . Divers confirmed this torpedo was without an exploder."

June 18: "Two torpedoes were located in the bilges and confirmed, one directly underneath the port side air flasks and a second approximately 8 inches to the right of the first (as facing the bow). Both torpedoes are without exploders." The next day they found two more torpedoes in the bilges.

Part of June 22 was spent exploring. "In the vicinity of the CO's cabin there is approximately 3 feet of clearance between the mud and sand level and the overhead. There is also a considerable amount of mud and sand in the mates compartment and the officers mess."

June 23: "Tubes one and four were drilled and probing revealed the presence of a torpedo in each tube. The two new torpedoes bring the total to ten torpedoes located thus far." So much for the veracity of the *U-352's* crew. They had stated that they started out with fourteen torpedoes and fired seven or eight.

"Divers reported the galley is approximately 2/3 full of mud and debris. The galley hatch door leading forward is present and partially open. Divers proceeded forward into the mates compartment and reported the space is approximately half full of mud and noticeably clear of debris, and that there is approximately five feet of clearance between the mud level and the overhead. A circular watertight hatch opens into the mates compartments and provides access into the conning tower control room. Divers then back tracked and proceeded aft through the engine room. However, the extreme starboard list, combined with the mud, debris and the port and starboard engines, made transit of the engine room very difficult. Divers continued through the engine room space and into the after torpedo room to investigate the two bars obstructing the after torpedo loading hatch. Investigation revealed the two bars appear to be securely in place and will probably require removal to allow easier access into the torpedo room. Like the forward torpedo room, the after torpedo room is full of a considerable amount of mud and debris. To complete a comprehensive survey all mud and debris will have to be excavated."

The next day they proceeded to torch through the bars, but then found that in MK II gear they could slip between them. After much excavation and time lost to bad weather, the determination was made on July 1 that no torpedoes were stored in the after torpedo room. Then they partially excavated the galley, where they removed the deck plates, and the CO's cabin. No unexploded ordnance was located.

July 3: "It was decided that any remote removal of the exploder from the torpedo in the stern tube is not considered a practical course of action." The next day "divers completed external excavation of sand alongside the entire length of the starboard side of *U-352.* No additional unexploded ordnance was found. However, communications problems developed with MK12 hats and diving had to be secured." When it developed that replacement communication assemblies were unavailable, survey operations were terminated.

July 6: "Divers recovered all 88MM and loaded them on board. Divers then placed the torpedo warhead section into a cargo net lowered to the bottom . . . lifted approximately 3 feet off the ocean floor and towed to a point 1500 yards away from the ship and submarine." Divers then attached an Incendiary Torch Remote Opening Device. "The first sign of the warhead burning was a large amount of smoke and bubbles on the surface. Approximately 5 minutes after commencing the burn, the warhead became buoyant and ascended to the surface engulfed in flames. The warhead was recovered and lifted onboard along with 5 lbs of raw explosive and 7 lbs of residual."

By July 7 it was all over. Navy divers had made one hundred thirty-seven dives for a total bottom time of three hundred sixty-one hours. A summary report stated that they had found numerous rounds from the ship's gun and an unexploded torpedo outside the submarine as well as eight torpedoes inside the hull (seven in the forward room and one in a stern torpedo tube)." Inexplicably, the report failed to mention the torpedo trapped outside under the starboard hull. "The torpedoes in the forward room do not pose a hazard as long as left undisturbed, i.e., if restricted from access they will not explode spontaneously but the torpedo in the aft tube does constitute a hazard as it can be approached from outside the hull."

The recommendation was made that the torpedo in the after tube be burned by ITROD, while gratings could "be welded on the entrances to the submarine to prevent access and accidental detonation of any of the torpedoes inside the hull or their associated exploders, six of which could not be located and could be anywhere inside the vessel."

The results of the survey were pondered for a year. Navy divers returned to the wreck on June 18, 1981, stayed nine days, and made sixty-seven dives. Using ITROD, they succeeded in burning the torpedo that protruded from the stern tube as well as the one trapped under the starboard hull in the bow. Then they proceeded to seal off the hatches. Instead of welding a grating across each hatch opening, as recommended, they opted to emplace on each a locking device that consisted of a steel T-bar that slipped inside the coaming and a smooth circular plate on the outside. The circular plate had a round hole in the middle, for the T-bar bolt, and two half-moon cutouts on opposite sides: so the T-bar could be held in place while the nut was run down the shaft from the outside. The nut was then welded in place. This was little more than an appeasement program for Weicker.

It took only weeks for recreational divers to remove the hatch covers. The wreck has been open ever since.

U-boat Reunion

George Purifoy maintained his fascination for the *U-352* throughout the years. After he started a charter service for divers, the U-boat became his most popular destination. In May 1992, he hosted a fifty-year reunion for surviving crewmembers. Purifoy invited me to participate. With the crewmembers on board his dive boat *Olympus*, we departed Morehead City for the two-hour trip to the wreck site. The Germans officiated an onboard ceremony for those who had died in action. Purifoy led a handful of divers (including this author) down to the wreck to lay a wreath on the conning tower.

U-853 (Type IX-C-40)

By the time the *U-853* was commissioned - on June 25, 1943 - the tide of the North Atlantic U-boat war was already swinging toward the side of the Allies. Previous U-boat successes were becoming overshadowed by U-boat losses. Allied countermeasures such as spy rings and decryption analysis enabled intelligence personnel to ascertain the departure dates of U-boats from captured French ports, and to track those boats along their routes. Anti-submarine detection devices such as radar and sonar enabled naval warships to locate U-boats before they struck at escorted convoys, and to follow their escape under water. Submersible interdiction weapons such as hedgehogs and depth charges enabled escort vessels and patrol craft to damage and sink arrogant U-boats that dared to attack against all odds.

It was into this losing battle that the *U-853* was flung. The first commander of the *U-853* was Kapitanleutnant Helmut Sommer. For the majority of his year-long command, the *U-853* operated as a training unit. By this time in the U-boat war, patrols were not exactly suicide missions, but the opportunities for making successful attacks against Allied shipping were remote, while the possibilities of being sunk were likely. Sommer was luckier than most.

In May of 1944, Sommer took the *U-853* on its first

war patrol - actually, a weather patrol, as his job was to report the weather rather than to track and sink enemy vessels. Whenever Sommer transmitted a weather report, Tenth Fleet intelligence personnel triangulated the U-boat's position. As a result, he was constantly hounded by aircraft that were dispatched to destroy him. The *U-853* successfully repelled one aerial attack that was made by three British Swordfish on May 25, and managed to damage one aircraft so badly that, after returning to its carrier, it was jettisoned.

On June 17, the *U-853* was not so lucky. Two fighter planes executed a brilliant surprise attack against the surfaced U-boat. They strafed the conning tower so severely that two men were killed and eleven others were wounded, including Sommer and his first officer, Helmut Fromsdorf. The *U-853* managed to submerge and evade pursuing warships, but so many of the crew were unfit for duty that the patrol had to be terminated prematurely. The *U-853* returned to its berth in Lorient, France for extensive repairs.

Brevet commander Oberleutnant Otto Wermuth turned over command to Korvettenkapitan Gunther Kuhnke. In July, the *U-853* proceeded to Norway for its second war patrol. During three fruitless months there occurred not a single incident worthy of note. No enemy contact was made. The *U-853* terminated the patrol and proceeded to Germany for refit.

The Snorkel

The *U-853* benefited from recent technological advances in submarine design by having a snorkel installed during the refit. The snorkel was invented by Dutch serviceman Jan Wickers. The submarine snorkel was a steel tube that was retractable (or foldable), and which permitted the ventilation of a partially submerged submarine. It housed air intake and exhaust pipes for the diesel engines. By "breathing" through a snorkel, a U-boat could proceed at the high speed provided by its diesel engines instead of at the low speed provided by its electric motors. When a U-boat was snorkeling, its hull and conning tower were completely submerged. The only part of a U-boat that was exposed above the surface was the snorkel head (and the periscope, if it was extended). The Dutch navy adopted the snorkel in 1936, the German navy in 1940.

The snorkel was small enough to avoid detection by early radar systems. It left a wake, however, that was clearly visible from the air during daytime operations. In the presence of the enemy, its use was confined to the hours of darkness. Eventually, electronic detection systems grew so sophisticated that the snorkel head could be detected by radar units that were mounted on both aircraft and surface vessels. Additionally, submerged U-boats were readily detected by sonar. Many U-boats were destroyed without ever being sighted visually.

New Skipper

Kunhke was detached from the *U-853*. He was promoted to commander of the 10 Flotilla. Command of the *U-853* then devolved upon Fromsdorf, who had recovered from the wounds he had sustained in the aerial attack.

The *U-853* remained idle until the end of February 1945. By that time the war in Europe was all but over. The massive bombing of German cities was a nightly event. Hordes of Allied aircraft flew under the cover of darkness to rain terror upon the Fatherland of Nazi occupation. High explosive and incendiary bombs devastated the cities and their occupants, creating an aerial spectacle that must have been horrific to behold: a deadly but magnificent stroboscope of gargantuan proportions.

In a last ditch attempt to relive the "happy days" of the early U-boat campaign, every operational U-boat was sent to sea. There was no longer any hope that Germany could win the war that it had started in its bid for world domination. All the U-boats could hope to accomplish was to prolong the strife before inevitable surrender. The deluded men of the U-boat arm were sent to a needless death. As far as German High Command was concerned, if they could take a few more innocent victims with them, so much the better.

Fromsdorf was ordered to operate in the Gulf of Maine, concentrating his efforts off of Boston. If conditions were unfavorable, he was given two alternative areas of operation: Halifax or New York.

The crossing of the Atlantic Ocean required nearly two months. The length of this passage contrasted starkly against the three-week passages of the *U-85* and the *U-352*. Most of the passage had to be made submerged, due to flocks of Allied aircraft that prowled through the air, and the fleets of warships that churned through the waves. It was a time of drudgery for the men aboard the *U-853*.

The exact date of the U-boat's arrival off the coast of Maine is a matter of speculation. However, it is almost certain that it scored the first success of its career on April 23.

Eagle 56

The *Eagle 56* was a patrol craft that displaced 640 tons. She was under the command of Lieutenant John Scagnelli. Sixty-six additional officers and enlisted men helped to operate the complicated warship. Without warning, a titanic blast ripped apart the Eagle boat's midship section, tearing the hull in two. The stern section sank within two minutes. The forward section rolled onto its side, and water flooded the interior compartments through the jagged opening. The stem pointed upward momentarily, then slid quietly beneath the surface of the sea. Gone to Davy Jones's locker were fifty-four American sailors. The skipper was among the thirteen injured and half-drowned survivors.

Men aboard the U.S. destroyer *Selfridge* observed the explosion from three miles away. They saw a geyser of water rise a hundred feet into the air; the geyser lasted as long as twenty seconds. The destroyer reversed course and steamed at flank speed for the scene of the tragedy. The *Portland* lightship followed in her wake.

When the vessels reached the field of debris they found men without life vests bobbing in the frigid water or clinging to pieces of flotsam. Both ships lowered lifeboats to rescue survivors.

While her boats were in the water, the *Selfridge* picked up a firm contact on her sound gear. She left the rescue operation in progress and proceeded to retaliate against the submerged U-boat. She dropped nine depth charges without achieving any positive result, then lost the contact. When she returned to the site of the sinking, she found that her boats had picked up ten men; the boats of the lightship had picked up three. All thirteen survivors were seriously wounded, requiring morphine and plasma, so the *Selfridge* rushed them to port for hospitalization.

Whether the *Selfridge* inflicted any damage on the *U-853* will never be known.

Black Point

The next emergence of the *U-853* occurred two weeks later, on May 5, when it torpedoed the *Black Point* off Point Judith, Rhode Island. This attack should never have taken place because, in anticipation of surrender, the German Navy had issued a cease-fire order to all its forces at sea. Whether Fromsdorf ignored the order or did not receive it has been the cause of endless debate.

The *Black Point* sank with the loss of twelve of her crew. Lookouts on a passing merchantman, the Yugoslavian vessel *Kamen*, observed the explosion of the collier. Her radio operator immediately transmitted an SOS. While a bevy of rescue vessels proceeded toward the site of the catastrophe, the transmission was also intercepted by a Naval task force that was operating thirty miles to the south.

The Search Begins

The destroyer escorts *Atherton* and *Amick*, and the Coast Guard frigate *Moberly*, cranked up their engines to flank speed and proceeded to the scene of the attack.

They fanned out as they approached the east side of Block Island, with the intention of boxing in the escaping U-boat. The destroyer *Ericsson*, having already entered Cape Cod Canal to the north, reversed her course and raced back toward the scene in a pincher movement that was intended to prevent the U-boat from escaping in her direction. Lieutenant Commander L. B. Tollaksen, skipper of the *Moberly*, was the senior officer of the three vessels that were the closest to the scene, so he was designated the Officer in Tactical Command.

As night closed in, the three warships from the south ran abreast, sweeping the darkened sea with their sonar gear. The *Atherton* possessed the best sound team and the latest equipment, so she took the position that was most likely to be used by an escaping U-boat. Two miles to the west ran the *Amick*, and two miles farther west ran the *Moberly*. With a precision borne of experience, the *Atherton's* course ran directly over the skulking U-boat. The propellers of the *U-853* were clearly discernible as Fromsdorf cruised slowly along the bottom at a depth of 125 feet, desperately seeking the safety of deeper water.

Massive Counterattack

The *Atherton* drove in for the attack, dropping thirteen magnetic depth charges. Only one exploded, but it could not be determined if the U-boat's hull had triggered the charge, or if it had been dropped on a shipwreck that was thought to be in the area. With the U-boat definitely pinned down, the *Amick* was called off to escort another merchantman through the narrows between Block Island and Point Judith.

The *Atherton* made another pass and launched a full load of hedgehogs. Hedgehogs detonate upon impact with a solid object. Geysers had just splashed down when a secondary explosion occurred a hundred feet off the edge of the pattern. This was evaluated as a depth charge from the first run - one that had been detonated by the hedgehogs. The *Atherton* worked over the area with another hedgehog attack. After that, because of the disturbance of the water, she lost contact with the U-boat and was unable to regain it.

Not knowing whether the original contact was a U-boat or a wreck, the *Atherton* left a lighted marker buoy at the site. The two warships then resumed the sonar search. By that time the *Ericsson* had arrived, and tactical control was passed to that vessel and senior Commander F. C. B. McCune. By 10 o'clock that night, the area was surrounded by three more destroyers and four additional escort vessels. The Navy was leaving nothing to chance.

It was nearly midnight before the *Atherton's* sonar operator heard pinging from a stationary object. No propeller noise was heard. The U-boat appeared to be sitting silently on the bottom. At this stage in the technology of sound navigation and ranging, a good listener could just about pinpoint a target. The *Atherton* fired a pattern of hedgehogs, which quickly brought to the surface a flurry of air bubbles, oil, and sections of freshly broken planks. The *Atherton* circled the spot. The sound contact was excellent, and unmoving.

The *Ericsson* did not join in the attack, but Commander McCune ordered the *Atherton* to make yet another run on the supposed U-boat, in order to split the pressure hull and ensure that the enemy did not escape in the resulting noise that might confuse the sonar equipment. The *Atherton* trounced the target again, this time with depth charges. Air and oil continued to rise to the surface. Searchlight beams from the *Atherton* and *Moberly* fell on water that was thick with oil and which was covered with cork and dead or dying fish. The *Atherton* recovered a pillow, a life jacket, and a wooden flagstaff.

The *Atherton's* sonar gear was temporarily disabled by the last pattern of depth charges. This was due to the shallow depth of water, which required commensurate depth settings to be placed on the detonators. The *Moberly* was ordered to make the next attack. If Commander McCune thought that the enemy was done for, and that the *Moberly's* attack was merely a coup de grace, the report from the *Moberly's* sound operator - that the target was again on the move - quickly dispelled that notion. The *Moberly* attacked at high speed, in order to distance herself from the blast of her own depth charges. Even so, the resulting concussion damaged her steering gear.

While the *Moberly* was recovering from her self-inflicted damage, the *Atherton* got her sound gear operational again, and discovered that the target was still on the move at two to three knots. The time was 4 a.m. The *Moberly* laid down a pattern of hedgehogs. After this, contact was lost due to reflections from the sandy bottom. The U-boat was soon detected by the presence of pools of oil that coagulated on the surface. For the next four hours the two warships drove back and forth over the site, constantly re-establishing sonar contact. The U-boat had finally come to rest - or had it?

Dawn of a New Era
As the sun rose over the smooth Atlantic swells, the stark yellow glow highlighted a huge field of debris that was filled with life jackets, escape lungs, emergency life rafts, a chart table, even the skipper's cap. Commander McCune had boats lowered to recover the floating material. "Sounders determined that the submarine moved again during the forenoon of May 6, but it is not known whether the craft tried to move under its own power or whether it had been knocked out and carried a short distance by the tide. To be on the safe side, more depth charges were dropped."

With the idea of cracking the sunken U-boat's pressure hull, McCune ordered all three warships to run depth-charge attacks in a cloverleaf pattern: each striking from a different direction while the others stood by awaiting their turn. In between each depth-charging, a boat went in to collect any loose items that floated up from the bottom. All told, more than two hundred depth charges and innumerable hedgehogs were dropped on the *U-853*.

Two blimps (the *K-16* and the *K-58*) lent assistance by dropping marker buoys, smoke bombs, dye markers, and sonar transponders over the site. They also took aerial photos of the oil slicks and attack operations. The *K-16* made a strong contact with her MAD gear. (MAD is the acronym for magnetic anomaly detection). "She marked this position on several successive sweeps and reported that the target was stationary. . . . The sonar operators in both blimps heard sound which they described as a 'rhythmic hammering on a metal surface, which was interrupted periodically.' About ten minutes later they heard a 'long, shrill shriek' and then the hammering noise was lost in the engine noise of the attacking surface ship." The blimps also "made attacks on the submarine with their 7.2" rocket bombs."

Diving for Certainty

Finally convinced that the U-boat had been completely destroyed, Commander McCune had the *Ericsson* drop a buoy directly on the wreck. That afternoon, the Navy salvage vessel *Penguin* arrived and established a four-point moor over the wreck. It was eight o'clock at night before the mooring was established. Three divers in turn descended through the cold water column, using the buoy line as a guide. Each landed right on the conning tower. Two more divers made examinations of the wreck after midnight. Diving operations were secured at 2:40 in the morning.

Diving operations recommenced after 8 o'clock on the morning of May 7. During the day, eight additional dives were made by as many divers. Three of the eight divers were officers: two lieutenants and one lieutenant commander. They found twelve unexploded depth charges around the wreck. They left the depth charges in place, but removed from the conning tower the body of a German seaman who was identified as H. Hoffman. The body was transferred to the *ATA-125*, which transported it to the submarine base at New London, Connecticut.

The divers reported that the pressure hull was pierced by gaping holes. They saw other bodies inside, but did not remove any of them. One conclusion was obvious: Fromsdorf and the entire crew of the *U-853* were dead: fifty-five victims of the obsolete German war machine.

The deaths of the U-boat's officers and crew, and those of their innocent victims, served no useful purpose in either winning or prolonging the war for Germany. The day after the sinking of the *U-853*, Karl Doenitz, former Grand Admiral and now Fuhrer of the Third Reich after Hitler's cowardly suicide, met with Allied commanders at Reims, France, and agreed to German capitulation. The Allied terms were unconditional surrender. The U-boat war was officially over.

Ironically, the last victim that was torpedoed by a German U-boat in the Eastern Sea Frontier sank only sixty miles from the spot where the first victim had been torpedoed: the Norwegian tanker *Norness*, on January 14, 1942. In between, an incredible amount of death and destruction had been wrought at the hands - or by the torpedoes and guns - of Hitler's aggressive U-boat arm.

Mercurial Salvage

The location of the *U-853* has never been lost. The wreck has been under continual public scrutiny, spawning uncountable articles in newspapers and magazines whenever national news was slow. Recreational divers began to visit the site almost as soon as scuba became available, in the 1950's. Commercial salvors have promoted plans to raise the U-boat intact for the purpose of display, or to leave it on the bottom but to retrieve its putative "treasure."

The treasure that is most often associated with U-boats is mercury (alias quicksilver). Mercury is a precious metal that is unique among elements on the Periodic Table in that it exists in the liquid state at room temperature. Time and again throughout the years, individuals have propounded the notion that U-boats employed mercury as ballast.

According to argument, because mercury has greater weight per unit volume than lead and iron, and because it is a liquid, it is the ideal movable ballast. Pumped forward, mercury could instantly nose down a submarine that was making an emergency descent. Pumped aft, the nose could be brought up quickly and efficiently.

This concept may sound good in theory but it is a practical absurdity. Mercury is so dense that an ordinary pump cannot move it. A pump that is capable of moving the amount of mercury necessary to affect the trim of a submarine, and that is capable of pumping the mercury at the required speed, would have to be incredibly massive and powerful, and quite possibly too large to fit inside the pressure hull. Anyone who claims otherwise is merely displaying his ignorance of scientific and engineering knowledge, and of U-boat history and construction.

As in all submarines, U-boats employed seawater for movable ballast. There has never been a submarine that employed mercury as ballast of any kind, and there never will be one. Mercury may not be as precious as gold, but it is far too expensive to replace the free and inexhaustible supply of seawater. Furthermore, due to its toxicity, mercury requires special handling procedures and storage containers: factors that mitigate against its practical usage.

I have often wondered how the belief in mercury ballast originated. I suspect that it is the result of a mixture of a handful of rare events, word-of-mouth misinformation, and wishful thinking. On several occasions during World War Two, U-boats transported mercury in stainless steel flasks, and rendezvoused with Japanese I-boats in order to trade for commodities that Germany desperately needed. From that came the conviction that *all* U-boats carried mercury in flasks - and, by extension, that the mercury was used for ballast. A minimal amount of research would have dispelled such rash credulity, but who wanted to be disillusioned?

Post-War Salvage

It is impossible to present a complete history of salvage operations on the *U-853*, because many of the enterprises were private in nature and the results were not recorded for posterity. Some proposals never got past the drawing board - or they failed to inveigle naïve venture capitalists into providing the funds for the undertaking. Many accounts were exaggerated by overzealous reporters. A few stories were completely bogus, such as the one that was released on November 19, 1968 by Wilhelm von Keudell, the German consulate in Boston. According to him, the Melvin Joseph Company had raised the *U-853* and was in the process of towing it to Lewes, Delaware. What follows are some interesting salvage highlights.

In 1953, Oswald Bonifay made a number of scuba dives on the *U-853* in search of gold bars and flasks of mercury. He found neither. He then hired a pair of commercial divers from Boston: William George and Bill Mercer. Wearing hard-hat diving rigs and breathing surface supplied air, they used explosives to blast open an access to the pressure hull. The pair explored some of the interior, again without success in finding mercury or gold. Their crowning achievement, however, was the removal of the bronze propellers by means of heavy explosives. The propellers were raised and transported to land.

Bonifay sold both propellers to J. T. O'Connell for their scrap value. O'Connell owned the fishing boat *Maureen*, which Bonifay had chartered for his salvage operations, as well as the Castle Inn and Resort, a hotel in Newport, Rhode Island. O'Connell wanted to exhibit the propellers in front of his hotel. O'Connell has since died. The hotel is owned by his descendants, and the propellers still grace the lawn of the hotel.

Question of Ownership

In 1960, Burton Mason and David Trisko commenced salvage operations on the wreck. Their avowed purpose was to recover Fromsdorf's logbook, in the hope of learning why he attacked the *Black Point* after German Naval Headquarters transmitted the order to cease fire. Mason and Trisko also hinted that they might even attempt to raise the U-boat in its entirety. They received a great deal of press, as well as some sharp censure from certain quarters - primarily German. The Bonn government adopted several contradictory postures: (1) that the German government owned the wreck; (2) that the government claimed 20% of the proceeds of the salvage; and (3) that the site was a war grave.

The claim for ownership was unsupportable. The government that originally owned the *U-853* was the Nazi government, or the Third Reich, which no longer existed, and not the West German government that was advancing its claim. The West German government had no better claim to the wreck than the East German government. Furthermore, according to the terms of unconditional surrender, the entire German fleet (including all U-boats) was turned over to the Allies. (Some German captains elected to scuttle their U-boats rather than to suffer the humiliation of surrender. Against official orders, a few U-boats proceeded to neutral ports for internment.) The Allies eventually scuttled the U-boats that were surrendered after the war: some singly, others in a mass disposal called Operation Deadlight. These acts of disposal of noncommissioned vessels were equivalent to abandonment as defined by maritime law. According to this thread of logic, there was no legal connection between the Nazi U-boats and any present or future German government, including reunified Germany.

The break in the chain of ownership invalidated the Bonn government's second claim to a percentage of the profits from salvage.

The third claim was not so spacious. War graves are recognized and respected by all major nations, including graves of the enemy. Military professionals adhered to a code of honor that was chivalrous in nature. Defeated soldiers were perceived as noble even if the cause for which they were fighting was not. Misguided causes notwithstanding, their bodies were revered because they died while fighting for their country - an ideal that followed from neither logic nor reason.

I suspect that the families of those who died on the *Eagle 56* and the *Black Point* might not feel so magnanimous toward the killers on the *U-853*. Fatherless children and wives without husbands are far less likely to perceive such nobility than the conquerors in combat. Certainly, there was no demonstration of respect for the living when the Navy warships blasted the U-boat's occupants to hell. So what was the justification for respecting the German sailors after they were dead? It is all a matter of perspective.

Grave Considerations

To a person who believes in God, the human body is but a vehicle for the soul, and means nothing after death. To a person who does *not* believe in God, the body after death is but a meaningless collection of bones and tissue that once housed a living personality that no longer exists. In either case, no significant emphasis is placed on skeletal remains or body parts.

Buried human remains were often disinterred for a variety of reasons, as I noted earlier in this Appendix and as I expounded upon in Chapter Two. There is no need to repeat those observations again.

Nonetheless, the treatment of aged human remains is a delicate subject for which no revelation is forthcoming. When all is said and done, each individual must let his conscience be his guide. And each individual must tolerate points of view that differ from his own - no matter how abhorrent those differences may appear. In the final analysis, it is more noble to be tolerant than to be adherent.

According to a local newspaper, Mason and Trisko found skeletons "with escape lungs draped about them. Apparently, the Germans were preparing to abandon the U-boat when concussions from the depth charges killed them where they stood. . . . Mason brought up one of the skeletons - all that was left of one of the six men a Navy diver had found in the conning tower the day after the attack on the *U-853*." These unidentified remains were presented to a representative of the West German government. The "unknown submariner" was buried in Island Cemetery in Newport "with full U.S. military honors." Nonetheless, German officials charged Mason and Trisko with "desecrating their war dead." They neglected to suggest how this second body recovery differed from the first (recovered by the Navy). Nor did they entertain the notion of commissioning a body recovery operation that was sanctioned by the Bonn government. Their attitude appeared to be, "Let sleeping dogs lie."

Mason and Trisko made many dives during the summer of 1960. What they accomplished and how many personal belongings and U-boat components they recovered went unreported. In 1961, Mason formed a company called Sub-Marine Research Associates. He and three associates planned to raise the hulk for exhibition. Mason later sold his interest to the other associates, after which the company faded into history.

In 1968, a treasure hunting outfit called Murphy Pacific Marine Salvage claimed that, according to the Seven Year Law, any salvage rights that SMRA ever owned had since expired. The outfit also claimed to have purchased the *U-853* from the German government. How much truth there was to these claims was never established. After the initial publicity campaign, little more was heard of MPMS.

Site Popularity

I first dived on the *U-853* in 1972. There was so much collapse in the after torpedo room that I could not locate the torpedo tubes. (Today, the tops of the inner doors are exposed.) Such was not the case in the forward torpedo room, where the upper two tubes were clear of the mud that covered the bottom two tubes. The German submariners had named the torpedo tubes in addition to giving them numbers. Stenciled on the inner door of the upper starboard tube was "Hannelore." A C-clamp was secured to the lower left of this door. According to local lore, German sailors who were trapped in the compartment had tightened the clamp in place in order to stop the door from leaking. It made a dramatic story - the last ditch attempt to survive the flooding. The truth was less dramatic: one of the salvors had placed it there in an attempt to make the compartment watertight for eventual dewatering. Today, the port tube door is open, exposing a torpedo inside the tube. A spare torpedo is secured to the port rack.

Years of deterioration have not treated the U-boat kindly. As I noted in Appendix One, the pressure hull now has so many rust holes and cracked welds between the plates that outside light peeks through in a number of places. The pressure hull looks like rotten Swiss cheese.

Increased current flow has washed out much of the burden of silt. And so many divers have penetrated the hull that most of the overhead scale has been cleaned away by two generations of exhaust bubbles. No penetration dive is perfectly safe, but penetrating the *U-853* has gotten a lot less risky than it used to be. It is now possible for an experienced wreck-diver to swim completely through the hull, from the forward torpedo loading hatch to the after torpedo room, in a matter of minutes. During this tour one will see such features as the remains of lockers in the forward and after compartments, the hand-wheels of the planesman's station in the control room, the attack periscope housing, the diesel engines, the electric motors, electrical panels, and numerous valves and hand wheels. Many of the interior partitions are rusted through.

Outside, the high-pressure compressed air cylinders are exposed because the outer skin has rusted away. The snorkel is also exposed. The diesel exhaust piping is evident on the stern, as is some of the steel decking (but not the wooden decking). The 37-mm gun mount is standing, but the flack shield is gone. The anchor is in place.

Thousands of people have dived on and inside the *U-853*. Many have seen bones and left them alone. The souls that once gave life to those bones have long since departed. That is as it should be.

APPENDIX FOUR
Deep-Water U-boats

"War is sweet to those who have not experienced it."
- Erasmus

Devil's Advocate

Winston Churchill was responsible for bestowing the designation by which the German submarine became known throughout the world. In order to distinguish the British sub from the dreaded unterseeboot (literally, "under sea boat"), he called the German submarine a U-boat.

Throughout the entire history of the world, prior to the Great War, the primary purpose of a warship was to engage other warships. World War One commenced with that objective in mind. But very quickly, Germany realized that the U-boat possessed a much greater potential: to destroy or disrupt the enemy's oceanic supply lines. Doenitz made this observation first hand, when he fought against the British as a U-boat commander during World War One.

While planning strategies for World War Two, Doenitz designed submarine tactics with one thought in mind: to sink Allied merchant vessels that transported the food, fuel, and materiel that were necessary to prosecute the war against German military expansion.

Merchant seamen looked upon the dreaded U-boat as the Devil of the sea: one whose new directive was to sink ships and send sailors to Davy Jones's locker. If the U-boat was the Devil incarnate, its crewmembers were his advocates.

The Devil and his advocates got more than they bargained for. Eighty percent of them went straight to perdition at the bottom of the sea.

U-157 (Type IX-C)

Doenitz deployed the *U-157* to the Gulf of Mexico, where traffic emerging from the Mississippi River was heavy. The U-boat had not yet reached its operational area when Korvettenkapitan Wolf Henne spotted a lush target in the Straits of Florida, which separated the Florida Keys from Cuba. On June 11, 1942, Henne's torpedoes sent the tanker *Hagan* to the bottom along with six of her crew and 90,000 gallons of molasses.

A bevy of patrol planes was dispatched to search for the enemy submarine. In the dawning light, an Army B-18 bomber detected a surfaced U-boat by means of radar. The plane dived on the *U-157* before it could escape by submerging, but the bomb bay doors jammed and thwarted the attack. The plane circled as frantic crewmembers freed the doors. Four depth charges were dropped in the second attack, but by that time the U-boat had submerged.

Navy warships swarmed into the area: six from Miami and nine from Key West. All fifteen vessels converged on the last reported position from opposite directions. They were attended in the air by Army bombers. By June 12, the Florida Straits was so thoroughly covered by anti-submarine forces that the *U-157* had little opportunity to poke its periscope out of the water without being spotted by alert airmen or sailors.

Radar and sonar were its nemesis. An Army B-18 detected the U-boat during the night of June 12-13. The *U-157* avoided attack by submerging. The Key West warships drove in with their sonar units sweeping. The Coast Guard cutter *Thetis* made definite contact on the afternoon of June 13. She ran over the underwater target and dropped nine depth charges in an enveloping pattern. The detonations produced air bubbles and oil. Five other vessels dropped twenty-two additional depth charges.

The *U-157* was never heard from again.

U-215 (Type VII-D)

The Liberty ship *Alexander Macomb* stood out on her maiden voyage, bound from New York to Archangel, Russia, with 9,000 tons of sorely needed military supplies: tanks, planes, ammunition, and explosives. She was traveling under escort with a convoy of forty-one vessels. Due to dense, nighttime fog and the fear of collision, she gradually fell behind.

At 0630 on July 3, 1942, a torpedo struck aft between holds #4 and #5, where the cargo of explosives was stowed. A titanic blast ripped the ship apart and spread fire along the decks and superstructure. Chased by flames, men were driven overboard in order to escape the fiery cauldron. Three boats and a raft were launched, and these went around and picked up men who clung desperately to floating wreckage.

Three escorts turned and proceeded for the conflagration.

With the fog lifting, the *Alexander Macomb* was clearly visible under the smoke and flames. As the HMS *Le Tigre* approached, she made a sound contact with a submerged object that was moving slowly across her bow. The echo remained strong.

Lieutenant C. Hoodless stated in his action report, "at three hundred yards Submarine turned towards and approached at very high speed. A pattern of depth charges was fired at appropriate moment. He did undoubtedly pass down our Starboard side but it seems probably he was damaged, as in the next attack, movement was nothing like so fast.

"Having run to 1100 yards only just maintaining contact we turned towards and ran in to attack, once again he appeared to pass to starboard and for this reason only the starboard thrower was fired. There seems no doubt that this was a direct hit or within two or three feet as submarine immediately became stationary and all H.E. ceased."

Three crewmen from the *Alexander Macomb* watched the counterattack from their raft, half a mile away. While columns of water and the smoke of the underwater explosions hid the departing armed trawler from view, they saw the U-boat broach, roll over, and disappear.

"Both these attacks were made very close to the survivors of the torpedoed ship, and they were all the time getting closer, so much that when we ran in to deliver the coup de grâce we were unable to fire as a life raft had drifted almost directly over the submarine."

The *Le Tigre* then picked up survivors, as did the HMCS *Regina*. Ten of the crew and armed guard were lost. With the men out of the water, the HMS *Veteran* detected a faint, stationary ping on her echo ranger. She dropped more depth charges.

The British antisubmarine trawlers did their job well. They sank the *U-215*, Kapitanleutnant Fritz Hoeckner, with all hands.

U-576 (Type VII-C)

By July 1942, nearly all shipping proceeded in convoy along the shore. U-boats were lured to shallow water like moths to a flame. They had to run the gauntlet of destroyers, patrol boats, and antisubmarine trawlers. When they came up for air, they had to search the skies with the intensity of prairie dogs watching for hawks. Army, Navy, and Coast Guard planes flew overlapping sorties that filled the sky with the noise of unmuffled engines.

U-boats could not relax their vigil for a moment. Whereas five months earlier they were enemies to be feared, now they themselves cowered in fear.

Attacks against U-boats became more aggressive. On the twelfth of July, Coast Guard plane #5772, piloted by Lieutenant E. B. Ing, drove down another U-boat off Cape Hatteras. He saw a disturbance in the water that he identified as the swirl of a diving U-boat. Ing figured that he had been spotted. Instead of pressing home an abortive attack, he lingered high over the area and waited patiently for the U-boat to reappear. He was rewarded by the wake of a periscope. Because the water off the Carolinas was so clear, once overhead he could discern the entire outline of the U-boat. He dived down at high speed, leveled off at two hundred feet, and dropped two 325-pound depth charges that straddled the cigar-shaped hull. He observed that the bow of the U-boat was kicked sharply to the side by the force of the blast, and later noticed a light film of oil on the surface of the sea. He had severely damaged the undersea marauder.

The next day, Army plane *B-17-E* patrolled the same sector. Captain A. H. Tuttle "established an instrument contact and almost at once sighted a submarine." It appeared to languish on the surface almost motionless. It was either the same U-boat that was damaged the day before by Ing, or another one that was caught completely off guard. Tuttle called to his bombardier to get ready. The plane swooped down from eight hundred feet, leveled off at two hundred, and, still traveling at one hundred sixty miles per hour, released six depth charges in rapid succession. The U-boat was straddled with explosives. The tail gunner saw the U-boat roll first to one side, then to the other, as plumes of water shot into the air.

After the U-boat submerged, Tuttle saw unidentifiable debris and a large oil slick staining the clear blue water. He circled the spot for five hours, keeping a visual as well as a radar check on the area. Despite the severity of the attacks, and the proximity of the depth charge explosions, the U-boat survived. But its patrol was prematurely ended. As it headed for home, it left behind an ocean that was lorded over by antisubmarine warfare units. Its report to Doenitz must have had nothing but a paralyzing effect on the future of the U-boat war in the Eastern Sea Frontier.

Into this angry wasp's nest charged the *U-576*, Kapitanleutnant Hans-Dieter Heinicke. On the night of the fifteenth, he surfaced in the middle of Convoy KS-520. The nineteen-vessel convoy had assembled in the Chesapeake Bay for the journey south. The escort consisted of two destroyers, two patrol boats, a Canadian corvette, and two Coast Guard cutters. In addition, a Navy blimp tagged along in the air, while patrol bombers offered fast offensive protection.

Heinicke had much to contend with. The heavily escorted convoy system offered very little opportunity for a sneak attack, much less a sustained assault.

Every Allied warrior knew his part and played it well. Even though the sun was still adorning the afternoon sky, Heinicke could not afford to let such a golden opportunity pass. He let loose a barrage of torpedoes that scythed through the parallel columns with deadly accuracy.

First struck was the *Chilore*, lead ship in the second column. At thirty-second intervals, the *J.A. Mowinckel*, second ship in the fourth column, and the *Bluefields*, third ship in the fifth column, were struck. This was the textbook convoy attack, shot from the leading forward quarter, so that any torpedo that missed the closest target had a prime opportunity of striking an overlapping target in the farther columns. Heinicke had delivered the attack flawlessly.

The *Bluefields* went down in four minutes. The USS *Spry* rescued her crew.

The *Chilore* suffered no casualties. Her forepeak was blown in and flooding, but not dangerously. The *J.A. Mowinckel* shuddered with the shock that tore a twenty-by-twenty-foot hole in her stern, and disabled the steering gear. One seaman was killed by the blast, twenty others were injured. Both ships lost way as the rest of the convoy dispersed.

Immediately following the detonations, the bow of the *U-576* broke the surface in the middle of the convoy. Perhaps Heinicke had not compensated adequately for the sudden weight loss of so many torpedoes. He might even have thought that the merchantmen would shield him from view of the escorts that surrounded the convoy.

In any case, the U-boat was spotted from the air by two alert Navy planes, and by the gun crew of the steamship *Unicoi*. As the planes dived on their target, the deck gun of the *Unicoi* burst into action: one well placed shot struck the U-boat aft. The *Unicoi* ceased firing as the planes dived in for the kill.

From the action report: "Ens. Lewis attacked immediately from ahead, dropping two Mark 17 depth charges in salvo with a fifty-foot depth setting which detonated in a perfect straddle of the conning tower. One charge actually slid off the starboard side of the submarine. At the instant of detonation the submarine's deck was just under the surface. The submarine's speed was about three knots at this time. After this attack the submarine was observed to veer to the right and to list to starboard. Black oil and bubbles came to the surface. Ens. Webb attacked shortly after the previous spray had subsided diving from the starboard quarter and dropping two Mark 17 depth charges in a salvo with a fifty-foot depth setting. Both charges detonated very close to the submarine on the starboard side just forward of the conning tower. At this time the submarine was sinking fast and was completely under at the time of the second set of explosions but with little headway. Shortly thereafter the scene of action was completely covered with oil and debris making it difficult to determine whether this was from the submarine or the sinking ship."

Sometime during the confusion, several merchantmen opened up with their deck guns against the exposed conning tower. Afterward, the U.S. destroyer *Ellis* made a well-defined sound contact, and drove in with two full patterns of depth charges.

The *U-576* went right to the bottom: no survivors.

The last reports that Doenitz received from Heinicke were "13/7/42 damaged from A/C bombs. Am attempting repairs, moving off to eastward," and, the next day, "Repairs not possible." It seems as if, this time, Lieutenant Ing got his man, and succeeded in weakening him for his final conflict.

Along with the destruction of the *U-215* and the *U-701*, three U-boats were sunk in twelve days. This was not just a turning point in the U-boat campaign against the American eastern seaboard. It was virtually the end. From this point on, U-boat action in the Eastern Sea Frontier was anticlimactic: a mere mopping up operation. Planes, armed merchant ships, and well-equipped escorts, all working in unison, were too well organized for the lone gray wolves.

U-166 (Type IX-C)

The *U-166* was dispatched to lay mines at the mouth of the Mississippi River (in the Gulf Sea Frontier). On June 11, 1942, the U-boat was slinking through the Florida Straits when a small sailing vessel hove into view. Oberleutnant Hans-Gunter Kuhlmann ordered his gun crew to action stations. They shelled and sank the helpless *Carmen*, which grossed a mere 84 tons, and left the crew to fend for themselves.

On July 13, Kuhlmann torpedoed one freighter out of a convoy of eleven vessels. After the *Oneida* sank, he stealthily avoided the attacks of the armed escorts. Kuhlmann did not always set his sights so high, for three days later his gun crew blasted apart the fishing trawler *Gertrude*, this vessel grossing only 16 tons.

Kuhlmann sowed his mines during the night of July 24-25. His efforts were wasted, for none of the mines ever detonated.

On July 30, some 45 miles from the Southwest Pass of the Mississippi River, Kuhlmann torpedoed and sank the passenger-freighter *Robert E. Lee*. Seventeen people perished, but 390 managed to get away in lifeboats and were later picked up by rescue vessels.

In harsh retaliation, the newly commissioned escort vessel *PC-566* charged into the fray, undaunted by the possibility of getting in the line of fire. Her sonar gear pinged off a hard target that was diving to deeper depths. The *PC-566* did not jump the gun like a novice might have done. She led the U-boat by the distance that was required for her explosive ordnance to sink to the depth of the U-boat before commencing her counterattack.

Nine depth charges were dropped in a pattern that straddled the target laterally and vertically. The detonations put paid to the *U-166*. It went down with all hands to a depth of 5,000 feet in the Mississippi Canyon.

As noted in Chapter One, credit for sinking the *U-166* was originally given to a Coast Guard amphibious plane that dropped its sole depth charge on a submerging U-boat off the coast of Louisiana on August 1. This

U-boat was likely the *U-177*, which escaped unharmed and returned to Germany.

The *U-166* was located in 1986 during a routine oil and gas survey, but it was not correctly identified until 2001. The wreck lay one mile from the site of the *Robert E. Lee.*

U-521 (Type IX-C)

Kapitanleutnant Klaus Bargsten cruised into the ESF at the end of the May 1943. He started his patrol off the North Carolina coast, then prowled northward until he was as close as a hundred miles to Virginia. On June 2, while Bargsten lay in his bunk reading a travel book, immersed in a chapter entitled "Middletown, U.S.A.", the sound operator reported propeller noises. Because it was daytime, and because of previous sightings of planes and warships, the U-boat maintained a depth of one hundred feet.

Overhead, Convoy NG-355 was proceeding from New York City to Guantanamo Bay, Cuba, when one of its escorts, the *PC-565*, made a sound contact. She veered off for a routine check, set her depth charges in accordance with her ranging gear to explode at one hundred feet, and dropped a standard five depth-charge harassment pattern.

Inside the *U-521*, the accuracy of the depth charges shattered instruments, knocked out breakers, blew out the lights, stopped the electric motors, and disabled the diving planes and rudder. Cold seawater spurted into the conning tower through ruptured pressure gauges. Amid the debris and darkness, Bargsten gave the order to dive for cover.

After a few seconds, Oberleutnant (Ing.) Henning reported that the boat was sinking. It was already down to five hundred feet and dropping rapidly. Even though it did not make sense to Bargsten that the U-boat could plummet so quickly on an even keel, he gave the order to blow all ballast. The main depth gauge must have been knocked askew by the depth-charge blast for, before he knew it, the *U-521* broke the surface. Bargsten snapped open the conning tower hatch and rushed outside to assess the situation.

The *PC-565* stood only a quarter mile away. She opened fire with her 20-mm gun, and turned to ram. Shells burst on and around the U-boat's conning tower. The *PC-565's* gun jammed. The USS *Brisk* let loose with her deck gun, but fired only one shot before the *PC-565* got in her line of fire.

Realizing that his boat was done for, Bargsten shouted down the conning tower to open the sea cocks and abandon ship. He saw Henning climbing up the ladder, but before the engineering officer reached the hatch, the U-boat suddenly sank from under the captain's feet. The last thing Bargsten saw was a maelstrom of water pouring into the open conning tower hatch. Then the *U-521* was gone, and Bargsten was left floating in the ocean.

With trained professional conduct, the *PC-565* turned as the U-boat slipped beneath the waves, ran a parallel course, led the swirl by a hundred feet, and dropped another depth charge. Huge bubbles of air rose to the surface, followed by iridescent slicks of oil. Chunks of freshly broken wood and pieces of vegetable fiber littered the sea.

Bargsten was the sole survivor. Several large chunks of human flesh were recovered, leading to the belief that other German sailors had been ascending to the surface when the last depth charge detonated among them.

U-550 (Type IX-C-40)

The ESF enjoyed a winter devoid of the baying of undersea wolves. With spring came the aggressors, and more death. Convoy CU-21, consisting of twenty-eight merchant vessels and six escorts, departed New York for England on April 15, 1944. Instead of continuing out of the swept channel for the Hudson Canyon as planned, the convoy steered due east in order to avoid an inbound convoy. Thick fog caused quite a bit of confusion, resulting in a collision between the *Aztec* and the *Sag Harbor*. As these merchantmen dropped out of the convoy, the rest proceeded for the grouping area that lay south of Nantucket.

The *Pan-Pennsylvania*, making fourteen knots, jockeyed for position among the local group. Around midnight, without warning, a torpedo struck her port side aft, blowing a fifty-foot hole in the side of No. 8 tank, ripping up the main deck, knocking out the steering mechanism, and destroying No. 4 lifeboat. No one was injured by the blast.

The ship settled slightly, and there was a fire in the boiler room as some of the cargo of eighty-octane gasoline seeped into the bilges, but the vessel was not in immediate danger of sinking. Nonetheless, a group of panicked crewmen and armed guard personnel jumped into a lifeboat and lowered away. Captain Delmar Leidy was unable to stop them. Because the tanker still had considerable momentum, the lifeboat swamped as soon as it touched the water, and all the men drowned.

Captain Leidy kept the rest of the men aboard, lest the flames in the boiler room ignite the gasoline-covered sea like a giant torch. Destroyer escorts converged on the burning tanker. The *Joyce* drove in to pick up survivors while the *Peterson* covered her.

The *Gandy* swung in a wide arc at flank speed and began a sonar sweep. A torpedo passed by the *Gandy* on a parallel course, missing the warship by seventy-five yards. The destroyer escort then stood erratically down the course for three miles, but failed to establish contact. Worse yet, her No. 4 engine destroyed her crankcase because of overheating cylinders; she was forced to a reduced and unbalanced speed.

The *Gandy* swept back toward the scene of the rescue operation then in progress. The *Pan-Pennsylvania* was slowly but surely settling by the stern, so Captain Leidy gave the order to abandon ship. Three men were crushed between No. 2 lifeboat and the tanker's hull. There were too many survivors for the *Joyce* to handle, so the *Peterson* was ordered to assist. Thirty-one survivors, including Captain Leidy, clambered aboard the

Joyce; the *Peterson* picked up another twenty. As the *Gandy* circled close to cover them, another torpedo track passed by her.

The wily U-boat was hiding under and close along-side the sinking tanker, masking it from sonar sweeps. With the last of the survivors safely on her deck, the *Joyce* got up speed and raced toward a target that her astute sound man heard on his earphones. She dropped a pattern of thirteen depth charges on shallow settings. The bow of the *U-550*, Kapitanleutnant Klaus Hanert, was blown to the surface by the force of the underwater detonations.

From the bridge of the *Gandy*, Lieutenant Commander W. A. Sessions shouted, "Right full rudder, come to 320, open fire, and stand by to ram." The U-boat's forward momentum was more than Commander Sessions anticipated, so he quickly ordered the rudder thrown back to port. Germans poured out of the conning tower hatch and rushed for the guns. At the last moment, with collision imminent, Lieutenant H. W. Perkerson ordered the sound head hoisted.

Commander Sessions aimed the *Gandy* at the after antiaircraft gun mount, but missed by twenty-five feet. The bow of the destroyer escort sliced through the U-boat just abaft the deadly armament. The rudder was kept at "left full" in order to throw the propellers clear. Accompanying the awful, grinding scrape of steel on steel was the cacophony of gunfire that was directed at the men on the U-boat. Several Germans fell under the hail of machine gun bullets, but others rushed to take their places at the guns.

Now the *Gandy* and the *U-550* ran along a parallel course. Guns from the destroyer continued to rake the conning tower and gun positions of the U-boat until Commander Sessions heard a voice "on one of our voice radios shouting something in a Germanic accent. Supposing it an offer to surrender, I ordered 'cease firing' which, after a few seconds delay, got through to the guns. Almost immediately the sub manned a machine gun battery and commenced firing on us. We swung left to bring guns to bear."

The deck of the U-boat was littered with the dead and dying. Aboard the *Gandy*, four men lay wounded. Tracer shells from the running gun battle struck the *Pan-Pennsylvania*, igniting the growing pool of gasoline that surrounded her. The sea erupted in a sheet of flames.

The *Peterson* cornered the U-boat from the other side of the *Gandy*, and fired two shallow-set depth charges from her starboard K-guns. Severely holed and damaged, the *U-550* became unmanageable. Hanert ordered abandon ship and scuttling charges set. An explosion ripped open her pressure hull aft. The U-boat sank by the stern, leaving only thirteen of her crew on the surface. The *Joyce* picked up the survivors.

The *Gandy* suffered the loss of four feet of her reinforced bow strake, had several antennas shot away, and had numerous .50-caliber and shrapnel holes. For a warship only eight days out of shakedown, her crew had performed their duties well under her baptism of fire.

The *Pan-Pennsylvania* capsized and sank.

Of the thirteen survivors from the *U-550*, one died of his injuries and was buried at sea the following day. Hanert and the other eleven men were imprisoned aboard the *Joyce*. All three escort vessels rejoined the convoy and completed the transatlantic crossing. The German prisoners were then turned over to authorities at Londonderry, Northern Ireland.

On May 5, fully nineteen days after the double tragedy, Coastal Picket Patrol Boat *CGR-3082* came across a body at sea: that of a German sailor wearing an escape lung. An autopsy report indicated no injuries except for burns on the head and face, probably from diesel oil; that the sailor had died prior to submersion, as though he had been on a raft; and that he had died only five days previous. The conclusion was that he had escaped from the submerged *U-550*, and had died on the surface.

Two other bodies were later found in the vicinity of

the sunken U-boat. The one picked up by the *SC-630* had been in the water for more than eighteen days. The one recovered by the *CGR-1989*, on May 11, was not only wearing an escape lung and a life jacket, but was still in a rubber raft: he was Wilhelm Flade, last of the *U-550's* casualties.

It was remarkable that so many men reached the surface from a depth of over 250 feet.

U-857 (Type IX-C-40)

Once again, the winter months were devoid of U-boat activity. But with spring, and with Germany's certain oncoming defeat, Doenitz made a last ditch attempt to wreak havoc off the East Coast of the United States. He sent five U-boats on virtual suicide missions, from which none returned. For a brief time only, after a hiatus of nearly three years, more than one U-boat at a time dared to operate inside the ESF.

On April 5, 1945, the *Atlantic States* was torpedoed by the *U-857*, Oberleutnant zur See Rudolf Premauer. The tanker was traveling alone and in ballast from Boston to Venezuela. As she passed Cape Cod, she was struck by a torpedo that blew in the boiler room bulkhead. Captain E. L. Lindemuth ordered abandon ship. Fifty-two crewmen and Naval gunners took to the boats, while the captain and four others remained on board. The USS *Guinivere* picked up all the men who had abandoned ship. Later, the Naval tug *ATR-14* towed the tanker back to Boston. The ship was duly repaired. There were no injuries.

While Premauer may have initially escaped, alerted antisubmarine units swarmed into action. The *Gustafson*, the *Eugene*, the *Knoxville*, and the *Micka* formed a scouting line with overlapping sound ranges, and swept the entire area north of Cape Cod. At 0212 on April 7, the *Gustafson* obtained a solid sonar contact. Like a well-oiled machine, the four warships split into a prearranged pattern, with the *Gustafson* making a dry run for evaluation, while the other three vessels conducted a box search around the point of contact.

The Navy analysis of the action was succinct: "At 0227 *Gustafson* made a hedgehog attack with negative results. At 0248 *Gustafson* made her second hedgehog attack, and obtained one explosion approximately 11 seconds after firing. An oil slick was seen at 0315 about 900 yards from scene of second attack. Four more hedgehog attacks were made by *Gustafson* at 0409, 0427, 0452, and 0503, with negative results. Contact was held until 0600 and subsequent efforts to regain it were not successful."

Each hedgehog attack consisted of twenty-four launched charges. The depth recorder indicated that the target was moving at a depth of 280 feet. The eleven-second flight time of the second attack, from launching to detonation, equated to a depth of two hundred seventy-seven feet. Yet, plotting room opinions varied from "probably sunk" to "slightly damaged" to "insufficient data." By this time in the war, the Navy had gained an incredible amount of experience not only in conducting attacks, but in understanding how much of a pounding the German machine could take and still survive.

The final recommendation stated, "It is considered that although a submarine, known to have been in this area, may have been lost, it was not lost as a result of this action."

Despite this conclusion, the *U-857* was never heard from again. In all likelihood, it was damaged beyond its ability to regain the surface, and slowly sank to the bottom at a depth of 750 feet.

U-879 (Type IX-C-40)

On April 14, Kapitanleutnant Erwin Manchen made his sole foray into the ESF about a hundred miles off Cape Henry. He cornered the *Belgian Airman*, running independently from Houston to New York, there to join a transatlantic convoy. Her cargo holds were filled with sorghum in bulk and dairy feed in bags.

The U-boat's torpedo struck the Belgian freighter on the starboard side opposite No. 5 hatch, blowing a gaping hole in her hull and damaging the main antenna and signal mast. The ship lingered for four hours, until 1600. The only casualty was a seaman who hit his head while jumping into the lifeboat, fell into the sea, and drowned. The *Harold A. Jordan* picked up the remainder of the crew.

The *U-879* did not make it home. Four days later it was trounced some two hundred miles east of Cape Cod, by the U.S. destroyer escorts *Buckley* and *Reuben James*. There were no survivors.

U-548 (Type IX-C-40)

Two U-boats remained in the ESF, but only because they had so far failed to reveal themselves. Now they took turns at sniping and hiding. First of this pair to attack was the *U-548*, Kapitanleutnant Erich Krempl, on April 18. The target was the *Swiftscout*, then about one hundred fifty miles off Cape Henry.

The *Swiftscout* was traveling independently from the Delaware Capes to Puerta La Cruz, Venezuela, in ballast. At 0925, a torpedo struck low in No. 6 tank, port side, and broke the ship's back. The bow and stern angled upward as the midship section slowly folded like a jackknife. No one was injured by the blast. Both bow and stern gun crews fired at what they thought was a U-boat, and managed to keep it submerged. Twenty minutes later, however, a second torpedo followed the path of the first, and completed the destruction of the midship area. The ship buckled and sank. Chief Engineer Alfred Brennan drowned during the subsequent evacuation.

Captain Peter Katsares sent a distress call using the emergency transmitter with which the lifeboats were equipped. The *Chancellorsville* intercepted the message and soon had all the survivors safely onboard.

The other U-boat was the *U-853*, which accounted for the loss of the *Eagle 56*. See Appendix Three for details.

On April 23, the *U-548* attacked the Norwegian tanker *Katy*. The tanker was en route from New York to

Houston, in ballast, when a torpedo slammed into her No. 1 tank. A distress call was transmitted immediately. Fearing a follow-up attack, the master ordered his merchant crew to abandon ship. He stayed aboard with his officers and the armed guard.

Although the *Katy* was so far down by the bow that her propeller stuck out of the water, those still onboard managed to shift enough water ballast to right the ship. Three lifeboats returned. The *Katy* proceeded unassisted at six knots to Lynnhaven Roads, Virginia, arriving early on the twenty-fourth. A Coast Guard cutter brought in the men in the other lifeboat. There were no casualties.

The *U-548* escaped undetected that time, but a week later it met its nemesis. On April 30, the U-boat poked its periscope out of the water, directly in the path of Convoy KN-382: thirty-six ships in nine columns headed north at eight and a half knots. Before the *U-548* could launch a torpedo, it was detected by the U.S. patrol escort *Natchez*.

The *Natchez* homed in on the sonar contact. Almost immediately she spotted the high wake of a snorkel tube and the clearly discernible feather of a periscope. *Natchez* altered course to ram, but did not realize how quickly the snorkel boat was moving. The *U-548* charged ahead on its diesels, feeding them air that was sucked in through the snorkel tube. The *Natchez* overshot the U-boat, which passed in the opposite direction close off the port side. The *Natchez* released an "embarrassing pattern of hydrostatically set Mark 8 charges," and reversed her course to pursue.

By this time, the entire convoy was bearing down on them. The *Natchez* was forced to take evasive maneuvers in order to avoid being run down by her own ships. The convoy executed an emergency turn to starboard, clearing the area where the U-boat had submerged. Three destroyer escorts turned back to hold the U-boat at bay.

As the *Natchez* cleared the rear of the convoy, she regained sound contact. The U-boat was dead ahead.

340   *Appendix Four*

Natchez backed down on her engines and made an ahead-thrown attack with her forward hedgehogs. Contact was temporarily lost in the noise of the underwater detonations. When it was regained, the *Natchez* drove in and delivered a depth-charge attack.

By this time, the destroyer escorts had arrived. The *Natchez* stood off while the *Thomas*, the *Coffman*, and the *Bostwick* took turns crisscrossing the position that was triangulated by the coordinated sonar scans. The U-boat "maneuvered radically during entire period of contact, turning in circles, fishtailing, changing speeds, backing down, and on two occasions firing pillenwerfers." (A pillenwerfer, or pill thrower, was a decoy device that ejected a calcium-zinc compound that dissolved in seawater to create bubbles to confuse enemy sonar.)

These concerted attacks continued for eight hours, until after dawn. Large amounts of oil were then seen on the surface. Breaking-up noises were detected on the sonar gear during the final attack. Eighteen minutes after the last set of depth charges had been dropped, a loud underwater explosion was heard. Then there was silence. The *U-548* had gasped its last.

Surrendered U-boats

According to the terms of Germany's capitulation, all U-boats that were still on patrol were ordered to proceed to the nearest Allied port and to surrender. Six U-boats that were operating in the Atlantic Ocean headed toward America shores. They were met offshore and escorted to the nearest port.

Shelburne, Nova Scotia received the *U-889* (Type IX-C-40)

Portsmouth, New Hampshire received the *U-234* (Type X-B), the *U-805* (Type IX-C-40), the *U-873* (Type IX-D-2), and the *U-1228* (Type IX-C-40).

Cape May, New Jersey received the *U-858* (Type IX-C-40).

All six U-boats were eventually scuttled in deep water off Cape Cod, Massachusetts.

APPENDIX FIVE
Niggling Inaccuracies and Misconceptions

"He occasionally stumbled over the truth, but hastily picked himself up and hurried on as if nothing had happened."

- Winston Churchill

Whole Cloth

On page X of *Shadow Divers*, it was written, "Everything was checked against multiple sources." If that statement were true, it would not have been possible to make such a large number of errors.

The purpose of this appendix is to emphasize for the uninformed reader the sheer wealth and magnitude of misinformation that *Shadow Divers* represented as fact. Errors range from sloppy research to shipwreck ignorance to internal inconsistencies to matters of omission to distortions of the truth - and everything in between.

In Chapter Three, I wrote at length about five major incidents whose accounts in *Shadow Divers* were grossly misrepresented. In Chapter Four, I wrote about two incidents in which I was directly involved. Here I will write about a number of topics of which I have personal knowledge. These examples will serve to demonstrate additionally how *Shadow Divers* was cavalier with the facts.

My faithful readers are warned that the number of factual departures in *Shadow Divers* was so overwhelming that this appendix might prove to be tedious for all but the aficionado of truth, justice, and the American way. On the other hand, this appendix provides a preponderance of evidence to support the argument that much of the material of which *Shadow Divers* was woven was merely whole cloth.

My Friendship with Bill Nagle

I first met Bill Nagle on November 19, 1972. After being introduced by mutual friend John Riley, we struck up a conversation as we loaded our gear onto Jim Dulinski's boat, the *Big Jim*. On the way to the *Hvoslef*, a small freighter that was torpedoed thirty years earlier by the *U-94*, we decided to dive together. It was the beginning of a long friendship.

Later, he was elected president of the Main Line Dive Club. I was elected vice president. His fiancé Ashley was the secretary. I was in their wedding. I was a constant visitor to their home. I was there when their son and daughter were born. Over the years, Nagle and I shared some tremendous adventures and two shipwreck discoveries (the U.S. submarine *Tarpon* off North Carolina, and an unidentified nineteenth-century steamer off New Jersey.

In addition to diving together locally, we carpooled on many, many trips: to New York, to North Carolina, and to Florida. Usually we drove together to the boat, but dived solo, then compared notes afterward. In 1980, he and I dived as buddies on the *Andrea Doria*. The following spring we dived as buddies on the *Wilkes-Barre*, off Key West, when Billy Deans first started to run trips to the World War Two light cruiser.

Of all the friends Bill Nagle ever had, I was his closest companion. I knew him better than anyone else except his parents and his wife. The people who met Nagle in the mid to late 1980's - after he embarked upon a lonely course through drug abuse and alcoholism - could not possibly have known Nagle as I knew him. They knew him as a drunkard on a downward spiral to perdition. I knew him as a person.

Nagle passed away on November 15, 1993. He was forty-two years old. I attended his funeral and cried like a baby. I miss Bill as much as I miss those wonderful carefree days that we shared when our world was a simpler place.

Finagling the Facts

On page 3 of *Shadow Divers*, it was written that Nagle had to be careful not to plunge through the rotten planks of a rickety dock. This was unlikely, as local ordnances mandated that public use areas be maintained in good condition for the safety of the public, under threat of penalties. I have departed from the very same dock for years, and never saw any rotten planks. Furthermore, divers walked along this dock carrying 100-pound sets of doubles in their arms or wearing their tanks on their back, without fear of plunging through the planks.

On page 6 it was written, "Early divers like Nagle had bad experiences every day." This statement is silly if not downright juvenile, and tends to impeach the book's acknowledged expert. Allowing that the quotation was a gross exaggeration, divers did not even have bad experiences on every *diving* day. In reality, bad diving days were few and far between, and a diver of Nagle's competence and experience almost never had bad diving days. Nagle was skilled but cautious and never overbold.

It was written on page 5, "Men died - often - diving the shipwrecks that called to Nagle." This sentence falls into the same category as the one in the preceding paragraph. Diving fatalities were fewer and farther between than bad days. By 1991 - the date of the *Shadow Divers* reference - there were fewer than a score of wreck-diving fatalities along the entire eastern seaboard since the inception of the activity in 1955.

On page 7 it was written that a photograph of Nagle hung in the wheelhouse of the *Sea Hunter* next to one of Lloyd Bridges. There were never any photographs hung in the wheelhouse of the *Sea Hunter*. A portrait of Karl Doenitz hung in the cabin.

Also on page 7, it was written that Nagle recovered two helms from the *Coimbra* in a single day. In fact, he recovered one helm in a single day. I photographed it under water, and helped to haul it over the transom and onto the deck. This photograph and the information were published in *Shipwrecks of New York.* Jon Hulburt and Rick Jaszyn were with us on the *Sea Hunter*, Captain Sal Arena. The date was July 31, 1981.

Again on page 7, it was written that Nagle recovered "a four-foot-tall brass whistle from the paddle wheeler *Champion.*" In fact, the whistle stood two feet tall and came from an unidentified steamship that I named Galimore's Cayru; it was not a paddle wheeler. Only three of us were on the *Seeker* that day: Nagle, John Moyer, and this author. I found the whistle on my solo tie-in dive, but was unable to extract it from under the heavy beam that pinned it to the seabed. I told Nagle where it was and how to get there. Because he outweighed me by fifty pounds, he was strong enough to lift the beam and pull out the steam whistle.

Contrary to what was written on page 4 of *Shadow Divers*, Nagle did not build the *Seeker*. He did not plan the boat's construction. The *Seeker* was commissioned by a man who designed the boat as a private yacht for his family. The man (whose name is unknown to me) died shortly after completion. The boat sat in the shipyard for more than a year before Nagle chanced upon it. He bought it, removed the luxurious chairs and sofas, pulled up the carpets, modified the interior layout, added a wheelhouse, and equipped the boat for diving.

When Nagle discovered the *U-869*, he was quoted as saying (on page 44), "This is deeper than I was expecting." This quotation implied that he did not know how to read a nautical chart. Any skipper who was worth his salt could plot a position on a chart to determine its approximate depth before going to that location.

Nagle was neither a reader nor a researcher. He did not devour academic texts, reference works, novels, blueprints, or any material that he could uncover on historical ships - despite what was written on page 6 of *Shadow Divers*. I never knew him to visit a museum, archive, or library. Nagle had very little interest in shipwreck history. His primary diving interest - practically his *sole* diving interest - was the recovery of artifacts. History was a distraction that he left for me to pursue.

Even after our falling out, in 1986, Nagle used to call me at odd hours of the day and night. Over the phone I could hear the clink of ice in his glass of alcohol, and the hissing inhale as he smoked. Seldom was he coherent. Mostly he wanted to rag about everything that was wrong with his life. But he never accepted advice on how to mend his ways.

Nagle called me after he discovered the *U-869*. Primarily he wanted to gloat, because by 1991 we had gone our separate ways. He told me that the loran numbers "came from Bogan," not a fisherman nicknamed Skeets (as it was written on page 15). By this he meant one of the local head boat skippers: a family that had been running charters since at least the 1930's. They were interested in knowing more about the wrecks that they fished. Because of the length of time during which the Bogan family had engaged in charter operations, they had collected a large number of "hangs" that were producible fishing spots.

Nagle certainly had his character flaws, but lying was not one of them.

He called for another reason. He wanted to pick my brain about U-boats that had been lost off the New Jersey coast. The only book that had that information was *Track of the Gray Wolf*, a copy of which he possessed. That was the "pile of research papers" that *Shadow Divers* claimed he had (on page 64). An appendix listed the latitude and longitude of every Allied and neutral vessel that was sunk by enemy action, and all the U-boats that were known to have been lost in the Eastern Sea Frontier. We went over the positions together. He was cagey about the actual location of the U-boat that he discovered. He told me only that it was "out by the Tower" (meaning the *Texas Tower*). No U-boat was known to have been lost closer than a hundred miles to the *Texas Tower*.

The attack reports that were mentioned on page 65 of *Shadow Divers* - reports of the *U-550* and the *U-521* - were described in *Track of the Gray Wolf*. Nagle had no other information on U-boats.

On page 206 of *Shadow Divers*, it was written that, in 1992, Nagle ran the *Seeker* to the *Andrea Doria* for three months straight, and that therefore the boat was unavailable for charter to the *U-869*. In fact, Nagle ran only two trips to the *Andrea Doria* that year, each of three days duration, and both in July. Otherwise, he had local weekend charters that were scheduled out of his homeport of Brielle, New Jersey. The rest of the time the boat was available for charter.

Shadow Divers neglected to mention that when the *Seeker* was not available, Chatterton joined divers who went to the *U-869* on other charter boats, such as the *Calypso* and the *John Jack*. The book gave the mistaken impression that only the *Seeker* was used for trips to the U-boat.

Tainted Idol

Chatterton did not meet Nagle until he had passed his prime as a diver and was on the decline. By 1986, Nagle had burned a hole through his nose from sniffing cocaine. His dedication had shifted from diving to drug abuse and alcoholism. All of his friends and family worked hard to redirect his misplaced energy, to no avail. He died sick and lonely in a lifestyle of his own choosing.

Shadow Divers went to great lengths to portray Nagle as an extraordinary person by exaggerating his audacity, accomplishments, and prowess; by misrepresenting him as a devoted shipwreck researcher; and by extolling virtues that he did not possess. I do not mean to besmirch my friend's reputation by correcting the conspicuous exaggerations and by denouncing the misconceptions that *Shadow Divers* promoted.

Nagle was a highly skilled wreck-diver - *but so were a number of others.*

Shadow Divers concentrated on Chatterton's fixation on Nagle for reasons that were never explained. In all the pages of obsessive preoccupation over Nagle, the book provided only three concrete examples of his diving expertise: the recoveries of a helm, a steam whistle, and the *Andrea Doria's* bell. The first two recoveries were doubly inflated, and the book neglected to mention that on the *Andrea Doria* bell trip, Nagle gave up the search after three fruitless days and went looking for knickknacks instead. Tom Packer and I were the only two who stayed focused on searching for the bell, and we found it.

Perhaps Chatterton truly idolized Nagle - or perhaps his hero worship was merely a bombastic plot device that was designed to create conflict between Nagle and Bielenda - between so-called good and evil.

Conflict is an important plot device in fiction. I have utilized the device to good effect in my novels. But make-believe conflict and affected characterizations have no place in a book that purported to be a "true adventure."

In *Shadow Divers*, Chatterton's overt adulation of Nagle rang patently false because, after Nagle died, Chatterton did not attend his funeral. I know, because I was there.

Andrea Doria Misinformation

On page 9 of *Shadow Divers*, it was written that no one had ever been to the stern of the *Andrea Doria*. On the contrary, the first half of *Dive to an Era* describes numerous explorations of the stern of the wreck, most notably on trips that were organized by Peter Gimbel, Frederick Dumas, Bruno Vailati, Don Rodocker, and Chris DeLucchi.

Gimbel explored all sections of the wreck on trips that he made during the first two years after the *Andrea Doria* sank. In 1956, Dumas made a dive to the propeller, at a depth of 215 feet. In 1967, Vailati filmed the wreck from stem to stern for his movie, *Fate of the Andrea Doria*. The brass letters on the curved fantail were clearly depicted in the film. Al Giddings worked as a still photographer on Vailati's film production; his photographs of the stern letters were published in Stephano Carletti's book, *Andrea Doria -74*. (Minus seventy-four referred to the depth in meters.) Rodocker and DeLucchi explored the stern in their 1973 saturation expedition.

On June 26, 1984, the *Sea Hunter* deliberately anchored in the stern because the skipper, Sal Arena, wanted to prevent his customers from accessing the First Class Dining Room, which was located near the bow. Jon Hulburt photographed Steve Gatto lying on the "Keep Clear of Propellers" sign as Gatto tied in. They and Dan Medleycott, Jim Medleycott, and Brad Sheard spent all their time under water exploring the Stern Wintergarten, a few feet from the grille that the *Seeker* divers torched open four years later. (The reader may recall from Chapter Four that Hulburt was a participant in the grille cutting episode.)

Shadow Divers neglected to mention that the *Seeker* anchored near the stern when Chatterton made his very first trip to the *Andrea Doria*, in 1987. On that trip, Steve Gatto recovered the auxiliary steering helm, which he had previously reconnoitered. Bill Nagle and Bart Malone recovered the "Keep Clear of Propeller" sign. Photographs of both of these items were published in *Dive to an Era* (which was published in 1989). An entire chapter of the book was devoted to the recovery of the stern bell, which took place in 1985.

On page 8 of *Shadow Divers*, it was written that in Nagle's day, the shallowest part of the wreck was 180 feet. The shallowest part of the wreck was 165 feet, as anyone who had dived on the wreck would know.

On page 9, it was written that five anonymous men shared with Nagle the ownership of the *Andrea Doria's* bell. In fact, six divers shared ownership of the bell with Nagle: Mike Boring, Kenny Gascon, Artie Kirchner, John Moyer, Tom Packer, and this author.

As part owner of the bell, I can state unequivocally that Nagle never insured the bell: not for $100,000 as it was stated on page 9, nor for any other amount.

On page 9, it was written that Ashley drove the bell home from the dock in her station wagon and, without explaining how, lost the bell. The Nagles did not own a station wagon, and Ashley did not appear at the dock upon our return from the successful recovery mission. Nagle drove the bell home in his diesel pickup truck.

The incident in which the bell was temporarily lost occurred many months later. Nagle placed the bell on the bed of his pickup because he was going to display it at an upcoming conference. After Nagle went to work in his Snap-On Tool truck, Ashley drove the pickup to visit a friend. When the tailgate unlatched, the bell rolled out of the bed onto a rural road.

Nagle did not call the highway patrol, as it was written on page 9. Ashley called the local police. By that time, a Good Samaritan had already recovered the bell, and had informed the police of its whereabouts. Ashley retrieved the bell - not Nagle, as it was written. This entire saga was described in detail in *Dive to an Era*.

Still on page 9, it was written that the ever anonymous "they" discovered the *Andrea Doria's* bell on the fifth day of the trip. In fact, Packer and I found the bell on the fourth day.

On page 133, it was written that John "Dudas had gone to 250 feet and had taken the binnacle from inside the *Andrea Doria*." In fact, he descended into the wheelhouse to 200 feet (not 250) and recovered the compass and its cover, not the binnacle (which is the stand or pedestal on which the compass is perched).

It was written on page 38, "Three quarters of all divers who have perished on the *Andrea Doria* died with a bag full of prizes." In fact, of the thirteen fatalities, only two divers had any artifacts at all: Craig Sicola had three plates; Matthew Lawrence had two rosaries.

Andrea Doria Ownership

On page 91 of *Shadow Divers*, it was written, "Chatterton owned the *Doria*." Such a claim was absurd. In actuality, the closest that anyone came to owning the *Andrea Doria* was when John Moyer filed a salvage claim to protect his ongoing search for the ship's forward bell, which was supposed to be stowed in a compartment near the bow.

Moyer funded two full-scale expeditions to the

wreck, in 1992 and 1993. Although the bell remained elusive, the second expedition resulted in the recovery of a pair of 1,000-pound ceramic panels from the Wintergarten. These were original creations of renowned Italian artist Guido Gambone. (See *Deep, Dark, and Dangerous* for full particulars.)

Chatterton had nothing to do with these expeditions, and he never had any claim of ownership.

Chronology, Geography, and Protocol

On page 88 of *Shadow Divers*, it was written that Chatterton started wreck-diving in 1985. Yet on page 17, it was written that Chatterton first met Bill Nagle on the *Seeker* in 1984, on a trip to the *Texas Tower*, during which Chatterton recovered the body of a diver. Then, on page 89, it was written that an anonymous dive shop owner suggested late in the summer of 1985 that Chatterton should dive with Nagle on the *Seeker*, which he commenced in 1986. On page 90, it was written that Chatterton recovered the body of the diver from the *Texas Tower* in 1986. Such internal inconsistencies are more than frustrating - they are obfuscatory.

The name of the anonymous clerk that was noted in the paragraph above was not given, yet his dialogue was quoted verbatim. If the dialogue was important enough to relate, then it should be important enough to name the person whose statements were quoted. Was this a real conversation, or just another fictional plot device?

On pages 300 and 301 of *Shadow Divers*, it was written that in 1997, Billy Palmer told Chatterton and Kohler that identification tags could be found on spare parts boxes in the electric motor room. This may be true but it is irrelevant. Palmer gave this information to Steve Gatto and Tom Packer five years earlier, in 1992. It was old news in the *Shadow Divers* chronology.

On page 40 of *Shadow Divers*, it was written that, when George Place attempted to climb the ladder of the *Eagle's Nest* in raging seas, a rung from the ladder uppercut his jaw and knocked him into the ocean nearly unconscious. Howard Klein, skipper of the *Eagle's Nest*, told me that the truth was less dramatic. Place got a cramp in his leg as he was climbing up the ladder, and fell off. The seas were not raging.

On page 60, it was written that Paul Hepler ran dive trips off Long Island, New York. Hepler has been a eminent fixture on the New Jersey coast for more than thirty years. It was common knowledge that he ran his boat out of Belmar, New Jersey. The name of his boat was the *Venture*.

On page 29, it was written that divers do not unpack their dive gear until after the tie-in team sends a foam drinking cup to the surface, as a way of communicating that the grapnel is secured to the wreck. In reality, by the time the cup hits the surface, most divers are already suited and chomping at the bit to go over the side. They hit the water as soon as the cup is sighted or they hear the announcement, "Cup's up!" This is routine wreck-diving convention.

On page 200, it was written, "He had become what divers called a 'dirt dart'." This alliterative phrase was a gratuitous invention of *Shadow Divers*. Not only has the phrase never been used by any wreck-diver of my acquaintance, but a survey of experienced wreck-divers failed to locate anyone who had ever heard it.

Shipwreck Ignorance

On page 19 of *Shadow Divers*, it was written that the *Corvallis* was "reputedly sunk by Hollywood for a 1930s disaster flick." This nine-word sentence contains six errors of fact and omits one important item of information; indeed, the only correct words were the two prepositions and the indefinite article.

There was nothing "reputed" about the fate of the *Corvallis*. The circumstances of her loss were reported in contemporary newspapers such as the *New York Times*, the *Washington Post*, the *Los Angeles Times*, and the *New York Maritime Register*. A full account was published in *Shipwrecks of New Jersey: Central*.

The *Corvallis* did not sink by accident; she was

scuttled. The name of the silent movie in which the scuttling scene appeared was *The Half-Way Girl.* First National Pictures, the producer of the film, was located in Burbank, not in Hollywood. The silent movie was released in 1925, not in the 1930's. The film was not a disaster flick, but a melodrama.

Anyone who possessed a moderate knowledge of local shipwrecks, or did a minimal amount of research, should either have known these facts or should have been able to ascertain them.

On page 53 of *Shadow Divers*, it was written that the *Texas Tower* was one of the darkest of the northeast's deep wrecks. Quite the contrary, the *Texas Tower* is one of the brightest of deep wrecks. It lies far enough offshore to be bathed in the warm, clear water of the Gulf Stream. Ambient light visibility is generally better than fifty feet, and often exceeds seventy-five. The constant penetration of bright sunlight accounts for the growth of kelp that graces the upper surfaces of the wreck.

On page 17 of *Shadow Divers*, it was written that the depth of the *Texas Tower* was 200 feet, that the wreck could be explored at 85 feet, and that it was a "very dangerous wreck." In actuality, the depth of the *Texas Tower* is 185 feet (although washouts may go a few feet deeper), and it rose to within 65 feet of the surface (although today, as a result of deterioration and gradual collapse, it does not rise as high). The shallow depth to the top of the wreck, coupled with astonishingly bright visibility, made the *Texas Tower* a perfect novice dive, and one of the least dangerous to explore. The actual depths and conditions are common knowledge, especially among those who have dived on the wreck.

With respect to the discovery of the U-Who? in 1991, on page 55 it was written that anonymous divers had searched for and researched the submarine *S-5* for years, and were certain that the wreck lay near Maryland. This sentence implied that the people on board the *Seeker* that day considered the possibility that the unidentified submarine might be the *S-5*.

It was common knowledge among northeast wreck-divers that Milt Herchenrider and Steve Sokoloff discovered the *S-5* in 1985, off the coast of Delaware. A full account of the discovery was readily available in *Shipwrecks of Delaware and Maryland*.

On page 15 of *Shadow Divers*, it was written that the *U-869* lies in a bad place, a dangerous place, near an edge where a huge current comes up over the continental shelf. The *U-869* is not near any drop-off. The continental shelf is thirty miles away. The wreck lies closer to shore than the *Texas Tower*. The *Texas Tower* is shallower because it was built on a sea mount. The currents in the vicinity of the *U-869* are no different than they are anywhere else offshore.

Anyone who dived consistently on the *U-869* should know this. The oceanographic information is readily available on the offshore nautical chart.

On page 9 of *Shadow Divers*, it was written, "A single day on the open Atlantic in a sixty-five foot boat will turn intestines inside out." Millions of certified can verify that this statement is totally absurd. Nearly every day on the ocean is a pleasant experience.

Marriage on the Rocks

Shadow Divers went to extraordinary lengths to describe how Kohler's and Chatterton's marriages were adversely affected by their so-called obsession with diving on and identifying the *U-869*, and how this obsession was directly responsible for each of their divorces. The book gave the impression that they passed every waking moment in the passionate pursuit of a single-minded goal and ignored their spouses and home lives.

Nothing could be farther from the truth. A handful of annual dives and a few days of casual research can hardly qualify as a time-consuming obsession, despite the fact that their short story was padded to the length of a novel in order to describe the situation. Their divorces had nothing to do with diving or with the *U-869*.

Both Kohler and Chatterton spoke volubly and angrily about their problems with their wives, not only as their problems arose but as they developed. The real reasons were well known to a small clique of wreck-divers. Kohler confided in me on more than one occasion about the true reason for his divorce, and why he did not want his wife to obtain custody of their children. Chatterton was just as open but less graphic.

In this instance, however, I prefer not to reveal what Kohler and Chatterton told me. Readers who wish to know the prurient details will have to obtain the facts elsewhere. The antiseptic *Shadow Divers* versions bore no resemblance to what I heard from the horses' mouths.

Going Postal

On page 146 of *Shadow Divers*, it was written that Chatterton received mail that was addressed simply to "John Chatterton - Diver - New Jersey." I pray that none of the readers of *Shadow Divers* was stupid enough to believe this. If any readers were that stupid, the world is in grave trouble.

Nonetheless, being the thorough researcher that I am, I invested the cost of first class postage in order to ascertain the delivery capabilities of the United States Postal Service. The letter was promptly returned to me, stamped with advice that read "Returned For Better Address."

Solipsism

Solipsism is the theory that the self is the only reality. A solipsist is one who believes that he is the center of the universe, and that everything else exists solely for his pleasure and convenience.

Shadow Divers presented a solipsistic view of wreck-diving in general and the *U-869* in particular. Time and again, the uninformed readers of *Shadow Divers* were given a one-man show in which no other participants appeared. The wreck-diving community was presented as a void, like the vacuum of space.

Uninformed readers who accepted the book at face value might have inferred that Chatterton was the only person who ever took affirmative action toward wreck research, body recovery, and lifesaving.

Those who made contributions to research were ignored. Divers whose assistance was invaluable were not mentioned. People who rendered first aid were disregarded. The result was a story that was practically devoid of essential group dynamics, which were sacrificed in order to spotlight a pair of devotional characters.

All too often, *Shadow Divers* brandished Chatterton and his sidekick Kohler as the only two people on a boat that was actually carrying ten to fifteen divers. Those others were given no existence.

Macho Man

The book was incredibly sexist. The word "man" was used almost exclusively instead of generic words such as "diver" or "person." I found this usage offensive because it implied that diving was some kind of manly competition in which women should not engage because of their frailty and fear.

The book named only one female diver, and that in passing. In fact, diving is a leisure time activity that is enjoyed by children and women of all ages.

Diving requires skill (like skiing), not brute strength (like weight lifting). The macho imagery implied that only the hardiest of "men" could hope to accomplish anything, and that Chatterton and Kohler were the hardiest of the hardiest.

On page 23, it was written that deep wreck-diving conspired to "attack a man's mind and disassemble his spirit." This was juvenile claptrap.

Anonymity

The plot of *Shadow Divers* was strung together by a thread of anonymity. Time and again, *Shadow Divers* referred to people and places without mentioning names. This literary vagueness gave the illusion of credence without providing the means to verify or confirm the statements that the uninformed reader was expected to accept.

On page 85, Chatterton attended an unnamed commercial diving school in Camden, New Jersey. On page 88, he spoke with an unnamed clerk. On page 89, he received advice from an unnamed dive shop owner. On page 173, he referred to an unnamed U-boat enthusiast. Other instances of anonymity are analyzed elsewhere in *Shadow Divers Exposed.*

Ouching the King's English

I will not bother to mention such minor but annoying errors as the continuous use of the word "grapple" instead of "grapnel." Every wreck-diver should know that a wreck is hooked with a grapnel (spelled with an "n"), and certainly every certified boat captain should know this. Nor will I mention the use of "speaker tube" instead of "speaking tube" (spelled with an "ing"). Niggling grammatical discrepancies appeared throughout the book.

There is no such astronomical body as a "sweltering moon," as described on page 77 of *Shadow Divers.* The Moon reflects the light of the sun but not its heat.

That's (Not) All, Folks!

But enough is enough!

I have left hundreds of additional flaws unaddressed, as well as numerous flaws that other readers pointed out to me. I have made my point. There is no need to beat a dead horse.

Whenever I opened *Shadow Divers* to quote a reference that was disputable, I found adjacent references that were in violation of the truth. Reading the book was like viewing a landscape through swirling mist: the scenery changed with each blink of the eye. The scene was never clear; it was always hazy and indistinct - as if something existed that I could not quite identify no matter how hard I squinted.

I think a more descriptive title for the book would

have been *Foggy Divers*.

I found it impossible to parse every passage because no passage told the full truth. I always found something that was distorted or inaccurate or embellished or inconsistent or omitted or imagined or misquoted or just plain wrong. It was a frustrating experience for an historian who has spent a large part of his adult life in researching and writing history by adhering strictly to the facts.

Shadow Divers was a travesty of misinformation. My faithful readers must decide for themselves how much chaff was lumped with the precious few grains of wheat.

Author's Biography

Of the thousands of decompression dives that Gary has made, over 180 of them were on the Grand Dame of the Sea: the *Andrea Doria*. He was the first scuba diver to enter the First Class Dining Room, from which he recovered many items of elegant china. He also recovered and restored hundreds of items of jewelry and souvenirs from the Gift Shop, located at a depth of 220 feet. More important, he discovered and recovered a number of ceramic panels that once adorned the walls of the First Class Bar. These colorful panels were the work of famed Italian artist Romano Rui.

In the early 1990's, Gary was instrumental in merging mixed-gas diving technology with wreck-diving. His 1990 dive on the German battleship *Ostfriesland*, at a depth of 380 feet, triggered an unprecedented expansion in the exploration of deep-water shipwrecks, and the advent of helium mixes as a breathing medium. He wrote the first book on technical diving. In 1994, he participated in a mixed-gas diving expedition to the *Lusitania*, which lies at a depth of 300 feet.

Gary has specialized in wreck-diving and shipwreck research, concentrating his efforts on wrecks along the eastern seaboard, from Newfoundland to Key West, and in the Great Lakes. In addition to diving on hundreds of known shipwreck sites, he has made more than forty discovery dives.

He has compiled an extensive library of books, photographs, drawings, plans, and original source materials on ships and shipwrecks. He has conducted surveys on numerous wrecks, some of which have been drawn in the form of large-sized prints that are suitable for framing.

Over the years, he has rescued many thousands of shipwreck artifacts from the ravages of the sea, making him a leading authority in recovery techniques. He has gone to great lengths to preserve and restore these relics from the deep, and to display them to thousands of interested people, divers and nondivers alike. Throughout the years, these artifacts have been displayed at various museums, symposiums, and club-oriented exhibitions.

Gary has written scores of magazine articles, and has published more than three thousand photographs in books, periodicals, newspapers, brochures, advertisements, corporate reports, museum displays, postcards, film, and television. He lectures extensively on underwater topics, and conducts seminars on advanced wreck-diving techniques, high-tech diving equipment, and shipwreck photography.

He is the author of forty-four books: primarily novels of science fiction and adventure, and nonfiction volumes on wreck-diving and on nautical and shipwreck history. The Popular Dive Guide Series will eventually cover every major shipwreck along the East Coast of the United States.

There is also another side of Gary's life: that of an outdoor adventurer. In this guise he has climbed rock and mountains, backpacked through country high and low, bivouacked in the snow, and paddled his canoe through rapids and down untamed wilderness rivers - often for weeks at a time. His longest trip lasted a month, when he and five companions paddled 380 miles down the George River in Labrador. For three weeks straight they did not encounter another human being, or see signs of civilization. Gary embraces total self-sufficiency in the wilderness.

He has captured on film all of these wonderful outdoor adventures, as well as the splendor of nature's colorful scenery. He has given slide presentations to dive clubs, hiking clubs, canoe clubs, elder hostels, church groups, cub scouts, power squadrons, Naval associations, Civil War societies, Masonic lodges, Mensa, corporate functions, scientific organizations, and many, many other groups too numerous to mention.

In 1989, after a five-year battle with the National

Oceanic and Atmospheric Administration, Gary won a suit which forced the hostile government agency to issue him a permit to dive on the USS *Monitor*, a protected National Marine Sanctuary. Media attention that was focused on Gary's triumphant victory resulted in nationwide coverage of his 1990 photographic expedition to the Civil War ironclad. Gary continues to fight for the right of access to all shipwreck sites.

Books by the Author

The Popular Dive Guide Series
Shipwrecks of Massachusetts: South
Shipwrecks of Rhode Island and Connecticut
Shipwrecks of New York
Shipwrecks of New Jersey (1988)
Shipwrecks of New Jersey: North
Shipwrecks of New Jersey: Central
Shipwrecks of New Jersey: South
Shipwrecks of Delaware and Maryland (1990 Edition)
Shipwrecks of Delaware and Maryland (2002 Edition)
Shipwrecks of Virginia
Shipwrecks of North Carolina: North
Shipwrecks of North Carolina: South
Shipwrecks of South Carolina and Georgia

Shipwreck and Nautical History
Andrea Doria: Dive to an Era
Deep, Dark, and Dangerous: Adventures and
Reflections on the Andrea Doria
The Fuhrer's U-boats in American Waters
Great Lakes Shipwrecks: a Photographic Odyssey
Ironclad Legacy: Battles of the USS Monitor
The Lusitania Controversies (Book One):
Atrocity of War and a Wreck-Diving History
The Lusitania Controversies (Book Two):
Dangerous Descents into Shipwrecks and Law
The Nautical Cyclopedia
USS San Diego: the Last Armored Cruiser
Shadow Divers Exposed
Stolen Heritage: Grand Theft of Hamilton and Scourge
Track of the Gray Wolf
Wreck Diving Adventures

Dive Training Manuals
Primary Wreck Diving Guide
Advanced Wreck Diving Guide
Ultimate Wreck Diving Guide
The Technical Diving Handbook

Outdoor Nonfiction
Wilderness Canoeing

Science Fiction
A Different Universe: Tales of Imagination
A Different Dimension: More Tales of Imagination
Entropy
Return to Mars
Silent Autumn
The Time Dragons Trilogy
    A Time for Dragons
    Dragons Past
    No Future for Dragons

Action/Adventure Novels
Memory Lane
Mind Set
The Peking Papers

Supernatural Horror Novel
The Lurking

Vietnam Novel
Lonely Conflict

Videotape (NTSC/VHS)
The Battle for the USS Monitor

Visit the GGP website for availability of titles:

http://www.ggentile.com

THE LUSITANIA CONTROVERSIES
THE TWO-VOLUME
HISTORY OF WRECK-DIVING

There is more to a book than its title. There is the subtitle. A subtitle is an explanatory device which describes the topic of a book more fully than its title. A case in point is *The Lusitania Controversies.* At first glance the title implies the sole subject of the *Lusitania.* But each of the two volumes possesses a subtitle which explains in greater detail the global premise of which the *Lusitania* is but a part.

Together, both volumes present the entire history of wreck-diving, from its meager beginnings in the 1950's to the advent of technical diving in the 1990's.

Book One is subtitled *Atrocity of War and a Wreck-Diving History.* One quarter of the volume is devoted to the construction, career, sinking, and aftermath of the *Lusitania.* Three quarters are devoted to the history of wreck-diving and to autobiographical experiences of the author, who became an essential element in wreck-diving and a pioneer in technical diving. Coverage extends to 1979, and includes a section on the author's first *Doria* trip, in 1974.

Book Two is subtitled *Dangerous Descents into Shipwrecks and Law.* This volume continues the history of wreck-diving from 1980; describes numerous dives on ever-deeper shipwrecks; a number of incredible penetrations into the vast interior of the *Andrea Doria,* including the recovery of two bodies; and details the beginning of mixed-gas diving to the point at which an expedition to the *Lusitania* became practical. The volume concludes with a detailed description of the 1994 *Lusitania* expedition (of which the author was a part) and subsequent legal activities.

The two volumes are larger than the sum of their parts. They comprise biographical content with incredible underwater adventures: some hair-raising, others deadly, all exciting: a fascinating excursion into the real world of wreck-diving and the evolution of the activity.

INDEX